IMAGINING SEATTLE

OUR SUSTAINABLE FUTURE

SERIES EDITORS

Ryan E. Galt
University of California, Davis

Hannah Wittman
University of British Columbia

FOUNDING EDITORS

Charles A. Francis
University of Nebraska–Lincoln

Cornelia Flora
Iowa State University

IMAGINING SEATTLE

SOCIAL VALUES IN URBAN GOVERNANCE

SERIN D. HOUSTON

University of Nebraska Press

LINCOLN

Claudia Castro Luna's "A Corner to Love" first appeared
on the Seattle Poetic Grid, https://seattlepoeticgrid
.com/, and is reprinted with permission of the author.

Library of Congress Cataloging-in-Publication Data
Names: Houston, Serin D., author.
Title: Imagining Seattle: social values in urban
governance / Serin D. Houston.
Description: Lincoln: University of Nebraska Press,
[2019] | Series: Our sustainable future | Includes
bibliographical references and index.
Identifiers: LCCN 2018053128
ISBN 9780803248755 (cloth: alk. paper)
ISBN 9781496216052 (epub)
ISBN 9781496216069 (mobi)
ISBN 9781496216076 (pdf)
Subjects: LCSH: Urban policy—Washington (State)—
Seattle. | Sustainable development—Washington
(State)—Seattle. | Seattle (Wash.)—Race relations. |
Seattle (Wash.)—Social conditions. | Seattle (Wash.)—
Economic conditions.
Classification: LCC HN80.S54 H68 2019 | DDC
307.7609797/772—dc23 LC record available at
https://lccn.loc.gov/2018053128

Set in Sabon Next LT Pro by Mikala R. Kolander.

For Ned, Susan, Zariah, and Will, with love

CONTENTS

MAPS

ACKNOWLEDGMENTS

Intellectual projects of a few months or several years invariably draw upon the help and expertise of many people. *Imagining Seattle* is no exception. I greatly appreciate all the assistance I have received along the way. First, heartfelt thanks to the many Seattleites who welcomed me into their work places and community spaces, shared their perspectives with me, provided access to resources and events, and believed in the importance of this research. The archivists at the Seattle Municipal Archives retrieved an untold number of file boxes throughout my months of fieldwork. I am grateful to them for their patience and help as I waded through these records. My thanks to Claudia Castro Luna for permission to use her poem "A Corner to Love" in the conclusion.

Sincere thanks to the National Science Foundation for the Graduate Research Fellowship that funded much of my fieldwork. Grants from Mount Holyoke College for research assistance, book publication costs, sabbatical leave, and research startup have been invaluable as well. A Postdoctoral Research Leave American Fellowship from the American Association of University Women (AAUW) supported the completion of this book. The opinions, findings, conclusions, and recommendations expressed here are mine and do not necessarily reflect the views of the National Science Foundation, Mount Holyoke College, or the AAUW.

The ideas of this book have germinated over multiple seasons and many people have nurtured, watered, and weeded them. I could not have reached this moment of full bloom without this support, guidance, and input. I warmly thank Mona Atia, Emily Billo, Adam Bledsoe, Alan Bloomgarden, Jenni Brown, Jen Cannon, Christine Chapman, Catherine Corson, Mark Davidson, Will Decherd, Mark Ellis, Melissa Fisher, Jen Jack Gieseking, Holly Hanson, Alice Hartley, David Hernández, Ned Houston, Seth Houston, Susan Houston, Jennifer Hyndman, Girma Kebbede, Kavita Khory, Elisa Kim, Jeremy King, Kirk Lange, Maria Lee, Kiana London, Cathy Luna, Michelle Markley, Caroline Melly, Lynn Morgan, Alison Mountz, Joe Nevins, Jackie Orr, Becky Packard, Eva Paus, Mary Ramsay, Swati Rana, Jill Riddell, Lauret Savoy, Preston Smith, Nicole Tsong, John Western, Jamie Winders, and Richard Wright for the stimulating conversations, productive feedback, useful references, and keen insights. I particularly want to thank Will, Jack, Holly, Ned, Girma, Kiana, and Caroline for astute comments on book chapters. Your collective close reads, probing questions, and enthusiasm for my ideas have been tremendously valuable and very appreciated. I also thank Kiana London and Quinn Wallace for excellent research assistance. Many thanks as well to the anonymous reviewers of my book proposal and complete manuscript for the useful questions and compelling feedback.

My colleagues in the departments of Geology and Geography and International Relations at Mount Holyoke College have provided incisive questions and thought-provoking conversations over the years. The maps of Seattle and Western Washington emerged through Eugenio Marcano's skills, patience, and attention to detail. I kindly thank Eugenio and the Mount Holyoke College Geo-Processing Lab for providing the space and technical support to create these maps. I offer deep gratitude to my colleagues in our Friday write-on-site group, my fellow small group members in the National Center for Faculty Development and Diversity "Faculty Success Program," and my online writing companions, especially Holly Hanson and Mary Renda, for inspiring, encouraging, and celebrating with me. I could always count on great progress during our shared writing times and knew I could depend on all of you for support.

My ideas have been clarified and sharpened through presenting aspects of this book in various venues. Thank you to co-presenters and audience members at American Association of Geography (AAG) conferences in Seattle, New York City, and Washington DC; the Kahn seminar on "Modes and Models of Making" and the "Race+Class" panel, both at Smith College; and the Wilbraham-Monson Academy "Cities" conference. Mount Holyoke College students in "Geography 202: Cities in a Global Context" invited me to think more deeply about social justice endeavors and systemic change.

I am indebted to Derek Krissoff, who sought me out as I was just starting my research and suggested I write a book about Seattle. It has been a pleasure working with everyone at the University of Nebraska Press. Bridget Barry improved my work with her keen editorial eye and graciously answered questions large and small during the manuscript preparation. Emily Wendell assisted with book logistics. Elizabeth Zaleski ushered my book through the production process. Sally Antrobus provided impeccable copyediting. Jackson Adams, Tish Fobben, Rosemary Sekora, and Andrea Shahan executed excellent design and marketing work. My sincere thanks to everyone at UNP.

Friends and family endured endless conversations about Seattle and believed in this project when I lacked energy to do so. I am humbled by the boundless support and honored to be a part of all of your lives. A particularly heartfelt thank you to my extended Farwell and Houston families, my extended Beck and Decherd families, and my Craftsbury community. Ana Bennett and Chaia Wolf provided incomparable support for my body and mind throughout this book journey.

With deep love and gratitude, I dedicate *Imagining Seattle* to three generations of incredibly important people who give meaning, purpose, and joy to my life: my parents, Susan and Ned Houston; my husband, Will Decherd; and my daughter, Zariah Decherd. My mom and dad have been my most longstanding and significant teachers, always encouraging my curiosity and willingly participating in robust conversations on innumerable topics. Thank you both for nurturing my spirit and providing unwavering support of me and my work. Your daily practice of living with purposeful engagement is continually inspiring. Special thanks to my dad for being my most consistent and longstanding interlocutor, and the person who has patiently read and commented on many drafts of this book. Dad's feedback and wisdom make every piece of my writing better.

Zariah's infectious laughter and imagination and awe with the great outdoors offer necessary antidotes to hours spent at the computer. She regularly invites me to acknowledge the rare gift of being alive, and for this I am extremely grateful. Finally, mountains of thanks to Will who has embraced and supported me through all phases of this project. From weathering distance while I did fieldwork to talking through ideas to keeping me nourished in body and soul, Will has been unflagging in his belief in me and this book. Will's hopeful vision for the future and ardent commitment to life and love are unparalleled. Profound thanks to you, Will, for being my rock.

While I extend gratitude and thanks for the assistance along the way, all errors and shortcomings in this book are my own.

ABBREVIATIONS

AYP	Alaska-Yukon-Pacific Exposition
CAP	Climate Action Plan
CLUE	Community Land Use and Economics group
CODAC	Cultural Overlay District Advisory Committee
DON	Department of Neighborhoods
DPD	Department of Planning and Development
EEI	Equity and Environment Initiative
ESJ	Equity and Social Justice
ESJI	Equity and Social Justice Initiative
eTOD	equitable transit-oriented development
GARE	Government Alliance on Race and Equity
GHG	greenhouse gas
HOLC	Home Owners' Loan Corporation
ID	International District
LGBTQ	lesbian, gay, bisexual, transgender, and queer
OED	Office of Economic Development
OSE	Office of Sustainability & Environment
POL	planning outreach liaison
RSJI	Race and Social Justice Initiative
SCVB	Seattle Convention and Visitors Bureau
SDOT	Seattle Department of Transportation
SLU	South Lake Union
SMT	Seattle Municipal Tower
SOCR	Seattle Office for Civil Rights
SPD	Seattle Police Department

SPU	Seattle Public Utilities
TDR	transferable development rights
TOD	transit-oriented development
UEC	Urban Enterprise Center
WMBE	women- and minority-owned business enterprise
WTO	World Trade Organization

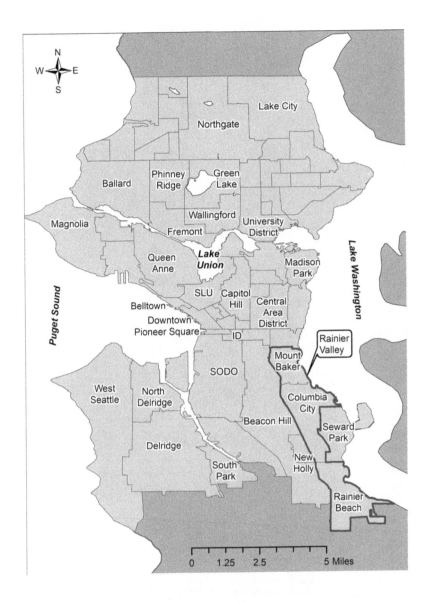

Map i. Seattle neighborhoods. Eugenio Marcano (2018) created this map
using ArcGIS® software by ESRI, and it is used herein under license.
Data sources: U.S. Census, USGS, ESRI, OpenStreetMap, and the
Mount Holyoke College GeoProcessing Lab.

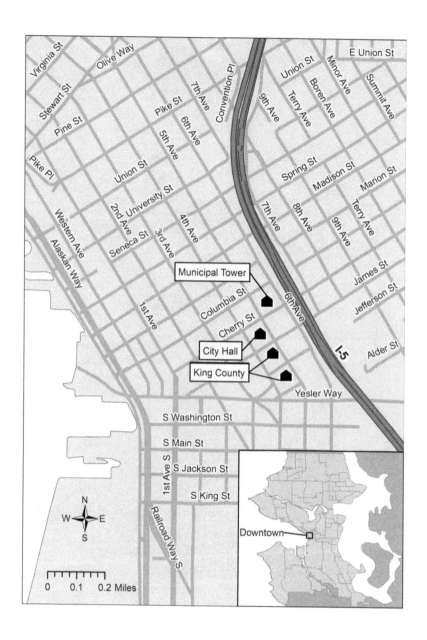

MAP 2. Downtown Seattle. Eugenio Marcano (2018) created this map using ArcGIS® software by ESRI, and it is used herein under license. Data sources: U.S. Census, USGS, ESRI, OpenStreetMap, and the Mount Holyoke College GeoProcessing Lab.

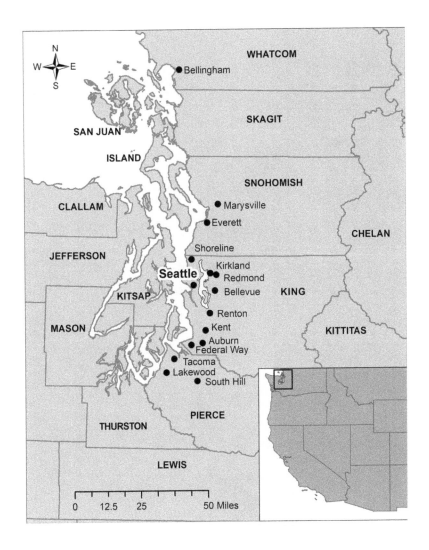

MAP 3. Counties of Western Washington. Eugenio Marcano (2018) created this map using ArcGIS® software by ESRI, and it is used herein under license. Data sources: U.S. Census, USGS, ESRI, OpenStreetMap, and the Mount Holyoke College GeoProcessing Lab.

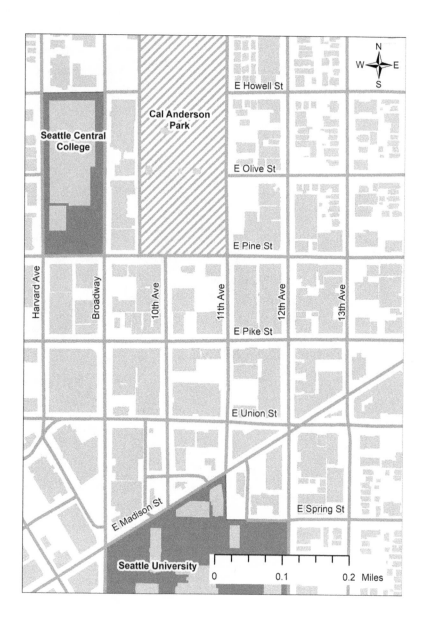

MAP 4. Core area of Capitol Hill Arts and Cultural District. Eugenio Marcano (2018) created this map using ArcGIS® software by ESRI, and it is used herein under license. Data sources: U.S. Census, USGS, ESRI, OpenStreetMap, and the Mount Holyoke College GeoProcessing Lab.

IMAGINING SEATTLE

Introduction

Seattle, "The City of "

An urban symphony purred, squealed, and rattled around me as I trod over pavement, concrete, discarded items, and occasional patches of grass on a fourteen-mile meandering transect through Seattle, Washington, a large city located in the Pacific Northwest of the continental United States. By the end of that October day in 2005, the contours of this urban context infused my body. The wonderment in my eyes reflected the array of façades and landscapes I had encountered during this walk. The savory aromas I smelled spoke to the multiplicity of people and cuisines populating Seattle. The dirt clogging my pores revealed the grit and grime of this mass of living and nonliving beings. The sounds of the lapping waters of Lake Washington, Lake Union, and Puget Sound emphasized the fluvial activity sculpting the city. The quickening of my heart rate beat out the fear and dislocation that often accompany dark city streets. The wincing of my feet reminded me of the many paths and travels that have brought people to and from this place. I had lived in Seattle for over a year at that time, yet I was experiencing the city entirely anew.

The long walk exposed me to profound juxtapositions: the social services office located next to the plush dog groomer in gentrifying Columbia City; the extended line outside the Salvation Army shelter practically reaching the doorstep of the sparkling new Starbucks in the Central Area District; and the array of compost bins dotting the porches of City Hall and the noticeable absence of such bins, and public trash cans for that matter, in parts of Rainier Valley (see maps 1 and 2). Through movement, I traversed spaces of inclusion and exclusion, and boundaries (mine and others) slipped in and out of focus. As I trudged the last few miles past the famous Lusty Lady, a now closed strip club, and the swanky bars of gentrified Belltown, I gazed at the sea of twenty- and thirty-somethings out carousing, and I felt viscerally the many divergent ways that we inhabit space. I was not part of their groups, and yet we shared the same sidewalks. Clearly Seattle as a city holds multiple meanings, experiences, and manifestations. It is a nexus of contradictions and assumptions. This evolving place emerges through and comprises varying social, political, cultural, environmental, and economic processes. By experientially occupying the liminality of the city, I became further attuned to a handful of the many urban realities that constitute Seattle. New sensory engagements with Seattle lodged themselves in my being just as I contributed to the ephemeral formation of the city. By the end of the day, I wondered more acutely: what experiences do Seattleites carry with them, and what stories do they tell about this place?

The sunlight refracting off the glass walls of Seattle's South Lake Union (SLU) Discovery Center added a blinding glow to this notable addition in the urban landscape (see map 1). My fingers curled around the solid metal handle of the front door, and with a pull I left the bustle of Westlake Ave and walked into a sparsely adorned entrance. Another doorway beckoned me farther into a circular viewing room where a handful of well-padded chairs sat waiting for occupants. No one else was discovering South Lake Union that July afternoon in 2009. As soon as I stepped into the round room, the door automatically closed, the lights dimmed, and I was ensconced in promotional visuality. Images of the five neighborhoods of the SLU filled the screen in front of me, and narratives about these new places burst forth on surround sound. Captivated by all the stated amenities, I momentarily forgot that something existed before a massive influx of corporate money powered extensive material changes in the SLU. The glitz and the glam—

and all the high-tech gadgets—started to feel convincing. Ah yes, it *would* be great to live, work, and play here.

Just as I was settling in for more enticing offerings about the up-and-coming neighborhoods of the SLU, the video concluded, the screen slid away, and I was set free to explore the rest of the Discovery Center. A model of Seattle commanded the middle of the next room. The white plastic skyscrapers, the mini trees, the empty roads—it all looked so tidy and coherent, a poignant contrast to my fourteen-mile walk through the city. Kiosks flanked the walls of the room. With titles like "creative + diverse," "urban + natural," and "swift + central," they helped orient me to a potential future in the SLU. A metal dog sculpture sat below a sign that outlined all the perks of the area for dogs (a nod to the stat that Seattleites are more likely to have a dog than a child). The potential reality for my life, replete with numerous lifestyle amenities, assumed tangibility as I followed the bamboo-flooring path to information and models about condos under construction in the SLU. The flow and format of the center told a persuasive narrative about this self-described innovative neighborhood redevelopment. The exhibit fanned expectations for what daily life would entail and offered a concrete mechanism for purchasing part of this dream. The near erasure of histories, contestations, and plural views of this place struck me. How innovative could a development project be if it rests on a tacit assumption that places are blank slates?

The perfect temperatures and bright sun of June 2014 welcomed me back to Seattle. I had returned to read recently released archival material. I was curious about how often I would become disoriented during my visit due to the seemingly frantic pace of redevelopment. Wandering 12th Avenue in the Central Area District on my way to the Seattle Municipal Archives in City Hall, I saw multi-colored street banners proudly proclaiming as they hung from street lamps, "12th Avenue, Live, Learn, Work, and Play." What did the people waiting for food, clothes, and household goods behind the banners at the adjacent St. Francis House, a non-profit that supports people in need, make of such depictions of 12th Avenue? What did these banners signal to the anticipated new residents and businesses that would occupy the buildings going up right next to St. Francis? A friend told me that the number of cranes on the Seattle skyline rivaled Dubai. I believed it. I was overwhelmed by all the construction. I felt the light and wind in different ways as I walked once recognizable streets; the new infill construction cast long shadows and sent the breeze whipping along the street. I turned off 12th Avenue and headed under Interstate 5 toward City Hall. A blue nylon tent sat askew under the highway. Access to the live/work/play new urbanist vision promoted on the 12th Avenue banners seemed distant and remote here. The contrasts were stark and painfully familiar.

As I passed by the encampment, a comment came to mind from an interview with Sebastian, one of the fifty-eight city and county employees, non-profit and for-profit employees, and community activists whom I interviewed for this research.[1] When I asked him about Seattle's attributes, he explained, "Seattle is 'the city of' whatever word you want to put back there. And I really mean that.... It's Seattle the City of Music.... It's Seattle the City of Business. It's Seattle, the city of. There's so much going on here that whatever people are identifying with or want to do, Seattle is accommodating that right now.... It's just the city of." For Sebastian, from his positional authority in municipal government and in the prime of his career, this depiction was clearly motivating. With palpable enthusiasm, he listed different endeavors unfolding in Seattle, "the city of." There was tremendous hope in this perception of the place.

Yet when he reclined in his office chair and kicked his leg onto his desk to describe Seattle as simply "the city of," I found myself both inspired and concerned about this vision. I too felt energized by the sense of possibility inherent in such a moniker, and I wondered about the acknowledgment of poverty and disparity in such renderings. I could not imagine Sebastian exuberantly stating, "Seattle: The City of Segregation" or "Seattle: The City of Gentrification," even though these realities are just as potent and significant as "Seattle: The City of Music" or "Business." Other questions began to demand my attention: How does the Seattle city government navigate the contradictions evident in urban space, particularly when prevailing representations of place leave little room for ambiguities? How do systemic inequities and discrimination fit into popular depictions of Seattle? How, and with what impacts, does the translation of social values into practice unfold in Seattle's urban governance?

Critical Conceptual Constructs

Imagining Seattle: Social Values in Urban Governance investigates how collective efforts to reimagine and remake a city according to specific social values—meaning the principles and judgments about what is important within and to the city—unfold through urban governance and with what effects. In particular, I analyze the translation of sustainability, creativity, and social justice from concept into practice and ask how it is that such translations often reproduce racialized and classed inequities amid efforts for substantive social change. The purpose of this research is not to offer a comprehensive review of all the ways different values translate into practice within Seattle's urban governance. Instead, I focus on a few particularly illustrative examples of actualizing sustainability, creativity, and social justice in Seattle to argue that the racism and classism built into current structures and systems of urban governance help perpetuate inequities, diminish the execution of social transformation, and produce divergences between values and practices within Seattle.

Empirically, examining these three social values together is unique and affords crucial insights into the structure and processes of urban governance. Conceptually, a geographic perspective and attention to hierarchies of power enable me to draw out how racism and classism often truncate the material realization of sustainability, creativity, and social justice. Taking place, space, and scale seriously affords opportunities to consider what social values currently mean in practice and what they could mean in the future. My goal with this analysis is to provoke further consideration of urban social transformation and to encourage a move toward greater engagement with equity-based and relational urban governance within Seattle in particular and in cities more generally, as they are the home to the majority of global humanity.[2] I hope Seattleites, policy makers, academics, urban residents, and activists alike will find insights woven throughout this book that advance their work and learning.

I understand urban governance as the process of governing and managing urban space via distinct actors, networks, negotiations, and institutions.[3] Power relations, formal and informal rules, and notions of quality shape urban governance as a process and constitute urban governance as an object of study (Gupta et al. 2015, 28). Consequently, through analyzing the translation of sustainability, creativity, and social justice from concept into practice, I glean insights into place making and the act of governing in Seattle. Translation in this context refers to the transition in form of an amorphous social value into material policies and programs. Put differently, translation constitutes a process, one that holds spatial and temporal aspects (Bassnett 2014). By investigating this shift, I also draw on translation to signify the powerful interpretative work undertaken to manifest tangibly a social value within urban governance.[4] Just as linguistic translation requires understanding a host of potential meanings embedded within a word or phrase and capturing this panoply within another language, I consider how city and county employees take the broad and multi-dimensional concepts of sustainability, creativity, and social justice and implement them within material practices for a wide range of urban denizens. I also underscore how racism and classism shape the materialization of social values because the process by which values move from the conceptual to the applied is not isolated from prevailing structures, hierarchies, and inequities.

Sustainability, *creativity*, and *social justice* are all capacious terms, subject to diverse applications and meanings. In the context of my research, sustainability refers to ecologically driven actions that reduce individual and collective use of resources, thereby diminishing impacts on biophysical systems and conceptually enabling future generations of all species to survive and thrive. Sustainability is also tightly bound up with the production of a green identity, one that enjoys popular support in narratives of Seattle and Seattleites, as I discuss in chapter 2. Creativity signifies both the entrepreneurship and innovation evident within various economic sectors in the city and the art making and cultural productions throughout Seattle that enhance the city's livability. Many research participants, and popular urban writers like Richard Florida, suggest that there is something special about Seattle (perhaps the rainy weather) that makes it a particularly creative place. I investigate in chapter 3 the translation of this value and place expectation into economic development proposals and policies.

Even though justice in the abstract is something many people view as important, what actually constitutes justice in practice can vary fairly dramatically. For instance, a libertarian view accents the ties between justice and merit. An utilitarian view, on the other hand, highlights what would be the most beneficial outcome for the widest number of people, whereas an egalitarian rendering of justice focuses on meeting individual needs (Agyeman 2013, 38). Distributional justice asks who bears the burdens and who benefits from actions and urban amenities. Procedural justice emphasizes inclusion and collaboration in decision making to unpack who has power in urban governance practices and how and why certain decisions are made. Attention to the plurality of needs, social identities, and experiences of residents reflects the concept of recognition justice (Walker 2012; Peters 2015). I primarily consider these last three understandings of justice as they coalesce within Seattle's Race and Social Justice Initiative (RSJI), which I examine in chapter 4. Addressing what assumptions underpin policy design and implementation, underscoring the benefits and burdens of various actions, and highlighting how city employees acknowledge assorted needs and experiences within Seattle illustrates how distributional, procedural, and recognition justice thread through the RSJI and its efforts to eliminate institutional racism and race-based disparities.

The RSJI foregrounds racial justice, which is one facet of social justice as a concept, organizing practice and goal rather than the entirety of what constitutes social justice as a value. Social justice generally refers to concerns with inequities, injustices, and persecution, but it is a contested term because what constitutes equality, for instance, is not universally agreed upon. The focus on equity within the RSJI, rather than presumed sameness as often espoused through equality, shapes the organizing strategies and methods of the initiative. Since I analyze the RSJI as the locus of how the municipal government strives to bear out social justice, I emphasize equity and racial justice. I do this while also recognizing—as recounted by Leslie, a county employee who self-identified as white and queer—that "the languaged nature of Seattle around social justice can be detracting or confusing because . . . racism and classism are still so thick in this city and displacement is happening at such a rapid pace in South Seattle and the Central [Area] District." She continued, "I think it [social justice] can be a bit of an empty signifier or a bit of a salve or balm for the guilt that's in the city." As a result, "there's lots of people doing really radical social justice work where there's deep and really rich meaning underneath that same vocabulary. It's just that it's been a bit co-opted. So you can't take for granted that knowledge of the language means commitment to the substance of the ideas," Leslie noted. My analysis of the RSJI delves into the content and context of the initiative to query the process of producing the conditions for social justice within Seattle's urban governance.

While I separate the values of social justice, creativity, and sustainability into distinct chapters so that I can analyze the particular translation they undergo from concept to practice, these values are clearly interwoven and mutually reinforcing. Expectations about the national leadership possibilities afforded by proposed environmental policy, for example, dovetail with notions of innovation and creativity. Tackling immense systemic inequities through the RSJI matches aspirations for directly addressing the tremendous challenges associated with climate change. Collaborating through the public art municipal plan to integrate arts into wastewater treatment and recycling plants, as city and county employees do, emphasizes the synergies of environmental issues, public art, and struggles for justice. Put simply, sustainability, creativity, and social justice are entangled, and the practices these values set in motion compound and constitute each other. Yet for the purposes of analytical clarity—and with recognition of how city departments parsed out their work during my research (the Office of Sustainability & Environment was in a wholly different location than the Seattle Office for Civil Rights, for instance)—I examine policy and program proposals and implementation that principally represent the translation of one social value into practice.

Inspired by ethnography, my research design consisted of participant observation within city government and neighborhood contexts, historical research in the Seattle Municipal Archives, and semi-structured interviews with fifty-eight people who at the time were employed in city or county government or local non-profit and for-profit entities or involved in community activism in Southeast Seattle (see appendix 1 for more on my methods). This methodological approach encouraged me to notice the ways in which expectations for, understandings of, and silences about place came to the fore and shaped practices of sustainability, creativity, and social justice at multiple scales, from the micro-geographies of daily life to the broader realm of policy implementation. All research participants volunteered and collectively represent a range of affiliations, years in a current position, and forms of engagement with social values. I take seriously interviewees' points of view and experiences because they help constitute urban governance. This does not mean that I avoid scrutinizing people's comments or juxtaposing divergent takes on a situation. Instead, I foreground the views of city and county employees, community members, and non-profit and for-profit employees to emphasize how these perspectives compose Seattle and illuminate the contemporary translation of social values from concept into practice. This decision allows me to focus on the context of participants' observations and their positionalities vis-à-vis efforts to envision and labor toward social change. I describe research participants according to information gleaned in the interviews, such as their roles in their communities, their work settings, or their histories within the city, to provide some context and materiality to their voices. I did not ask people about personal identities, such as how they self-identified racially, their class background, their pronoun, or their educational attainment.

Some participants shared their racial identities as African American, Asian, black, person of color, white, or woman of color during interviews. In such cases, I include this information. Outside of direct quotes from interviewees, I use the umbrella term *black* to refer to people who may self-identify as black Africans, African Americans, and/or black. The general silence about racial identities during interviews with people I read as white follows broader trends wherein people in positions of power, in this case racial power, often do not explicitly name identities of privilege (Tatum 2017). Race, as a social construct, is not biological, and yet it is persistently reproduced with material consequences and contains economic, political, emotional, ideological, and social power (Goodman et al. 2012). Thus, to acknowledge the freighted reality of this social construct, I use racial signifiers without quotes. I by no means want to suggest some sort of static or all-encompassing metric for any of these identities. On the contrary, I understand them as dynamic and tenacious categories, which are influenced by history and geography.

Examining racism is fundamental to my analysis. Within the U.S. context of my research, I understand racism as a spatialized form of oppression that draws on contemporary and historical practices, structures, and processes. Through the linking of power and prejudice, racism accumulates benefit and opportunity to a dominant racial group (Golash-Boza 2015; Bonilla-Silva 1997; 2018). In the United States the dominant racial group is white people. Racism contours all aspects of daily life, from individual interactions to national systems, and operates as the "ordinary means through which dehumanization achieves ideological normality" (Gilmore 2007, 243). Dehumanization and the associated rationalizations for such ideologies often have fatal consequences. Rather than viewing racism as an aberrant behavior of a few "racists," I recognize institutional, structural, and interpersonal forms of racism and grapple with the intersectionality of racism and other categories of difference in my analysis. In brief, institutional racism references the ways in which institutional policies and practices indirectly or directly generate outcomes that benefit white people and discriminate against people of color. Examples of institutional racism include racial profiling in policing and redistricting. Structural racism speaks to the systemic inculcation of race and racism throughout the development of the United States and within every facet of society today, from health outcomes to educational opportunities to rates of incarceration. Interpersonal racism refers to the individual interactions, such as derogatory jokes and the dismissive treatment of the successes of people of color, that perpetuate racialized hierarchies. These different forms of racism coalesce to produce the systemic racism and racialization evident experientially and conceptually throughout the country in the past and the present (Omi and Winant 1994; Feagin 2014; Elias and Feagin 2016).[5] Through my analysis of social values in Seattle's urban governance, I particularly address different forms of racism as they emerge through white privilege and whiteness.

Critical whiteness studies, an interdisciplinary field, further informs my examination of the translation of social values into practice and the racialized and classed impacts of such efforts. Conceiving of whiteness as a generally unmarked system of power and propertied asset that accrues privilege to white people, literature in critical whiteness studies unpacks the implications of white supremacy on the preservation and production of racialized inequities and racialized privilege (Harris 1993; Pulido 2000; Ahmed 2007; Sensoy and DiAngelo 2017). *White supremacy* as a term refers to the extensiveness of white privilege and normative racial dominance rather than only the extreme actions of racially motivated hate groups (Sensoy and DiAngelo 2017, 143). Critical whiteness studies also examines how people racialized as white understand racial categories and are complicit with systems and structures that justify the naturalness of prevailing racial hierarchies (Hartmann et al. 2009; Houston 2009; Bush 2011; DiAngelo

2011). Addressing the presumed naturalness of whiteness prompts analytical consideration of assumptions about class differentiation as well because, as law professor Cheryl Harris (1993, 1714) explains, "whiteness and property share a common premise—a conceptual nucleus—of a right to exclude." The exclusionary practices borne out through classism and whiteness are key features in my analysis of the translation of sustainability, creativity, and social justice into practice in Seattle's urban governance. Examining whiteness and white privilege helps me recognize and think through dominant forms of power that shape how institutional changes does and does not happen. Unpacking why and how actions undertaken in the name of progressive social values do not fully bear out their intended goals requires close engagement with insights gleaned through scholarship on whiteness and racism in the United States. As geographer Laura Pulido (2000, 13) cogently reminds, "If we wish to create a more just society, we must acknowledge the breadth and depth of racism."

I further animate my analysis of social values and urban governance through a concerted focus on imaginative geographies, place, scale, and the co-constitution of society and space. Imaginative geographies signal the assumptions about people and place that circulate within and outside groups. These representations reveal social coding and carry political, emotional, and ideological gravity. They often transmit through discursive and visual registers, yet incite material consequences. Imaginative geographies gain power and legitimacy through repetition and frequently become taken-for-granted presumed representations of truth. They sustain expectations and assumptions about the world and as such influence actions taken (Hoelscher 2006; Gregory 2009a; Driver 2014). English and comparative literature professor Edward Said (1978) wrote about imaginative geographies in *Orientalism* in his examination of constructs of the West and the exoticized and othered East; the concept has traveled widely since then. In the context of my research, the frame of imaginative geographies helps me parse out how narratives of Seattle as a particular kind of place have gained traction and contributed to expectations for and assumptions about the city. Imaginative geographies "are not simply colorful mental maps confined to the world of ideas. Rather they are active participants in the world of action" (Cresswell 2006, 21). As such, imaginative geographies pervade expectations for, associations with, and practices in Seattle. Indeed, the frequently repeated stories of Seattle as creative, sustainable, and progressive helped guide my examination of how values funneled through imaginative geographies assume tangible form.

The geographical imagination is related to imaginative geographies but accents some slightly different points. Geographer Paul Cloke and colleagues (2014, 927) define the geographical imagination in the singular as referring to core intellectual contributions from the field of geography. They note that the plural— geographical imaginations—encapsulates the many ways in which people develop geographical sensibilities and awareness or, as geographers like to say a-where-ness. Geographer Jen Jack Gieseking (2017) offers a different take and summarizes the geographical imagination as an analytical window for unpacking assumptions and stereotypes associated with spaces and places. The geographical imagination as such draws attention to the constitutive production of space and place (Gregory 2009b). I use the frame of the geographical imagination not to describe contributions from geography but rather to depict the constitutive work of imaginative geographies. Put differently, the concept of imaginative geographies helps me underscore how assumptions about Seattle gain and maintain legitimacy in popular interpretations of the city, and the geographical imagination alerts me to the ways in which these representations constitute spaces within Seattle. Thus, while I mostly focus on imaginative geographies, there are times when I intentionally call upon the geographical imagination to scrutinize practices and processes in the city.

Building on this geographic perspective, I understand place to signify more than a mere designation of location on the surface of the earth. Place can be marshaled as an ideological force to normalize practices and actions through suggestions that something or someone is "in" or "out" of place. Engaging with place as the context for everyday life and as a site imagined to be singular, but clearly inhabited and experienced in multiple ways, helps draw attention to the contradictions evident within Seattle between espoused values and material practices. Places convey meaning and serve as repositories for memories (Agnew 1987; Cresswell 2014). Such salience of place is poignantly evident as people narrate stories of change in familiar spaces throughout Seattle and wonder about future belonging. I center these emotional and affective landscapes through interpretations of a sense of place. I think it matters what stories are told about a place for promotional reasons, for political gain, for internal community referencing. As conduits for articulating the intangibles of a place, narratives materialize power relations and implicitly and explicitly specify goals and anxieties. Cities are unrepresentable in their entirety, so people craft and share narratives about urban spaces to give them shape and tangibility. Indeed, as geographer Patricia Price (2004) expounds, places are "thoroughly narrative constructs" (xxi). She continues that places "would not exist *as places* were it not for the stories told about and through them" (Price 2004, xxi, emphasis in the original). Put differently, places emerge through narratives, and narratives shift and evolve in response to transformations evident in places and people. Such discursive interventions feed into material decisions and inform built and perceptual landscapes, as my analysis of various policies and proposals repeatedly shows.

The co-constitution of society and space and the spatial relations within and beyond Seattle that shape the city are other geographical concepts that I lean on in this book. Space is not a fixed and flat backdrop. Moreover, it is neither a container nor static. Instead, just as events, movements, or buildings, for example, spatially happen somewhere, the qualities and experiences of space vary and are informed by societal pressures, norms, and expectations. There is a recursive relationship, in other words, between society and space. They are mutually constituted and always cocreating (Harvey 1990; Lefebvre 1991; Massey 2005; Thrift 2009). This relational understanding of space enables me to underscore

how societal pressures, such as a demand for greater accountability from government officials, can lead to different spatial
patterns in how and where meetings are held, for instance. Similarly, the arrangement of furniture, style of decorating, and flow
of physical movement through a space can signal whether or not
residents are really welcome within city departments. The imbri-
cation of society and space is a significant conceptual lens for my
analysis of the translation of social values into practice as I consider the many kinds of messages sent through discursive, material, and spatial formats.

Articulating spatial scale as a unit of analysis, ranging from the
individual or body to the neighborhood, city, state, and so on, helps
demonstrate how and why expressions of social values can vary
in meaning and practice. For instance, the retail redevelopment
strategy that I discuss in chapter 3 might appear well constituted
if one is principally thinking about how to have a neighborhood
economically contribute more to the city's bottom line. Yet shifting scales of engagement to the individuals and households living and working within the neighborhoods suggests a different
interpretation of the plans. Drawing upon spatial scale in this way
helps me identify and think through the seemingly unintentional
reproduction of inequities in the translation of social values into
policy prescriptions and program development.

Delving into the discursive frames of the *City* and the *city* inter-
sects with my geographic perspective as well. The City refers to the
imagined broad-scale collectivity known as Seattle. It is both the
locus for aspirations of city boosters, various actors who work to
promote stated perks of a place internally and externally, and the
object of frustration ("if only the City would resolve the persistent
parking issues!"). In contrast to the homogeneity often implied
within articulations of the City, the city denotes the intricate webs
of power that constitute a place, the divergent and at times conflicting priorities and practices evident within governance, and the
array of living and nonliving beings and experiences that charac-
terize Seattle. Neither of these specifications focuses principally
on the formal statistical designation of Seattle's metropolitan area

or the city proper. They are instead perceptual renderings of the place. Examining the translation of values into practices means that I routinely tack back and forth between expectations and expressions of the City as a contained, definable center of power and the city, a messy, heterogeneous, dynamic, and shifting urban space.

I was not alone in considering City and city dynamics. For example, Whitney, a city employee who has spent much of her professional life in city government after moving to Seattle from the East Coast, spoke to the tension between neighborhood and citywide pride as she discussed broader patterns of segregation throughout Seattle. She noted, "On the one hand, you want people to identify and invest in your neighborhood because it really takes people committing to their neighborhood to make it great, right? . . . But on the other hand, we really need people to identify with Seattle rather than little fiefdoms that are just a federation! [*Laughs*] We need to understand that we *are* a city, and so how do you do both?" Whitney's query about how to encourage a connection to and investment in the success and well-being of all residents in the entirety of Seattle *and* manifest ties to local neighborhoods reflects this dynamic between the city and City. The positioning of Seattle as a singular monolith managed by a municipal government emerged in people's exasperation with policies and practices undertaken by city departments. Interacting with city employees and spending time in the Seattle Municipal Archives, community meetings, and neighborhood spaces, however, demonstrated the heterogeneity, dynamism, unpredictability, and contestations that comprise Seattle. It is far from a uniform space or place. Blending awareness of the city and City discursive dichotomy with a geographic perspective and critical race literatures helps illuminate how assumptions about and articulations of place take root and circulate and how social values shape urban governance.

To illustrate this point, let's turn to an account from Amiko, a former community organizer and now a city employee in the arts department. Amiko explicitly invoked her personal biography as a born and raised Seattleite while responding to my question about examples of social justice work within city government. She commented,

> Every neighborhood has a certain personality, and from the time you're little, you know ... Ballard is the place where all the Norwegians are [*laughs*], the Central [Area] District is where it's primarily African American. ... Magnolia and Madison Park are the ritzy neighborhoods where wealthier people live. And if you live on Beacon Hill or Rainier Valley, it's where the poor people—I mean these are things that, they're stereotypes, but they are what every kid in Seattle growing up, just you know it. ... It just gets passed down through everything. And so coming into the city, and working here in the government level, you realize oh, well, the city actually kind of builds on that kind of already distinction between the different neighborhoods ... everything is based on kind of these geographic areas. ... The city government structure has built on the fact that the City of Seattle, just as a culture, has divvied up its geography into different sectors based on actual physical space.

Amiko's account of Seattle speaks to the persistence of dominant imaginative geographies about people and place because, for example, many African Americans have been gentrified out of the Central Area District, but it is still commonly known as the black neighborhood. As she acknowledges, these associations with places are longstanding and the imaginative geographies are routinely reproduced. Admitting that she has grown up with prominent narratives about neighborhoods requires Amiko to try to avoid replicating engrained place stereotypes in her professional city employee capacity and instead to open up space for alternative conceptualizations of neighborhoods. This is challenging given the structure of municipal government with its department designations and the delegation of employee focus areas by region of the city. Such practices can unintentionally reinscribe patterns of segregation that have a long reach in the city, as I discuss in chapter 1.

Amiko's comments also indicate how significant it is to recognize the personal biographies of decision makers within city and county government. It matters where people grew up, how and what they learned about the city, and what pathways led them to city or county government work. For instance, Anna, a relatively recent addition to city government, shared much of the idealism and enthusiasm that I witnessed in other city officials. She was also soft-spoken and judicious about her words. She seemed to take her role as a public servant very seriously, as she reserved a conference room for our interview so that we had an official place to meet and answered all my questions in a forthright manner. She was clear about what could be said in her official capacity as a city employee, going so far as to say, "Now I'm not speaking with my city hat on, but just as an individual," to remind us both of her multiple identities. When I asked her about expected defining features of Seattle in ten to twenty years, Anna paused, folded her hands on the conference room table, and replied,

> I think there really is an opportunity for Seattle to become known as one of the greener, greenest cities. When I think of sustainable, I think of not only the ecological part of sustainable, but also the sustainment of the community. From the level of the sustainment of a family to the sustainment of the neighborhood, of a community of a larger—you know, then not to be too hokey—but of the world. . . . I would hope in my most optimistic and hopeful times, that Seattle will really be known for being sustainable on a lot of different levels, on the environmental level, on the human level, on services, and on maintaining a diversity. . . . I think that's a real richness that can [*pause*] really improve and enhance the city by recognizing and bringing everybody to feel like there's a sense of ownership and investment in this city, and that the city is theirs. So they look at the city, and nobody feels like an outsider.

As she shared her vision for the future of Seattle, there seemed to be some weaving together of Anna's responsibilities as a city employee and her individual ideas. She affirmed the centrality of sustainability within Seattle by starting with a reference to being green. She quickly tacked to a broader understanding of sustainability than what I generally found within city government as she

talked through sustainability environmentally, socially, and economically. Anna hoped these would be the expressed values by
which Seattle becomes known in the next couple of decades. The
passage ended with her vision of shared belonging and inclusion
within Seattle, thereby hinting at a blend of social justice and
sustainability values. This is a compelling narrative of place and
demonstrates how social values thread through and shape plans
and aspirations for Seattle. Anna's comments also underscore why
I focus on sustainability, creativity, and social justice. These were
values repeatedly mentioned by city employees, in policies, and in
the popular press. They influence and contour the work done by
the individuals who constitute city government and enact urban
governance. As oft-mentioned values, they give purpose and meaning to the imaginative geographies of the City and city.

Why Seattle?

Seattle is frequently heralded by city boosters and external reviewers alike as a leader among urban areas. "First of its kind" enterprises, along with economic and social innovations, enhance this
status and add to the recognition that the city enjoys and elicits.
For instance, Seattle's public utility City Light used a variety of
practices, including conservation, carbon offsets, and renewable
energy, to lead the country as the first major electric company to
become and remain carbon neutral (Seattle Climate Protection
Initiative 2009, 2). On a related front, former mayor Greg Nickels
championed the U.S. Conference of Mayors' Climate Protection
Agreement in 2005, a nonbinding contract that committed mayors to reducing city carbon emissions to the Kyoto Protocol levels
(see appendix 2 for a list of recent Seattle mayors). By 2009 nearly
one thousand mayors and cities had pledged to lower emissions
accordingly (U.S. Conference of Mayors 2018). The Seattle Central
Public Library draws wide acclaim for its unusual design and its
symbolic representation of the high levels of literacy in the city.
Phrases such as "cutting edge" and "ambitious" often follow descriptions of these and other enterprises and activities within Seattle.
A pervasive sense that Seattle has been and remains a place that

takes risks and pushes the envelope also emerged in the archives and interviews, as I discuss in chapter 1. Thinking through how sustainability, creativity, and social justice assume tangibility in Seattle, therefore, sheds light on innovations and challenges evident in the enactment of social values in urban governance.

Many bodies of salt and fresh water, Mount Rainier to the south, the Olympic Mountains to the west, and the Cascade Mountains to the east surround the city and imbue it with stunning encounters with the biophysical world. These landscapes also contribute to perceptions of Seattle's uniqueness and advantages as a place (Karvonen 2011). To this point, as he reflected upon the special qualities of Seattle, Wes, who works in the non-profit sector promoting Seattle and its attributes, commented, "You can kayak by day, and see the opera by night, and you can attend a convention, go to sessions by day, but go night skiing. Not every other city affords that opportunity." These tourism draws and lifestyle amenities feed into imaginative geographies of Seattle as a place to be, making it an especially dynamic urban context for considering the infusion of social values within governance.

A common perception of Seattle as a site of liberal politics exists within and beyond the city limits. As evidence of this point research participants routinely mentioned how Seattle voters repeatedly pass levies for parks, public transportation, libraries, and housing. For example, Beth, who has worked in community organizing, non-profit and for-profit organizations, and city government during her three decades as a Seattleite, enumerated many of Seattle's assets in our conversation, including the physical geography, the neighborhoods, and the people. She then reflected that Seattle "elected a black mayor when it had such a small percentage of people of color. The city has voted for housing levies for so long, since the early eighties, willing to tax themselves to make sure that there's gonna be housing for folks." She took these points as indications of the progressiveness of the place. At the same time, she quickly noted that despite these seemingly liberal politics, the city "proclaims to be very progressive—sometimes I think it's not at all." Raquel, a county employee who previously worked in the affordable housing sector, concurred and stated, "you have people getting on board [with equity issues] because that's the politically correct thing to do. That's where the money is flowing, that's where the funding is. That's where the attention is being paid. Once it shifts, someone just shifts to the other political issue." Put differently, expressed commitment to bearing out social values within municipal and county government can be largely driven by political ambitions rather than substantive investments in particular values.

On the other hand, Sierra, a city employee who volunteered that she is "a person of color in this community, but I'm also a dyed in the wool Seattleite," stated, like many of her colleagues, that while some programs are "flavor of the day, or theme of the month or whatever," a portion of Seattle's municipal government work is "for real and has had impact, and it's very serious." Sierra's emphasis on the significant work happening in certain quadrants suggests that collective and sustained efforts are transforming urban governance. The contradictions between presumed political liberalness on the one hand and political ambitions on the other makes Seattle an especially fascinating site to examine how the social values of sustainability, creativity, and social justice—all of which could be incorporated into radical social transformation or more status quo liberal action—translate into material practices, policies, and processes. Focusing on these three social values within Seattle's urban governance offers an illuminating case study of contemporary urban practices within a place perceived to be in the vanguard of advancing a politically progressive agenda.

Several research participants attributed the perceived political progressiveness of Seattle to the educational attainment of many residents. For instance, Matt, an idealistic thirty-something who worked in a sustainability-focused organization, described the city this way: "Seattle is a really educated city. It's got the highest per capita of college graduates, Master's degrees and PhDs." He then acknowledged that Seattle is "a wealthy city. It's got a lot of money. So, having the politics supported and the financial resources to kind of make stuff happen, it's like Seattle's the perfect sort of laboratory." Matt was referring to Seattle as the perfect laboratory for building a model sustainable city because it has three crucial ingredients: the necessary politics to articulate such a sustainability goal; the educational degrees to help professionally translate the value into practice; and the money to bring goals to fruition. This connection between politics, education, and wealth is relevant to the enactment of the values of creativity and social justice as well. This urban context matters because the rapid wealth generation in Seattle makes some resources available for social change and exacerbates inequities. The program developments and policy proposals and plans that I examine underscore this very tension between aspiring to social transformation and deepening racialized and classed divides between residents.

As national politics become ever more contentious and divisive, local municipalities are wading more deeply into the enactment of social values in the name of progressive politics. Seattle is a ripe case study of such endeavors. For example, newly elected Mayor Jenny Durkan exclaimed in her State of the City address in February 2018, "To the lesser Washington, let me be clear: When the lives of people and the environment we cherish in Seattle are under attack, we will never, ever back down. . . . You won't win against the City of Seattle" (Derrick 2018, 17). Such powerful statements reveal the impulse to confront national politics and ideologies through local urban governance. While many efforts to amplify urban governance in these ways stem from divergences between local and national politics, the decentralization of state governance activities from the federal level to the regional and local ones through the expansion and recapitulation of neoliberalism is also a factor. Neoliberalism refers to the political-economic ideology, policy influence, and system of governance based on open, competitive, and unregulated economic markets (Larner 2000).[6] Within cities, the shift away from a managerialist approach to urban governance in the 1970s created space for the rise of urban entrepreneurialism, a particular manifestation of neoliberal policies and practices. As a result, a focus on public-private partnerships, expanded consumption landscapes and market competition and enhanced speculative transactions that grow capital accumulation accompany neoliberal practices within urban governance (Harvey 1989). The devolution through neoliberalism of the federal state's responsibilities, particularly in terms of social welfare, clearly contours conditions in Seattle. This context has also intersected with platforms and actions in Seattle that expressly contrast with federal policies.

In addition to the key insights afforded by Seattle's contemporary context, the city is also relatively young, and it offers different takes on urban development and evolution than older, more established places. City employee Sierra described various stages of urban development and the associated histories etched into city landscapes. She noted, "When I visit East Coast cities, ... it's like being [with] an elder ... I also see the scars and the worn [*pause*] the worn physique, the exhaustion, in some ways, and the frailty. I mean, I very much see that. But you cannot miss the wisdom and the teaching and the richness that wisdom, that age, brings. And that's what East Coast cities have, and that's what's attractive about those older cities. . . . Our potential? That sense of potential that we have? It's adolescence. That thinking that we know it all? [*Laughs*] That's adolescence!" Sierra outlines how the built environment conveys the layers of memories and events sustained in a place. She contrasts the depth of history in East Coast cities with the notional youthfulness of Seattle. Likening Seattle to a teenager marks a fascinating discursive move in which the city is represented as temperamental and boisterous, a singular entity with agency that is ready to march in the streets one day and sleep until noon the next. The described adolescence of Seattle underpins imaginative geographies of the city as an innovative and daring frontrunner. In a different vein, city employee Whitney also described the youthfulness of Seattle as she tied urban development to racism and race. She commented, "For the most part people get along across different cultures, not necessarily interact completely, but there's not some of the tension and anger and fear, or at least it's not so overt as it is in some of our bigger, older cities." Whitney then reflected upon the shorter time frame within which Seattle has contended with "race conflict" and noted that this history contributes to the specific forms of racism that thread through the city.

Frustrations about the purported teenage years of Seattle also emerged. For example, Xavier, who had worked for the city and was currently employed in non-profit sustainability work, compared Seattle to other U.S. cities on various sustainability benchmarks. With exasperated sighs, he expressed his impatience with how the city handled the World Trade Organization ministerial meetings and riots in 1999 (discussed in chapter 1). He chalked up the debacle to the developmental stage of the city, stating, "I think we're kind of in our adolescence as a big city." He then gloomily predicted, "We may never get out of that adolescence." Sierra, Whitney, and Xavier accented different attributes of adolescence in human development and mapped those qualities onto actions undertaken and ethos alive within Seattle's urban governance. These factors, matched with the purported prestige of Seattle and the imaginative geographies of progressive politics, illuminate why Seattle marked a productive case study for the examination of social values in urban governance.

Other books have focused on Seattle as well and chronicled, for instance, the environmental history, fluvial management, cultural representations, and indigeneity of the city (Lyons 2004; Klingle 2007; Thrush 2007; Karvonen 2011). *Imagining Seattle* contributes to this multi-disciplinary urban scholarship by drawing on qualitative methods, a geographic perspective, and understandings of racism, particularly whiteness, and classism to examine what happens when a city government strives—in clumsy and ineffective ways at times and in elegant and brilliant manners at others—to admit to and learn from the past to build a more equitable present and future. While I consider the impacts of race and class throughout my study, the arc of my analysis flows from an accent on class in my assessment of sustainability initiatives to attention to the racialized and classed effects of creativity endeavors to an emphasis on racism and race-based disparities in social justice work. This trajectory illuminates various examples of the translation of social values into practice from the greatest separation to the most closely aligned.

The realities of climate change, economic globalization, growing disparities between people, patterns of inequities, and widespread migration necessitate a thoughtful and considered appraisal of how social values assume material form in urban governance. As municipal governments increasingly articulate platforms on these issues, they constitute rich sites for investigation. Linking a dynamic urban setting like Seattle with a geographic perspective and attention to racialized and classed inequities makes this book an important addition to understandings of social change in Seattle in particular and urban governance more generally.

Situating Seattle

Seattle is the largest city in King County and the state of Washington (see map 3). It has a full-time mayor and a City Council of nine members, seven of whom represent electoral districts and two of whom represent the city at-large. The term length for the mayor and councilmembers is four years. According to the 2010 U.S. Census, Seattle had a total population of 608,660. The April 2017 population estimate for the city was 713,700 (Office of Financial Management 2018). Ten percent of the city's population was over sixty-five and 15 percent under the age of eighteen in 2010. This distribution remained through 2016 and shows that the majority of Seattle residents are of working age. These numbers are lower than national trends. Higher than nationally, 94 percent of Seattle residents over the age of twenty-five had earned a high school diploma (compared to 87 percent nationally), and 60 percent of this same group had received a bachelor's degree or higher by 2016, a number that is double the national count (U.S. Census Bureau 2018). The 2010 median household income in Seattle was $66,273 (Office of Economic Development 2018), compared to $49,445 nationally (U.S. Census Bureau 2011). In 2016 the median household income in the city was $74,458, compared to $55,322 nationally (U.S. Census Bureau 2018). The median home value in September 2010 was $379,000, and as of September 2018 the median home value had soared to nearly $739,600 (Zillow 2018a). The expectation is that these numbers will continue to increase.

In the 2010 Census 69.5 percent of Seattle residents self-identified as white, 13.8 percent as Asian, 7.9 percent as black or African American, 6.6 percent as Hispanic, 2.4 percent as some other race, 0.8 percent as American Indian or Alaska Native, and 0.4 percent as Native Hawaiian or Pacific Islander (the demographic distributions are about the same in 2016 data). The 5.1 percent of respondents who identified in 2010 as being two or more races was virtually the same percentage as the 2000 Census report for mixed-race individuals in the city (U.S. Census Bureau 2018). The percentage of people in Seattle who identify as black or African American or American Indian has decreased since 1990. The percentage of white people has also decreased, and the number of Asian and Pacific Islander people has grown. Still, overall, Seattle is a predominantly white city. Within this broader context, the racial demographics vary throughout the city. For instance, in 2010 in South Beacon Hill and New Holly, neighborhoods both in Southeast Seattle, half of the people identified as Asian, 28 percent as black or African American, and 13.1 percent as white. In contrast, Madison Park in Capitol Hill was nearly 92 percent white the same year (see map 1; City of Seattle 2011a).[7] The historic residential dividing line of the city has produced a racialized landscape wherein many people of color live south of downtown and many white people reside north of downtown. I discuss these dynamics further in chapter 1.

The hostility toward and exploitation of people of color throughout Seattle's history have made it a place that, accordingly to several interviewees, discourages many people of color from relocating to and staying in the city. Lance, who advocated for social change through business and helped facilitate more people of color entering the business sector in Seattle, observed, "If you are a person of color, black person, let's say African—you are probably not gonna move to Seattle." For Lance, there were not many reasons why people of color would move to Seattle given the demographics of the city and the histories of systemic and individual racism.

He did acknowledge, though, that "Seattle didn't have the racial experiences that Mississippi had or New York had or Pennsylvania had or Virginia had or Kansas had. You know what I mean? So even though, when I talk to guys—black guys, brown guys, Native American guys, and ladies—in Seattle, to them it was rough. To me, it was not . . . when I got here, I licked my lips. I'm saying, is this all you guys are dealing with? I mean, I love it here. . . . This is easy." While Lance understood why many people of color would not move to Seattle, he had personally found the city an easier place to reside as a person of color than other areas of the United States. The racial politics and exclusions were less of an imposition on his daily life.

Within the mix between Lance's perceived sense of relative ease in Seattle and his understanding of why people of color would not move to the city, Lance spontaneously posed and answered the following question, "Who are the people of color that stay here? Usually, upwardly mobile, middle-class people that speak big time Caucasian . . . and have relatively good rapport interracially." Lance's reference to speaking "big time Caucasian" signals how whiteness shapes social power, codes, and relations in Seattle. He points to the close ties between race and class in this comment and suggests patterns for who generally thrives in the city and who does not. Scholarship in black geographies helps unpack these comments from Lance because it critiques pervasive and oppressive racism and structures of racialization and highlights innovative forms of resistance and the "unique political practices and sense of place" (Bledsoe et al. 2017, 8) of black and brown communities. The spatiality of blackness and anti-blackness is a core consideration in this scholarship as well (McKittrick and Woods 2007; Ramírez 2015; Bledsoe et al. 2017). Lance outlines a prominent feature of whiteness, as a forum for anti-blackness, as delimiting possibilities for success in Seattle.

Structures of segregation and patterns of disenfranchisement, also indicators of whiteness, matter in other ways too. For example, some of the sustainability, creativity, and social justice policies and programs I analyze were intentionally citywide in scope (although the application of these interventions varied around the city); others were more geographically targeted in intended implementation. A primary place of focused attention for the municipal government is Southeast Seattle, which includes Rainier Valley (see map 1). The boundaries of Southeast Seattle are not universally agreed upon but generally extend east of Interstate 5 to Lake Washington and south of Interstate 90 to the city's southern boundary. Extensive infrastructure changes in the area, namely in the form of an at grade light rail line, and the possibilities and challenges of such development are notable preoccupations for many city officials.

Southeast Seattle is also the most racially and ethnically diverse part of the city. By way of example, in the far southern neighborhood of Rainier Beach, the racial breakdown in 2010 was about one third black and African American, one third Asian, and one quarter white. The remaining residents identified as some other and two or more races (City of Seattle 2011a). Many residents in Southeast Seattle are immigrants, and dozens of languages are spoken in the neighborhoods. For instance, one afternoon after walking through community centers, gardens, and neighborhoods in Rainier Valley, I stopped by a local restaurant. My field notes from this day reveal some prominent characteristics of the area: "I went to lunch in a Vietnamese restaurant right on Martin Luther King Jr. Way. It was small and packed. I was definitely the only white person and the only one who didn't speak Vietnamese. Very little English floated around the room" (October 2009). Southeast Seattle is also home to the largest share of low-income households within Seattle and has a high rate of poverty. In parts of this area unemployment rates reach 20 percent. About 80 percent of children attending public schools in Southeast Seattle qualify for free or reduced cost lunch. While the citywide average household size for owner-occupied and rental units hovers around two, in Southeast Seattle households are generally much bigger. Almost a third of the residents in Southeast are under the age of eighteen (South-East Effective Development 2018). This part of Seattle stands in marked contrast to other neighborhoods in North Seattle, for instance, where schools are more fully funded, unemployment rates are lower, and the majority of residents identify as white.

Underlying prominent imaginative geographies of Southeast Seattle are assumptions of crime and public safety issues. When I asked city employee Sal about these factors, she replied, "In Southeast there just seems to be this [*pause*] predominant sense of it's not a very safe place to live, work and play here, . . . yes, we do have crime issues just like everywhere else . . . but I don't know [*pause*] if that's the way that the Southeast should be known to the rest of the city." Similarly, Southeast Seattle resident and business owner Joanna states that prevailing imaginative geographies emphasize the violence, poverty, and employment instability of the area. Yet, with some exasperation and irony, she said, "This is a community. It's a neighborhood. People live here. It's not just like this dead valley." Joanna's pithy statement points to the racist and classist portrayals of the Valley in circulation and hints at how such assumptions can contribute to structural inequities, such as the differential allocation of financial resources throughout the city. Foregrounding a perspective of common humanity, Joanna continued, "Once you realize that people just live here, then it's just 'oh, okay.' They might be wearing their national garb or whatever, but that's just what they wear. They're not like thugs." Once again Joanna digs right into the dominant stereotypes of people and place that emerge within the media and conversations in the white-majority city of Seattle. The policy and program focus on Southeast Seattle and the prominent imaginative geographies of the area matched with the overall demographics of the city frame the translation of social values into practice in Seattle's urban governance.

Overview of the Book

In chapter 1, "Urban Ambitions and Anxieties: The Quest for World-Class Status," I examine historical events that set the stage for my contemporary analysis of social values in urban governance. I suggest that many past status-seeking endeavors and economic development efforts stem from a concern with noted ties between

Seattle and provincialism. I recount how the desire to distance the city from such affiliations—and strengthen links with global and world-class city titles instead—contributes to specific booster activities that inscribe inequities into the physical, social, and built environments. For instance, the clashes at the World Trade Organization (WTO) ministerial meetings in 1999 in Seattle punctured the appearance of a politically progressive city government and brought to light the extent to which people in positional authority sought to prove that Seattle embodied the qualities of a world-class city. The debacle that unfolded shattered this façade and created space for alternative narratives of the place to set roots and flourish. Recovering from the WTO via a public focus on the values of sustainability, creativity, and social justice has made for positive press and some striking examples of social values in urban governance. Simultaneously, given historical patterns in the city, current endeavors launched in the name of social values have also contributed to racialized and classed inequities.

Chapter 2, "Exclusive Inclusion: Choosing Sustainability and Being Green," analyzes the movement from the lofty value of sustainability to actual policies to underscore how marginalization can emerge alongside "green" urban interventions. Using the frame of exclusive inclusion, I argue that sustainability policies and programs in Seattle pivot on assumptions of choice, a presumption steeped in latent class privilege that impinges upon the widespread applicability of programs and policies. I analyze such patterns in two examples that were prominent focal points during my fieldwork, the Way to Go transportation initiative and the Green Fee debate. After identifying the ways in which inequities emerge in tandem with these sustainability practices, I conclude the chapter by discussing some of the recent equity-focused work in the Office of Sustainability & Environment

I shift my attention to expressions of the frequently mentioned concept of creativity in chapter 3, "People, Products, and Processes: Creativity as Economic Development." Here I examine the differences in economic development policy proposals and prescriptions when creativity is mobilized as an attribute linked to specific people, products, or processes. A cultural district designation, a retail revitalization proposal, and an equitable transit-oriented development plan frame this analysis of the translation of creativity as a social value into practice. These examples show that using creativity to guide processes provides a higher likelihood for equity as an outcome. Drawing on creativity as linked to people and products, on the other hand, often contributes to the commodification of certain bodies within urban space and can unwittingly augment patterns of gentrification and displacement.

Investigating the conceptualization, development, and implementation of the Race and Social Justice Initiative constitutes chapter 4, "Unsettling Whiteness: The Race and Social Justice Initiative and Institutional Change." As a government-wide commitment to eliminating institutional racism and confronting race-based disparities, the RSJI demonstrates how the distillation of the value and ideal of social justice assumes tangible and varied forms. I suggest that a key part of what makes the RSJI transformative and able to produce equity—more so than the sustainability and creativity work—is the persistent unsettling of whiteness. Recognizing that Seattle is a majority-white city built on deeply racist practices (as I discuss in chapter 1), the RSJI interrupts patterns of whiteness and confronts racialized hierarchies of power. These strategies are crucial, I argue, to the transformative possibilities and processes of the RSJI.

The conclusion, "The City Lives in Us," reflects upon the challenges of social transformation through urban governance as I summarize how the city government both espouses and works toward politically progressive goals of social change and further entrenches racialized and classed inequities within Seattle. This is not an uncommon situation for individuals or institutions. Accordingly, I outline some key reasons for the institutional movement toward greater justice exacted through the RSJI as compared to the wider gulf between value and practice in the sustainability and creativity examples. I also affirm the critical insights generated through close analytical attention to racism and classism, a geographic perspective, and narratives to amplify the key findings and contributions of this book. I draw out the ties between this case study of Seattle and broader macrostructural considerations as well. Finally, I review a variety of frameworks from systems thinking to the Great Turning that inspire actions and suggest possible pathways toward substantive social change. Inasmuch as inequities persist, institutions do evolve, and possibility and motivation are embedded within the acknowledgment that the city resides within and is constituted by "us."

Seattle, as "The City of," is important to analyze because popular imaginative geographies suggest it is a city that believes in and manifests social transformation. A common assumption may be that progressive social values inherently produce more equitable policies and programs. My research demonstrates, however, that just because a policy proposal focuses on sustainability or creativity, for example, does not mean that it will avoid contributing to disparities. Any faltering between value and practice is not due only to neoliberalism and its extensive reach. Similarly, the distance between value and practice is not necessarily due to people lacking aspirations for change. Instead, as my analysis underscores, the architecture of policies and programs often undermines stated goals and enables latent classism and white privilege to truncate opportunities for social transformation. Drawing attention to such processes and outcomes, I hope, will encourage shifts in urban governance and will enable greater sustainability, creativity, and social justice in theory and in practice in Seattle and beyond.

1

Urban Ambitions and Anxieties

The Quest for World-Class Status

The sixty-two-story Seattle Municipal Tower (SMT), home to the majority of city government offices, is a striking edifice in the physical landscape (see map 2). A commanding structure of steel and glass, the SMT symbolizes the centrality of municipal government in the urban context. Gazing at the looming tower from nearby or afar conjures up images of weighty decisions being made in this monolith. While I initially felt intimidated by the SMT, I quickly became a recognizable figure there and in City Hall. Entrance guards at both buildings would acknowledge me knowingly and comment, "You here again?" The visitor sign-in sheets at a few city departments indicated that I was often the most frequent and sometimes the only visitor during 2009. Encounters within the SMT moderated the grandness of the physical form and emphasized human dimensions. For instance, after passing the overstuffed couches and perfectly placed potted plants in the main entryway, I routinely witnessed city employees and constituents meeting in coffee shops scattered throughout the complex, chatting in the elevators, gathering in hallways, and populating the conference rooms. These points of contact endowed the SMT with an air of accessibility. Dialogues, debates, and discussions were commonplace and represented a key pulse and purpose of Seattle's urban governance.

By way of example, people filled every seat and then some at the Starbucks coffee shop in the lobby of the SMT one afternoon in June 2009. Roger, a city employee focused on urban planning and design, and I had emailed about our movie star look-alikes (mine is Julianne Moore). With this info, we easily located each other amid the crowd, much to our mutual surprise. As no seats were available, we ended up propped up against the floor to ceiling windows just steps away from the long line of people awaiting their cappuccinos, chai lattes, and macchiatos. Roger only had thirty minutes to talk so time was of the essence. During the interview he candidly reflected upon the innumerable challenges facing Seattle as the city strives to bear out its commitment to social values. His comments blended pragmatism and optimism. Roger enthusiastically noted, for instance, how translating all city documents into many languages enabled a broader array of Seattleites to engage with the municipal government. At the same time he expressed concern about the financial impacts of such practices and mused about the seeming economic impossibility of doing such extensive translation over the long term. Near the end of the interview when I asked how he described Seattle to others not in the city, he looked out the window at the buses, trucks, and cars rumbling down the street and the pedestrians enjoying the wayfaring signs and public art and then said:

> Seattle has, traditionally, and I think even more today, had a two-sided image. One is this extraordinarily diverse, extraordinarily world-focus connection . . . because of our place on the Pacific Rim a connection to Asia, a connection to Europe because of our settlement patterns . . . very much a world city, a cosmopolitan place and likes to see itself as such. A technological leader, both in airplane manufacturing and software manufacturing, and companies like Amazon and Starbucks. Really this world connection.
>
> And then on this other side, we still want to see ourselves as a comfortable, small-scale, return to your quiet neighborhood, leafy green, simple town without pretension. And I think we grapple with that two-sided nature all the time: what are we and what are our aspirations? I think Vancouver BC has very much modeled itself into that cosmopolitan place. I think Portland to the south has modeled itself on a small scale, comfortable city without the kind of global aspirations. And I think we're torn a little bit between those two.

The dual pulls toward recognition as a global city and comfort with the neighborhood feel of Seattle have a long history, as I show in this chapter, and consequently shape contemporary urban governance and the enactment of social values. For instance, a desire to be viewed as a global city can distort holistic implementation of sustainability practices, as examined in chapter 2, and the craze about the creative class can undermine efforts to produce economic stability for local artists, as demonstrated in chapter 3. Other times, actualizing values in response to the Seattle context, such as the RSJI's work on social justice discussed in chapter 4, can begin the process of repairing from legacies of injustice and building structures for a more equitable present and future. Such social justice actions have positioned Seattle as a leader, so that in this case, focusing on neighborhoods, residents, and daily life in the city has produced widespread recognition.

Still, this question of image and place essence is one that has nagged city bureaucrats and boosters, the people who promote a place, for decades. For example, a 1965 report titled *Designing a Great City* included a quote from architect and urban planner Charles Blessing. Blessing described how a city "is a center of commerce, industry, government and culture" (as quoted in Urban Design Advisory Board 1965, 1) and then offered: "The truly great cities—the *definable* cities—also have an 'image.' What is the 'image' of Seattle?" (Urban Design Advisory Board 1965, 1, emphasis in the original). While city officials have struggled to answer this question definitively over the last century and a half, as Roger's comments about the "two-sided image" suggest, in this chapter I demonstrate that there has been a consistent focus on trying to secure Seattle's place in the pantheon of global cities and a concurrent effort made to distance ties between Seattle and provincialism. In this case provincialism refers to a narrow focus on local happenings at the expense of engagement with broader cultural, political, and intellectual activities. The anxiety about Seattle being labeled as provincial has power because, as geographer Tim Cresswell writes, "Place suggests simultaneously a geographical location and a position on a social hierarchy" (2014, 250). In other words, if Seattle is provincial, too focused on the small-town ambiance of city neighborhoods, and ignorant of wider trends, then it will lose its assumed status in the hierarchy of reputable and powerful cities. The concern about provincialism, therefore, has compelled material and discursive investment in the stated global relevance of Seattle. Indeed, city employees and boosters alike have repeatedly contributed to the imaginative geographies of Seattle as cosmopolitan, globally connected, economically robust, and eminently modern. Such representations gloss over poverty and inequities, as these facets of Seattle do not advance a powerful world-class characterization, although stark disparities are present in all contemporary world cities. The juxtapositions and contingencies of the city have been persistently swept aside to assert Seattle's world-class qualities.

The purpose of this chapter is to provide historical context for the next three chapters on social values. Current governance practices clearly have legacies, and I offer this selective urban history to highlight how past race relations, urban spectacles, and economic development efforts set the stage for current engagements with social values. I follow the urban ambitions for world-class city status and the concomitant anxieties about provincialism through these themes to emphasize how imaginative geographies of Seattle and the naturalization of racialized and classed disparities have cohered over time. I focus on events, practices, and policies both unique to Seattle and reflective of broader patterns within the United States to shed light on some prominent urban trends. With these themes in mind, I move through the Eurocentric founding of Seattle in 1851 to examples from the turn of the twenty-first century to demonstrate how the forces of world-class ambitions and anxieties of provincialism shape the city and the City.

Whitening the City

The most commonly circulated origin story for Seattle focuses on the 1851 landing of twenty-four white settlers, mostly from the U.S. Midwest, on Alki Point in what is now West Seattle (Lyons 2004; Thrush 2007). Yet as historian Coll Thrush (2007, 20–22) notes, indigenous peoples had already been settled in the Seattle area for hundreds of years. Moreover, white people, propelled by desires of conquest and empire, had previously visited the area, by some accounts as early as 1792. British captain George Vancouver and U.S. captain Robert Gray are two well-known figures in the early explorations of Washington and what later became known as Seattle. Still, 1851 marks the Eurocentric founding date in many official narratives of Seattle's origin (Sale 1976). The city's name purportedly honors Seeathl, the Suquamish and Duwamish chief linked to the famous "Chief Seattle" speech, and the 1850s treaty negotiations between Territorial Governor Isaac Stevens and the Duwamish and Suquamish tribes. The name Seattle therefore tacitly acknowledges the building of the city on indigenous lands (Crowley 2003; Thrush 2007, 5).

Urban development on indigenous lands reflects a pattern that historian Carl Abbott has chronicled throughout western U.S. cities. Abbott suggests that from the 1840s to the 1880s western cities focused on establishing urban infrastructure on newly occupied lands in order to show power and control (as cited in Barraclough 2011, 6). Within the Seattle context, in an effort to create what politicians called "the white man's country" (as quoted in Taylor 1994, 23), the 1850s treaties with indigenous peoples in the Puget Sound region explicitly focused on removing indigenous people from ancestral lands, creating reservations near blossoming industries (since many relied upon the labor of indigenous people), and lumping together into named tribes various groups of people who did not necessarily view themselves as collectives (Klingle 2007, 35–36). These actions of settler colonialism helped promote imagery of Seattle as a modern city since indigenous peoples were framed as antiquated and tied to the environment, while clearing the land and asserting territorial control exemplified innovation and progress (Klingle 2007; Thrush 2007). Such actions helped stave off associations between Seattle and provincialism. At the same time, expulsion from traditional lands and resettlement to reservations prompted warfare between whites and indigenous peoples in 1855 and 1856 and ongoing resistance since then in the form of nonviolent protests to raise awareness about discrimination and racialized disparities in education, health, employment, and housing (Klingle 2007, 36–37). Working against the tides that seek to invisibilize and principally commodify indigenous peoples in Seattle is another forum of continued struggle.

Reflecting mentalities common in settler colonialism, early city employees and boosters alike described the presence of indigenous peoples in Seattle as an indication of social ills and urban disorder. They vocally positioned indigenous peoples as violators of the desired racially pure city space and as aberrations to the urban landscape. As a result, in 1866, Seattle passed ordinances that formally restricted the living spaces of indigenous peoples and increased disparities between racial groups (Thrush 2007, 39). Previously, the Color Act of 1855 voided existing marriages between white and indigenous people in Washington State, and the Marriage Act of 1866 denied legitimacy to common-law white-indigenous relations. Such prohibitions, alongside residential restrictions, effectively helped produce and sustain a segregated and whitening Seattle deeply shaped by racism.

Paralleling these discriminatory practices exacted upon indigenous communities, in 1886 local mobs chased Chinese individuals, primarily former laborers on the railroads, out of town and forced them onto boats departing from Seattle (Nelson 1977, 147–48). This action followed the 1882 passage at the federal level of the Chinese Exclusion Act, which prohibited Chinese laborers from entering the United States and declared Chinese immigrants ineligible for naturalized citizenship (Ueda 1994, 169). In 1907 the federal government passed the Gentlemen's Agreement with the Japanese government, thereby initiating a policy that shrank the emigration of Japanese laborers to the United States (Ueda 1994, 169). The tides turned further against Japanese residents in Seattle in a profound manner with the advent of World War II and the internment in 1942 of nearly 6,000 individuals from Seattle and over 110,000 Japanese individuals from the U.S. West Coast. Although some Japanese residents eventually migrated back to Seattle after the war, the community stayed relatively small until the late 1900s. The removal of the Japanese community facilitated the expansion of urban development to lands on the fringes of Seattle that had previously been used by Japanese families for agricultural purposes (Sanders 2010). This shift in land use marked broader transformations in the built environment of the city and made visible prominent assumptions about who belonged in Seattle and who had rights to property and economic enterprises. Given these actions, historian John Findlay (1997, 46) sums up race relations in the region accordingly: "Whites in the Pacific Northwest have discouraged African-Americans from coming; coerced Indians onto reservations and away from economic opportunities; lobbied the federal government to restrict or halt Asian-American immigration; pressured Chinese immigrants to leave, sometimes violently; prevented Japanese immigrants from owning land; and supported both the internment of people of Japanese descent during World War Two and their continued exile from the region after the war."

Alongside the colonization of the area that became Seattle, in the name of modernization, economic possibility, and city recognition, "city workers erased Seattle's mounts to make new real estate, remove unwanted residents, and cleanse neighborhoods" (Klingle 2006, 199) in the wake of the 1889 fire that destroyed much of the downtown business district. Physically altering the landscape revealed the power of humans to dominate and exploit nature (Karvonen 2011). The flattening of the hills, the filling of the swamps to make the harbor, the damming of rivers, and the displacement of lower-income and black, indigenous, and Asian communities characterized the late 1800s through the early 1900s and demonstrated the investment in gaining recognition as a noteworthy city (Klingle 2006; Thrush 2007; Karvonen 2010; 2011). On this point, alongside the extensive transformations in the biophysical environment for economic enterprises arose the desire for parks and sites of leisure. Accordingly, the Olmsted Brothers were hired to create master plans for Seattle's parks in 1903 and 1908 as part of the national "City Beautiful" movement (HistoryLink and Friends of Olmsted Parks 2004; Friends 2009; Mitchell et al. 2011). John Charles Olmsted and assistant Percy Jones created the proposed "emerald necklace" of parks and green spaces—only partially realized then and today—which called for the inclusion of green and open spaces and purposely interwove settled and natural areas within the city. The Olmsted Brothers worked for the city of Seattle until 1941 and designed many of the parks and green spaces throughout the city (Williams 1999). Two primary rationales emerged for the parks: (1) enriching the aesthetics of the city and cultivating spaces for quiet contemplation; and (2) providing opportunities for invigorating public health with designated recreational areas.

To these points a 1902 article in the *Seattle Post-Intelligencer* explained, "Physicians say that the peculiarly local malady is the various forms of dyspepsia.[1] And they attribute its cause to the influence of the climate, accentuated by the lack of exercise. It therefore behooves every man, who knows that he has a liver, to get out in the open and do something" (*Seattle Post-Intelligencer* 1902). In other words, parks were necessary for health and well-being in the modernizing city. The inclusion of substantive parks within Seattle was not totally seamless, however. Indeed, the codification of green spaces subsequently raised the question of who could legitimately occupy such places. Were these outdoor spaces for wealthy people to engage in healthy leisure pursuits (as described in the *Seattle Post-Intelligencer*) or shared spaces where squatters could spend time (Klingle 2006; 2007)? This was a contentious debate replete with class and race overlays. Divergent opinions notwithstanding, at the forefront of city boosters' minds was the important point that the parks plan developed by the famous Olmsted Brothers connected Seattle's transformed biophysical landscape with renowned places, such as New York's Central Park, and consequently elevated the image of the city. Partly "tamed" and partly "wild," parks provided a key site for leisure pursuits, a use of the land that purportedly emphasized Seattle's economic modernity.

Spectacles and Structural Disparities

John Charles Olmsted designed the fairgrounds for the Alaska-Yukon-Pacific Exposition (AYP) at the University of Washington campus as well. After the discovery of gold in Alaska, Seattle city boosters and local industry elites conceived of and executed the AYP from June to October 1909 to showcase Seattle as a global gateway city (Sparke 2011). To position Seattle publicly as a city of repute and a leader on the West Coast, exposition organizers chose to emphasize the international nature of the exposition (and by extension Seattle itself) and the geographic placement of Seattle as a portal to U.S.-Asian commerce and trade. The exposition emblem featured three women, one Asian and two white (representing Alaska and America), holding a steamship, brick of gold, and locomotive and looking toward one another in presumed expressions of friendship (Lee 2007). This seal sought to depict visually the ties between Seattle and the economic activities of Alaska and Asia, particularly Japan. The discursive linking of the "Occident" and the "Orient" was an important theme for the AYP. Such bonds, alongside invited exhibits from around the world, aimed to separate Seattle from provincial associations. Part of this explicit focus on relationships between Seattle and Asia was also an affirmation and assertion of white racial superiority. For example, a reconstructed Bontoc Igorrote Village, populated by Igorrote people from the northern Philippines, deepened the ties between Seattle and Pacific Rim nations within imaginative geographies and furthered assumptions that Seattleites were civilized and the Igorrote indigenous people were primitive with their loin cloths and purported eating of dogs (Duncan 2009; Huberman 2009).[2] A Chinese Village, with spectacles like rickshaw rides, furthered Orientalist stereotypes (Lee 2007).

As Washington's first World's Fair, the AYP saw originality, risk taking, and largesse claiming center stage. Huge trees were felled just to show the size of their trunks. Figures such as a life-size elephant made out of pecans reminded visitors of the region's agricultural bounty. An Alaska exhibit with gold nuggets and bricks rumored to be worth one million dollars made visible the spoils of the gold rush and linked Seattle with this economic possibility. Pleasure boats built just for the event provided riders with views of Mount Rainier. New buildings constructed on the University of Washington campus (many of which were torn down immediately after the fair) sought to represent an erudite and learned populace, while a Model T race from New York to Seattle symbolically linked eastern and western areas of commerce and signaled technological prowess. Live premature babies were housed in incubators and set up for preview to demonstrate scientific progress. The national American Suffrage Association convened its forty-first convention at the fair and raised awareness about women's rights. Each day of the fair had a special theme, such as fish day, octogenarians' day, Japan day, and free entrance if your last name was Smith day. Nearly four million people traveled to Seattle to participate in the AYP spectacle during its run (Duncan 2009; Huberman 2009; Zajac 2009). Alongside the drive for global recognition, much of the grandiosity of the exposition was compelled by urban competitiveness and the desire to elevate Seattle's status compared to San Francisco, California, and Portland, Oregon (Lee 2007). This was a tremendous place-branding endeavor and represented a significant achievement in 1909. How could anyone depict the city as provincial after such a phenomenal event?

Despite such efforts, according to journalist Lancaster Pollard, Seattle was still described as "the most provincial city of its size in the United States" by the mid-1930s (Pollard, as quoted by Lee 2007, 277). In an attempt to challenge this association one more time, in 1936 a group of city boosters began a promotion campaign based on discourses of cosmopolitanism. The series "Cosmopolitan Seattle" in the *Town Crier*, a local paper, sought to shed the frontier image that had become linked with Seattle during the gold rush and to elevate the city's status by amplifying the trade connections with Asia once again. New to the booster repertoire, the series also endeavored to reveal Seattle's cosmopolitan nature by portraying the racial and ethnic heterogeneity of the city. The Cosmopolitan Seattle articles profiled different communities, extolled the greatness of the AYP, and invigorated commitment to the revival of the International Potlatch festivals. These summer festivals, initially held from 1911 to 1913, ran again from 1934 to 1942 in an effort to bump up tourism in the wake of the Great Depression and to confirm the internationalism of Seattle. The festival included sporting tournaments (often with different indigenous communities competing against each other as a key spectacle for the predominantly white crowd), a powwow, a parade, fireworks, and the crowning of the Potlatch queen. Purportedly inspired by the Potlatch tradition of different indigenous peoples, the Potlatch festivals drew upon indigenous iconography and symbols while adding the layer of trans-Pacific relations to declare publicly the cosmopolitan image of Seattle (Lee 2007, 277, 296–97).

Appropriating traditions is a common strategy of domination, and these festivals, largely organized by the white elite, followed this practice. As historian Shelley Lee (2007, 301) elucidates, the Cosmopolitan Seattle campaign and the International Potlatch festivals said more about the aspiration for recognition and status as an internationalized City of acclaim than they did about everyday realities in the city. Specifically, these events further accumulated status and privilege to the white elites who stood to gain financially from any additional prominence Seattle gleaned through the branding campaign and festivals. Moreover, the International Potlatch festivals and Cosmopolitan Seattle series showed the great lengths to which city boosters went to counter stated ties between Seattle and provincialism. In this work of skirting provincialism, the racial and ethnic diversity of the city emerged as a public asset and part of the appeal of the city, as long as it did not disturb the overarching privilege and power of the dominant group.

Behind the boosterism of the Cosmopolitan Seattle campaign lay structural and interpersonal disparities that countered the public celebration of a multiracial city. Indeed, during the first half of the twentieth century, racial covenants—restrictive agreements that limited who could own, rent, or generally occupy property in certain neighborhoods—truncated living options so that most people of color in Seattle concentrated in the Central Area District and International District (ID) east of downtown (see map 1, center right). Examples of such covenants include this one used in the North Seattle neighborhood of Ballard in 1929: "No part of said property hereby conveyed shall ever be used or occupied by any Hebrew or by any person of the Ethiopian, Malay or any Asiatic Race" (Seattle Civil Rights and Labor History Project 2018). Another covenant from the North Seattle neighborhood of Queen Anne, also from 1929, stated, "No person or persons of Asiatic, African or Negro blood, lineage, or extraction shall be permitted to occupy a portion of said property, or any building thereon; except domestic servants may actually and in good faith be employed by white occupants of such premises" (Seattle Civil Rights and Labor History Project 2018). Seattle was not alone in its use of racial covenants to solidify residential segregation as towns and cities around the United States applied these restrictions.

Starting in 1933 the Home Owners' Loan Corporation (HOLC), a product of the New Deal, created color-coded maps of U.S. cities that categorized lending and insurance risks according to racial criteria, thereby compounding existing segregation. Affluent and white areas received green color coding to show they were the "best." Next came the blue areas, which were "still desirable." In contrast, black, brown, and poor white neighborhoods were colored as yellow, to mark them as "definitely declining," or red, to mark them as "hazardous." This practice of coding, which became known as redlining due to the color designations, entrenched segregation in urban spaces throughout the United States. In particular the Federal Housing Administration, created in 1934, used the HOLC's methods to assess locations for federally insured new housing construction. Furthermore, banks and insurers adopted the HOLC's maps to guide lending and underwriting decisions, and real estate agents used the maps to decide what properties to show clients. Explicitly tying together mortgage eligibility and race meant that 98 percent of federally backed home loans between 1932 and 1962 went to white homebuyers (Lipsitz 2006, 107). Racializing neighborhoods and consolidating wealth through home ownership for white people produced urban economic expansion, which often got parlayed into the perceived economic robustness of a city. Therefore alongside the Cosmopolitan Seattle campaign, the city practiced redlining and allowed for racial covenants. Clearly, social equity was not considered in the ambitions for or evaluation metrics of world-class status.

Even though the U.S. Supreme Court ruled in 1948 against the use of racial restrictive covenants, strategies of exclusion, such as redlining, persisted for several more decades and further installed neighborhood-level concentrations of communities of color in Seattle (Silva 2009). The federal Fair Housing Act in 1968 outlawed redlining and eventually forced the city to change, at least legally, its housing strategies. Still, Seattle residents in the 1960s enforced racial restrictions that were written into property deeds throughout the city, such as the aforementioned covenants, and used tactics of intimidation to maintain segregation (Taylor 1994). The persistent employment discrimination also meant that many members of the black community were confined by economics to predominantly black neighborhoods, such as the Central Area District (Taylor 1994). Finally, in 2006 Washington State passed legislation to assist in the elimination of racial restrictions in property deeds (Seattle Civil Rights and Labor History Project 2018).

The use of redlining and racial covenants in specific Seattle neighborhoods embedded spatial patterns of segregation that are still evident. By way of example, Rick, a self-identified global citizen and active member of his Christian church, explained that in the 1990s when he used to ride bus number 7 north from his home in Southeast Seattle, "right in the middle of downtown Seattle, all the people of color would get off, and the white people started getting on as they went to the university. It was always just amazing to me." Rick's account of changing demographics on his bus route to work illustrates one of the many implications of persistent racialized separation. Jill, a more recent resident of Southeast Seattle than Rick and a self-identified white, Jewish idealist, also reflected upon segregation in Seattle. She locates the current segregation as partly stemming from "the heritage. We definitely have a Scandinavian heritage, and there's a lot of that kind of provincialism that created the culture." In her view, provincial mentalities exhibited by early white settlers cohered a focus on whiteness and structural racism within the city. Urban spectacles have repeatedly emerged as key sites for challenging such associations with provincialism and working toward recognition as a world-class city.

The hosting of the Century 21 Exposition, commonly known as the World's Fair, in 1962 demonstrated once again the push for global city status. The months of fair activities brought more than 10 million visitors to Seattle and, much like the AYP, showcased the innovative and daring nature of the city (in a relative sense because, as a point of comparison, the New York World's Fair in 1964 and 1965 ran for a longer period of time over two years and hosted more than 51 million visitors). The global prestige of Seattle, measured by the contributions to the fair from over thirty-five other countries, was on display, and the space age and science focus elicited exhibits about computers and the development of Boeing's Spacearium, a new space motion picture system that enabled visitors to view the stars on a massive hemispheric screen. As part of the space race, the U.S. government committed over $9 million to construct the NASA-inspired United States Science Exhibit (which was later recast as the Pacific Science Center). The Alweg monorail served the practical purpose of transporting fair attendees from downtown Seattle to the exposition site and made visible the futuristic "World of Tomorrow" focus.

Perhaps the most important enduring part of the 1962 Worlds' Fair iconography is the Space Needle, a defining feature of Seattle's skyline silhouette. The Space Needle added material height to the city's global ideals and prominently translated the foci of progress, ingenuity, and science into the built environment (Sparke 2011). Significantly, the Space Needle endowed Seattle with distinction and raised the bar, literally, on the city's competition with Portland and Vancouver for global status (Morrill et al. 2011, 4). Not only is the Needle futuristic in form; it also provides a commanding view of the region. The act of surveying and admiring the view from the Needle affirmed the power of human domination over nature while concurrently showcasing the natural beauty of the place. The 1962 fair helped Seattle shed some of the associations with provincialism and align the place more closely with the coveted status of world-class city within imaginative geographies.

The fair additionally provided a proving ground for ideas about urban renewal, which became a core focus of U.S. cities in the 1960s and 1970s. The status of Seattle as a global city became embedded within ensuing debates about how to manage changes in the urban core precipitated, in large part, by suburbanization and shifts in the global economy. The fair tested plans that urban renewal enthusiasts envisioned for Seattle's downtown, notably "efficient monorail transportation, soaring singular modern architecture, and a perfect mix of private and federal funding for development" (Sanders 2010, 18). While a group of business elites and developers sought to capitalize on the successes reaped by the fair and to overlay such development schemas on the downtown core of Seattle, grassroots groups organized to offer a different perspective on what kind of urban environment mattered the most. Underpinning these conflicting views about how to address urban challenges were questions about the kind of city Seattle wanted to be: a global city of consequence or a small city with local charm. Roger reflected on this internal struggle when we spoke nearly fifty years after the World's Fair. In the 1960s and 1970s, though, developers and business elites in Seattle proposed a significant redevelopment of the downtown core to craft an economically prosperous city of global reach. The demolition and redevelopment of the existing Pike Place Market was a fundamental step in this plan. Proposed high-end condos would flank the renovated Pike Place Market. The breath-taking views of Puget Sound and the Olympic Mountains from the market would be leveraged into a built environment funded by federal money allocated for the elimination of urban blight. Private enterprises sought to derive large returns from these vistas through this proposed public-private downtown redevelopment plan.

In contrast, grassroots groups spoke of the value of preserving vernacular architecture, the assorted enterprises of the Pike Place Market, and the grittiness of the area (Sanders 2010). The activists noted that although economically described as poor, the communities in the downtown area were socially and culturally rich. The debates about redeveloping Pike Place Market bore out the tensions between the City and the city. Advocacy for the vernacular architecture and dynamic affect of the market as indicative of the heterogeneity of the city did not match with the sought-after image of Seattle as a globally relevant city. Ultimately, the push for historic preservation won out, and the subsequent renovations of the downtown area did not include the demolition of the Pike Place Market or the immediate construction of luxury condos (such housing stock joined the downtown more recently). In this period of urban history, Seattle as a place amassed status through the sights and smells of the quotidian as epitomized by interactions in the Pike Place Market. The emphasis on the vernacular architecture and neighborhood aesthetic of the market has become firmly integrated into prominent imaginative geographies of Seattle. Promotional materials of Seattle frequently showcase the market, and a stop to watch the vendors throw fish is virtually mandatory for visitors. The initial calls for respecting the heterogeneity of the city have become folded into the iconography of the City.

By the 1990s, after a period of intense economic decline, the desire for commercial advantage and renewed recognition as a noteworthy city surged to the foreground in Seattle once again.[3] Whereas past status-seeking efforts focused on innovation, cosmopolitanism, futuristic developments, and funky, authentic neighborhoods, in the 1990s the call was for renewed credit as a global urban leader. Longstanding city employee Sebastian was not a fan of this period of urban history. He recounted, "I hated the mid-to-late '90s in Seattle because what we kept hearing over and over again was, 'We need to be a world-class city.' There was this big chip on its shoulder from our leadership. 'We need to be a world-class city, world-class city.'" One of the primary outcomes of this drive for world-class status was the fraught decision to host the 1999 World Trade Organization (WTO) ministerial meetings. Sebastian continued, "The leadership definitely brought the WTO here as, 'We are the world-class city.' It was kind of like the World's Fair. 'Come here. We are *the* city of the future.'" The business elites and city government believed forecasts that hosting an international trade meeting of such consequence would finally assure Seattle's status as a global city rather than a provincial one. To this point, geographers Katharyne Mitchell and colleagues (2011, 182) state, "Seattle aspired to become the Geneva of the West—a small but world-class city hosting high-level meetings with significant outcomes."

Yet the WTO ministerial meetings did not unfold as city officials and business leaders intended. On the contrary, from November 29 to December 5, 1999, Seattle commanded international attention as members of the Seattle Police Department (SPD) clashed with anti-globalization protesters opposing the WTO meetings. The confrontations between the SPD and the estimated 40,000 to 60,000 protesters resulted in the use of tear gas and rubber bullets, widespread arrests, vandalism, imposed curfews and no protest zones, the calling in of the National Guard, and the declaration of a state of emergency for the city (Wainwright et al. 2000; Herbert 2007; WTO History Project 2018). The "Battle of Seattle," as the sets of confrontations were called, helped spark the vibrant anti-globalization movement because after the events in Seattle, the political and social agendas underlying free trade and globalization were laid bare (Wainwright et al. 2000, 2). It became evident, in other words, that neoliberalism was a chosen path, not an inevitable one. The days of clashes ultimately left Seattle as an embarrassed example of how not to respond to and manage thousands of protesters filling city streets (Compton et al. 2000). In the aftermath of the WTO, previous perceptions of Seattle as potentially world-class crumbled under the weight of martial law and violent restrictions on free speech.

While the conflicts between the SPD and the protesters produced significant press coverage, these encounters also rattled the imaginative geographies of Seattle. In particular, the confrontations raised questions about the city's ability to maintain and protect free speech and the right of assembly. The clashes tarnished the city's reputation, produced a host of lawsuits, and resulted in significant financial burdens through property damage and the loss of consumer business (Compton et al. 2000, 3). Many panels and review boards carefully assessed why and how such a debacle unfolded in Seattle (Burgess et al. 2000; Citizens' Panel 2000; Compton et al. 2000; Kelsey et al. 2000; McCarthy and Associates 2000; Seattle Police Department 2000; World Trade Organization Accountability Review Committee 2000). The planning and organization of the meeting along with weak oversight and leadership emerged as primary areas of critique. A citizen panel found a lack of careful attention to possible financial costs as well, which ultimately left the city government footing a bill of over $9 million (Compton et al. 2000, 3). Another panel indicated that the promotional fervor of Seattle as the meeting site overshadowed good fiscal decision making: "Whether because all the effort was focused on promoting the city as the conference location, or because officials believed that Seattle's odds of being selected as host were small, there is no record of any city official expressing concern or interest about the potential costs to the city" (Citizens' Panel 2000, 5). The lurking specter of provincialism underpinned many of the critiques about Seattle's inability to manage this global event successfully.

Critiques of the push for world-class city status explicitly surfaced in reports as well. For example, according to the accountability committee, "Holding the conference in Seattle was portrayed as a coup that would bring millions of dollars in revenues to local business owners. More importantly, hosting the WTO Ministerial Conference would solidify Seattle's reputation as a 'world class' city and place us at the hub of international trade. Unfortunately, none of the publicly stated benefits would come to pass, as the WTO Conference became one of the most disruptive events in Seattle's history" (Kelsey et al. 2000, 3; see also Moody 2003). The reactions to the WTO protests certainly ruptured associations between Seattle and the world-class city label. Ultimately the evaluators and panels concluded that the city needed to put into place (a) policies to ensure that another unraveling akin to the WTO would never happen again in Seattle, and (b) strategies to ensure that individual rights were safeguarded in the city (Compton et al. 2000, 16). The disillusionment with Seattle city government after the WTO protests provided a crisis that opened up space for the social values of social justice, sustainability, and creativity to emerge as prominent focal points for urban governance. These were welcomed counterbalances to the WTO debacle; these new foci within municipal government also stemmed from years of community and neighborhood activism that finally made its way more prominently into the Seattle Municipal Tower and City Hall. Urban ambitions about global recognition and anxiety about provincialism assumed some different forms as a result of the loss of prestige that Seattle experienced after the WTO spectacle.

Economic Enterprises and City Branding

Efforts to achieve acclaim as a world-class city rather than a provincial place have emerged within the framing of the city's economic development as well. For example, Brian, a self-identified white middle-aged man who moved to Seattle as a young adult for work in the sustainability field and then shifted to county government, spoke to this point: "When you talk about Seattle, you also can't help but talk about certain industries like Microsoft." Miranda, who worked in neighborhood advocacy, added, "I think the perception is still there that big business can run Seattle....'If we lose Boeing, the whole thing will go to hell. Microsoft calls the shots.' Some of that's true, but not completely." Miranda's comment reflects a lingering anxiety that the prominence of a handful of corporations, such as Boeing, Amazon, Microsoft, Starbucks, Costco, and Nordstrom, shows that Seattle is a bona fide company town, which is read as a veneer for provincialism. City employees and boosters, therefore, often try to position Seattle as a wealthy place owing to its economic diversity and involvement in the global economy rather than due to ties with a small number of super successful corporations.

Still, the economic and perceptual significance of these corporations cannot be underestimated. They are largely the reason that Derek, a three-decade resident of Seattle and city employee in sustainability efforts, stated, "We don't really have a lot of poverty here. We have some poverty here, but it's not a crushing poverty like you have in other places.... I would say it's actually relatively [*pause*] prosperous." The wealth generation from these corporations augments statistical and experiential accounts of the city as one where many people are economically well off. Lance summed up the economic status of Seattle more bluntly: "Seattle is a rich town. It's got some of the largest corporations in the world here—some of the richest families in the world here. It's got a deep seaport out there that's second to none. You know what I mean? It's got a world-class airport. It's got one of the biggest medical centers in the world—University of Washington. . . . I mean, do you see any ghettoes here? Do you see any slums? I mean, you have got to run a long time around here to find any poor, p-o-o-r, neighborhoods. Seattle is a very wealthy town." Lance works in economic development, so he is well attuned to the wealth distribution and the overall class status of the city. He excitedly discussed the possibilities for gaining wealth in Seattle by hinting that the success of people like Bill Gates and Jeff Bezos was somewhat attributed to Seattle as a place. Wes, who also works in economic development, shared this view as he commented, "There's something in the air in Seattle. There's some mystery element that allows creative thought and pop phenomena to happen here, and by being here you can kind of tap into it." Historically, people moved through Seattle to strike it rich with gold mining in Alaska. Now, the imaginative geographies of the city suggest that people develop enterprises in Seattle and then amass tremendous personal wealth.

Many interviewees pointed to the "entrepreneurial spirit" of Seattleites as a key reason for the innovation and subsequent wealth generation apparent in the city. For instance, when asked to describe her home city, community organizer turned municipal government employee Amiko spoke uninterrupted for over five minutes about many different facets of Seattle. She repeatedly referenced the individualism of residents and that "Seattle's always been known for that kind of entrepreneurial thing." She attributed this entrepreneurial spirit to "why everyone's a little bit more segregated than together in terms of community" because "it's easier just to kinda start your own thing than just build on a legacy of what's already been established." The links Amiko forged between the economic standing of Seattle, the racialized and classed segregation of the city, and the historical legacies of these patterns poignantly contextualize my analysis in chapter 3 of creativity as linked to people, products, and processes. Amiko suggested that the focus on entrepreneurialism has been around since white Europeans arrived in the area:

> When Europeans came over [to the United States], they originally established in the East Coast, and then . . . the more adventurous ones, the ones who were willing to take risks, the ones who were more entrepreneurial, the ones who weren't satisfied with the establishment, tended to move out west. . . . And Seattle is the furthest west you can go. . . . I mean Seattle is really the last place in the United States in terms of that entrepreneurial spirit. So, I think [these are] a lot of the reasons why we have such independent creative minds. These are people who were not satisfied with the establishments where they were born and kept pushing out west, west, west, and then, finally, from San Francisco up north. . . . The last people coming here were in a sense, the most, biggest risk takers, the biggest entrepreneurs.

This rendering of why there is a prominent association between entrepreneurialism and Seattle, to the extent that people talk about something special in the air, furthers the imaginative geographies of risk taking and innovation as key essences of the city. Amiko was not alone in telling me that the European settlers of Seattle were people motivated by the possibilities of forging new enterprises and pushing intellectual and economic boundaries. The political and economic structures that fueled the settling of the West and the resource extraction and commodification that shaped these population migrations are largely left out of such interpretations. While some contemporary migration to Seattle is described as an exodus from San Francisco for the quality of life and reduced expenses in Seattle, this was not the case historically. Still, and more central to my point here, Amiko's perceptions about entrepreneurialism as related to the European founders help show how and why racialized discrimination persists. Her explanation also frames how risk taking and innovation have been crucial to many city booster activities, as people continually seek to parlay the entrepreneurialism of Seattle into a metric of global recognition.

The focus on entrepreneurialism and wealth generation—in actuality and in perception—produces some significant blind spots in interpretations of and stories about Seattle. Indeed, the positive and celebrated aspects of capital growth frequently mean that the implications of the unequal distribution of wealth and the lack of opportunities for all residents do not surface in common characterizations of Seattle. As Leslie, a self-identified white and queer person who works in county government, cogently expressed, "There's [an] incredible amount of wealth in Seattle, particularly, and a real investment in that wealth not being the problem for poverty" when I asked about why there is a powerful narrative of progressive politics in the city. She continued, "If there's a lot of poverty and there's a lot of investment in wealth not being the problem, then you're gonna have a kind of split consciousness." Leslie's description of a "split consciousness" speaks to the broader debates within Seattle about how inequities become written into structures and practices and why inequities emerge and persist. The split consciousness also relates to how much Seattle's identity as a global city or provincial company town rests on its relationship with specific corporations and related economic largesse. Do these corporations signal an over-reliance within Seattle on specific sectors, or do ties to companies, such as Microsoft and Amazon, indicate the world connections of Seattle? Returning to the description of Seattle given by Roger, is Seattle a cosmopolitan city or a neighborhood-focused place?

According to cultural theorist James Lyons (2005), many of the well-known businesses in Seattle took off because of touted links between products and Seattle place imagery, suggesting that global businesses have made a global city. For example, in the case of Starbucks, the associations produced between coffee—a global commodity—and Seattle—a place where beans are not grown but a hip image and lifestyle existed—was crafted through "a series of carefully circumscribed narratives of 'origin'" (Lyons 2005, 15). Connecting coffee with Seattle as a way to promote Starbucks revealed the status enjoyed by Seattle in imaginative geographies and the value of assumptions about the place for marketing agendas. There is a pervasive sense in Seattle that economic success is both feasible and anticipated in large part due to the particularities of the place. Given the number of companies that have exploded onto the international scene in addition to Starbucks, there is a belief that something significant happens on the global stage when a business starts in Seattle.

Corporations are not the only ones trying to leverage imaginative geographies of Seattle in order to help sell products. In fact, a turn of the twentieth century city branding campaign sought to identify Seattle strongly with the tech sector in order to rebuild the city's image post-WTO. In 2001, as tech money began to reshape the urban and suburban landscape visibly, the Seattle Convention and Visitors Bureau (SCVB) rolled out a new city tagline—comprised of a stylized eye, the @ symbol, and a capital L, which phonetically represented "See-at-L"—with the hope of literally capitalizing on the groundswell of tech companies and the innovation, creativity, and success attributed to this sector (Moody 2003).[4] In describing the branding history of the city to me, Wes said, "[See@L] was tied to the tech world, and the boom of the mid and late '90s . . . I'm not sure that it really ever encapsulated the visitor experience as well as it could. . . . I think it addressed better the business and innovation side." Wes freely admitted that this brand did not have extensive purchase in the tourism markets and worked better as an image reset within economic sectors in Seattle. He noted, "It's hard to even say, See@L," which caused limited uptake of the brand. Importantly, the constrained interpretation of place represented by this brand also re-ignited fears about Seattle as provincial. When Boeing went through a bust period in the late 1960s and early 1970s, two local realtors put up a billboard stating, "Will the last person leaving Seattle—Turn out the lights?" (Lange 1999). This sign reflected the tight relationship and company town associations between Boeing and Seattle's general economic viability. These kinds of ties persist, as the See@L brand demonstrates. Even though tech companies have global reach and thus could position Seattle as similar by association, a primary underlying concern with See@L was the explicit focus on one economic sector. Such a move too closely mirrored past company town affiliations.

Metronatural replaced See@L in 2006 as the city brand. Deemed a moniker that foregrounded the presumed lifestyle amenities of the urban cultural infrastructure and the biophysical environment, SCVB defined Metronatural as the following: "adj. 1: Having the characteristics of a world-class metropolis within wild, beautiful natural surroundings. 2: A blending of clear skies and expansive water with a fast-paced city life. n. 3: One who respects the environment and lives a balanced lifestyle of urban and natural experiences 4: Seattle" (Seattle's Convention and Visitors Bureau 2006, 4). The fusion of urban and natural spaces in Seattle was the focal point of this brand (Karvonen 2011). Emblazoning Metronatural on the Space Needle and promoting the brand globally signaled efforts to affirm affiliations between Seattle and world-class urban amenities. Such a framing distanced the proximity between Seattle and depictions of the city as a provincial company town.

Seattleites voiced concern after the launch of Metronatural primarily because of the similarities to the word metrosexual and the British Columbia tourism brand of "Super, Natural." Sheila, who works in branding and economic development, added that the "biggest problem with it [Metronatural] is that everybody's made fun of it. Nobody's taking it seriously." At the same time, regardless of local perspectives, Wes, who was also well acquainted with city branding endeavors, stressed that Metronatural thrived in the international marketplace because it effectively encapsulated the urban and the biophysical environmental aspects of Seattle. He opined, "Regardless of how you feel about Metronatural, it's kind of true ... and there aren't a lot of other cities that grant you that." From Wes's vantage point, Metronatural summed up the best of Seattle as a city with myriad cultural attractions, economic opportunities, and lifestyle amenities, including ready access to the great outdoors. He carried on to say that visitors and residents alike "all want to go on float-plane rides, but they also want to go to the theater." Without the high quality outdoor opportunities, Seattle's environmental landscape could be viewed predominantly as an impediment (as people who mention how steep the hills are for walking around downtown frequently complain). Underscoring the biophysical environment as a lifestyle amenity, on the other hand, incorporates nature "as [an] 'urban appendage'" (Lyons 2004, 43). This representation of nature clearly generates economic benefit for the city as the prestige of Seattle's status grows through the commodification of these outdoor attractions.

An avowed outdoor enthusiast, city employee Derek echoed the biophysical environment as a lifestyle amenity perspective when he discussed the appeal of life in Seattle:

> We like the place because it's got a mild climate.... Kind of like Goldilocks, just right.... We get spoiled by that.... We like the fact that there are trees here even though we're trying to get more.[5] ... We like the fact that there's lots of water.... I think it's a visually appealing place to live. As human beings, we do a lot of living through our eyes and through our ears, so we can hear the birds, we can hear the trees, and we can see the water. We can see the mountains.... Many people like to be here because there's access to all the natural things.... In an hour you can be in the middle of really deep woods all by yourself.

Derek touched upon the scenic topographic features of Seattle as he celebrated the climate of the city. He spoke with clear reverence of the multi-sensory ways that Seattleites engage with the biophysical environment. These were important features of living in Seattle for him and presumably many others. The snow-capped mountains, the sweeping moss-drenched forests, and the cerulean ocean expanses certainly are impressive. He then mentioned how quickly one can escape the urban trappings into a vast forest. Although usual traffic probably extends that one-hour escape time to more like two hours, the point Derek made was clear. A significant perk of Seattle is that residents and visitors have access to urban and outdoor landscapes. The two are deeply interwoven within the quotidian and imaginative geographies promulgated through the Metronatural branding initiative. The repetition of this narrative of Seattle as the best of both worlds—"urban" and "natural"—helps naturalize this "truth" about the city. Importantly, the "marketization of nature" (Heynen et al. 2006, 4) and the production of cities through the containment of nature also work to confirm Seattle's status as urbane and a leader in green (Kaika 2006). Such positioning, as I discuss more in chapter 2, foregrounds urban standing and limits associations with provincialism.

Conclusions

As our interview drew to a close, I asked Roger what he thought the future of Seattle would entail—would this place become more like Vancouver and unquestioningly embody world-class city attributes, or would the city mimic Portland and become more resolutely known for its neighborhood-focused familiarity? In response to my question, he stated: "I think there's a happy compromise between those two things. I think the place where you can walk down the leafy green street to your Ethiopian restaurant. You can have a job in the day that's connecting you globally, but return home at the end of the day to, if not the single-family detached home, a quiet, comfortable slower speed, leafy, leafy neighborhood. I think that's a model that's enticing and can hopefully lead us into the future." Considering the possibility of a future compromise between the seemingly disparate expectations for Seattle as a city of global reach and one of local focus requires contending with historical events and patterns that have shaped the contemporary place. Thus, in the scene that Roger outlined, I wonder about the people who own and work within the fictive Ethiopian restaurant. Where do they live and what access to resources do they have?

Tracing how anxieties about provincialism and the ambition for recognition as world-class drove actions to affirm modernity and prestige within Seattle helps frame the recent upwelling of interest in municipal government on the social values of sustainability, creativity, and social justice. These efforts work to suggest that Seattle is not provincial. Yet many of the actions taken out of fear of such a label have helped secure whiteness and solidified inequities into the built and experiential environments of the city.

Given the persistent racialized and classed segregation in the city and the stark divergences in education, employment, and health outcomes for people of color and white people in Seattle, it is important to consider how the interweaving—as compared to the opposition—of world-class and small-town aspirations has unfolded and will yet unfold, particularly in the context of social values in urban governance. Without such inquiries, the desire for a multicultural city replete with lifestyle amenities could further instantiate liberal whiteness rather than the progressive politics often celebrated in imaginative geographies of Seattle. As historian Quintard Taylor (1994, 193) observes: "Seattle's liberal image masked deeply held racial antipathies and anxieties." Shifting this reality toward equity and crafting urban experiences that contain the middle ground that Roger outlines, therefore, invites examination of how recasting the label of world-class city to a place imbricated within global flows of capital and information, which Seattle clearly is, could alter urban processes and discrimination. Moreover, rather than focus on hosting lavish affairs, such as the AYP, the World's Fair, and the WTO meetings, to achieve recognition as a global city, striving for meaningful social change within Seattle could bear out the middle path that Roger describes. Such shifts might ease up some of the booster language about the relevance and prominence of Seattle, although many contemporary resolutions emerging from City Council begin with a statement that Seattle is a national leader on any given issue. The desire for recognition seems to be a longstanding feature of the City. Still, attending to a broader set of dynamics and goals, including social values, could more effectively represent the city in all its complexity and vitality.

When I asked Geneva, a longstanding city employee and self-identified person of color, what draws people to Seattle she replied, "We're the portal to Asia, but we're also the Microsoft capital of the world. So, it's a creative haven. It's gorgeous. And there are enough people of color to make it interesting." This comment captures the central themes examined in this chapter. Geneva depicts Seattle as the entry point to Asia, a position that indicates some global ties and connects with past city booster activities, and as a hub for the tech sector, an affiliation that conveys economic might.

This portrayal both locates Seattle within a global framework and represents the tension between economic success and being a city defined by one company or corporation. Geneva mentions creativity, analyzed in depth in chapter 3, and extols the beauty of the Seattle landscape and surroundings, discussed in reference to sustainability in chapter 2. She closes on an ironic note as she states that there are just enough people of color in Seattle to give the city some intrigue and difference. A tacit nod to racism and racialization accompanies this assessment of the city, as discussed further in chapter 4. Geneva's observations indicate that city status, economic activity, and race and racism remain central features of imaginative geographies of the City and city and provide the complex context for the contemporary translation of social values into practice in Seattle's urban governance.

2

Exclusive Inclusion

Choosing Sustainability and Being Green

A smiling and blinking animated sun peeks over a mountain range to a lush garden and orchard. Lyrics pour forth—"Last summer was great, though it's up for debate" (Office of Sustainability & Environment 2013a)—and waft over this pastoral scene. Suddenly, wilting leaves, dropping fruit, and a browning of the landscape emerge as the vocalist croons, "Eighty days with no rain is kind of insane." Thus begins the 2013 video *We're So Green* created by Capitol Media and Punch Drunk for the Office of Sustainability & Environment (OSE) as a way to engage Seattleites with the Climate Action Plan (CAP) under review at the time (Office of Sustainability & Environment 2013a; 2013b; see appendix 3 for the full lyrics). At just over two minutes long, the video *We're So Green* includes a multi-age, multiracial cast and an array of iconic Seattle landscapes, ranging from the skyline with the Space Needle and Mount Rainier to community gardens to the signature dark teal and yellow city buses. The cartoon primarily extols Seattle's environmental accomplishments as evidence of the sustainability measures enacted by both individuals and policies. For example, the video uses audio like "We make use of the rain," mixed with visuals of residential rain barrels, and "We got it wired by using our wires," with images of electric buses. Practices and processes meant to demonstrate sustainability, such as "We grow our own food," "We recycle our trash," and "We plug in our cars," further underscore the content of being green. The lyrics of "We are Seattle, and we're leading the change" suggest a kind of exceptional and first-in-class mentality, one that Seattle city government and boosters have cultivated in a variety of ways for decades, as discussed in chapter 1.

After commending the laudable green work under way in Seattle and tacitly celebrating the people engaged in these activities, the *We're So Green* video concludes with the acknowledgment, "There's so much more we can do." An invitation posted on a placard and written in computer-simulated handwriting states, "Tell us what the City should do. Find out what you can do," as the repeating chorus "We're so green" fades away. This video and final request for feedback were key strategies used for soliciting comments from Seattleites on the then in-process CAP (as discussed in City of Seattle 2011c, 4). Successfully convincing Seattleites to value the status of being green and adopt certain personal practices, such as the ones detailed in *We're So Green*, helps expand the seemingly reasonable jurisdictional reach of the city government. The premise is that if one wants to be seen as green, and wants the city to be recognized as such, one must accept a potential increase in government regulatory actions and involvement in the now deemed quantifiable and governable climate and environment (Rice 2010). In exchange, one receives positive affirmation and inclusion within an esteemed group of Seattleites, people who bear out the desired identity of green. As I show in this chapter, however, not everyone has access to this green social capital.

We're So Green is musically catchy. Like a bad pop song, the lyrics for the video get stuck in my head. I find myself walking down the street singing the tune. If I had lived in Seattle at the time of the cartoon's release, I would have felt compelled to submit my feedback. And I might have added a little pep in my step because this song is clearly talking to me as a white, educated, upper middle-class, and cisgender woman. Of course, just like the characters in the video, I bring my bags to the store and recycle my trash; I am *so* green. This kind of assumed affinity indicates how *We're So Green* worked as a venue for connecting the city government with residents. The video promoted a familiar and purportedly shared identity, one endowed with positive accolades. As Derek, who works in the sustainability field within municipal government, blithely stated in his description of Seattle, "We like that we are a 'green' community." Journalist William Yardley (2008) adds, "Gray and green may be the colors most associated with this forward-focused city." Emi, when talking about successes in her county government department with regard to the sustainable communities initiatives, added that in the Seattle area, "If you're not on the green train, you're missing out."

The term *green* is a slippery signifier, though. Simultaneously a designation of behaviors and practices described as environmentally responsible, and by tacit assumption sustainable, and a status achieved through specific actions, *green* is more than a name of a color. It is, as cultural historian Bruce Smith (2009, 1) explains, "a relationship." He continues, "'Green' invites us to consider that subjects, especially *thinking* subjects, don't exist apart from the objects amid which they live, move, and think" (Smith 2009, 1, emphasis in the original). In other words, Smith asserts that the meaning of *green* arises in relationship with facets of Seattle's context that reflect assumed greenness. This context of green within Seattle includes myriad city policy documents, programs, evaluation measures, and popular press articles about sustainability from the past twenty-five years. The video *We're So Green* joins this lineage as it articulates the parameters of the city as a green place at the forefront of sustainability activities and serves as a textual declaration of Seattle's longstanding relationship with a green and sustainable identity. Geographer Julie Cidell describes such perceptions and associated actions as part of the "*sustainable imaginary*," which is "'a society's understanding and vision of how resources are being used and should be used to ensure socioenvironmental reproduction'" (2017, 2, emphasis in the original). Cidell examines the sustainable imaginary of the city as a garden in Melbourne and Chicago.

I build upon Cidell's ideas to suggest that the *We're So Green* video does crucial work for translating the value of sustainability into practice and constructing the sustainability imagination within Seattle. The cartoon offers normative assessments and affirms the

intended audience within Seattle's sustainability imagination—
"you know who you are, and we're talking to you, we're so green!"
(Office of Sustainability & Environment 2013a). The construct of a
green Seattleite and sustainable city is a key focus in this chapter,
alongside the analysis of the voices, experiences, and perspectives
brought to the foreground and pushed to the sidelines through
the imaginative geographies that cohere into the sustainability
imagination. Specifically, I examine the Way to Go transportation challenge and the Green Fee debate—the two most prominent sustainability programs and policies put forth by ose and
Seattle Public Utilities during my fieldwork—to illustrate the perceived pathway to achieve green status for individuals and the city,
the desirability of sustainability, and the exclusionary practices
set in motion through the inculcation of the green identity and
associated assumed choices within Seattle's urban governance.[1] I
argue that the latent class privilege and logics of choice embedded
within the Way to Go program and Green Fee helped secure sustainability and greenness as classed aspirations in Seattle, despite
the seemingly progressive veneer of these sustainability endeavors. My analysis of these two cases exhibits the iterative production of hierarchical social differentiation through the emphasis
on choice within the exclusive inclusion of Seattle's sustainability programs and policies.

I take inspiration for the frame of exclusive inclusion from
legal scholar Devon Carbado. He examines naturalization as more
than a formal process for gaining citizenship within the United
States and demonstrates how naturalization is significantly also "a
social process that produces American racial identities" (Carbado
2005, 637). Furthermore, he asserts that racism is an operative lens
that determines belonging within the United States and that U.S.
identity is consequently distinct from citizenship. In teasing out
the relationship between citizenship and identity, Carbado puts
forward the idea of "inclusive exclusion." Reading inclusion and
exclusion not as opposites but as entangled and mutually constitutive processes, Carbado shows how racial naturalization means
that certain people are simultaneously included in the category

of citizenship and excluded from U.S. identity or vice versa, hence inclusive exclusion.

Rather than examining how exclusion helps solidify a racialized hierarchy, I analyze the exclusivity, meaning the limited access to a select few, of inclusion within the normative discourses of sustainability and green. I draw upon the frame of exclusive inclusion to illustrate how boundaries are erected to demarcate and center the eco-conscious and "good" residents and exclude the "bad" non-green practices and people who undermine sustainability endeavors by their representational status or actions. Such an articulation of the city as green and sustainable celebrates certain activities and implicitly sidelines others. To ascertain who is sustainable and green, members of this ascribed community need to self-identify as such and be legible as such to the wider populace. The *We're So Green* video contributes to this project. The collective identity of green relies upon individualized choices and actions publicly coded as sustainable. Given the co-constitution of society and space, this means that specific uses of space and enactments of spatial relations have more social power and legitimacy within Seattle. Being seen putting food waste into a compost bin, for example, is more acceptable than gleaning fruit off a city tree. Driving a hybrid car garners greater recognition than driving a 1980s sedan with almost the same gas mileage. In an effort to include certain Seattleites—"you know who you are" (Office of Sustainability & Environment 2013a)—within the green identity, exclusionary boundaries are drawn. Indeed, the intertwining of inclusion and exclusion in sustainability practices shows how exclusivity is critical to generating purported inclusion. Such are the ways that exclusive inclusion contours communities and spaces throughout Seattle, a place that is deeply attached to its sustainability imagination.

To specify the classed assumptions and overtures embedded within sustainability practices and show how these help confirm exclusive inclusion, I delve into the premise of choice in sustainability initiatives and practices. I identify what choices are articulated and gain visibility and what choices are situated as holding weight and necessitating recognition within Way to Go and the Green Fee to reveal the classed dimensions of these sustainability activities. Teasing out choice as I see it embedded within past and current sustainability initiatives and policies helps underscore the ways in which class differentiation and exclusion prop up sustainability endeavors. Highlighting choice in concert with the production of exclusive inclusion suggests one reason why inequities persist in the translation of sustainability as a value into practice in Seattle's urban governance.

The language of choice emerges within many sustainability actions in general. For example, Xavier, who has worked in the sustainability field within non-profits and city government in Seattle, explained that in order to navigate the tension between new urbanist developments and neighborhoods made up of single-family homes, sustainability advocates had to highlight consumer choices. He stated: "We have to communicate that [sustainability] in terms that Americans can understand, which is flexibility, choice, opportunity . . . so you don't say 'well, okay, we need to take more density,' which I've heard used by people frequently as 'take more density.' Sounds like 'take your medicine,' 'eat your spinach.'" Xavier articulates how the idea of choice often makes sustainability goals more palatable and possible. Choice grants individuals a sense of having control and options. Through careful research and thoughtful assessment, individuals can choose to support greater density, for example. This approach sounds less draconian and less like a directive or governmental requirement. The idea of choice also corresponds to the future beneficiaries of current work. In other words, individuals can purportedly choose to provide the context for success and happiness for future generations or can choose to destroy the local climate and environment now. Yet not all people have access to the kinds of choices and opportunities that Xavier implicitly describes. Indeed, the terms *flexibility*, *choice*, and *opportunity* convey and embed latent classed assumptions within sustainability undertakings because of the presumed uniformity and ubiquity of choice. The privilege to make choices that ostensibly benefit the planet and future generations attains center stage. The attendant sustainability imagination, therefore, rests on practices of exclusion.

It is vitally important to elucidate the inequities produced through exclusive inclusion and matters of choice because Seattle is widely touted as a green and sustainable city. For instance, in 2014, then President Barack Obama recognized Seattle as one of sixteen climate action champions in the United States based on the city's efforts to reduce greenhouse gas emissions (Office of the Press Secretary 2014). In 2015 Delta Airlines' *Sky* magazine designated Seattle one of the world's "greenest, most sustainable cities" (Gilliam 2015). WalletHub, a personal finance company, ranked Seattle the eleventh "greenest" large U.S. city (Bernardo 2017) in 2016 and 2017, and the *Seattle Post-Intelligencer* saw this recognition as fit to reprint (DeMay 2016). The accolades continue, even though the criteria for emerging as the "greenest city" usually rely on changes that can be measured, such as building materials, bike lanes, and recycling programs. The social sustainability facets of such efforts, and related structural and systemic shifts that can generate longstanding equity, frequently fall by the wayside in such evaluations (Davidson 2010). Seattle's urban governance of sustainability has followed such patterns, as I show in this chapter, and these elisions contribute to the exclusive inclusion of sustainability in the city.

Defining and Developing Seattle's Sustainability

In 1994 the municipal government titled the city's comprehensive plan *Toward a Sustainable Seattle*. This plan both addressed the growth mandates dictated by Washington state's Growth Management Plan and outlined the vision for how Seattle would grow and develop sustainably during a twenty-year time frame based on a variety of performance standards (Portney 2013). The comprehensive plan detailed four core values as guides for Seattle's development: "community, environmental stewardship, economic opportunity and security, and social equity" (City of Seattle 1995, vi). Both the 1994 comprehensive plan for Seattle and the related Environmental Action Agenda borrowed quite directly from the United

Nations World Commission on Environment and Development report *Our Common Future*, also known as the Brundtland report, in their working definition of a sustainable city (United Nations World Commission on Environment and Development 1987, 16). The Brundtland report operates within an extended time frame and defines sustainability as ensuring that the actions of the current generation do not undermine the possibilities for future generations to meet their basic needs. Extending this logic indicates that choices made in the present day can either enable or harm future generations and the planet. The long-term view within sustainability indicates a different type of engagement for city government with the temporal. Indeed, the emergence of sustainability within urban development strategies shifted the terrain and scope of urban planning as the future became conceptualized as a *"definable object"* that had assumed materiality and could be "controlled, ordered" (Raco et al. 2008, 2655, emphasis in the original). As a result, the logic of choice became central to the meaning of sustainability; choices made today should conserve opportunities in the future.

Since the 1994 comprehensive plan and vision for a sustainable Seattle, many people working within municipal and county government and non-profit entities have focused on the social value of sustainability. A consequence of the broad uptake of sustainability is that, as Xavier stated, "Sustainability has now officially crossed into buzzword territory and everybody wants sustainable this and sustainable that.... I think it's now become kind of an empty vessel. It means whatever people want it to mean." Furthering this point, Emi added that in county government, "When we say sustainable, it's kind of like everything under the sun." The flexibility of the term *sustainability* renders it a floating referent, one that becomes attached to countless and disparate endeavors and actions throughout Seattle. This reality undercuts the possibilities for systemic social change coordinated around a core set of practices that exemplify a social value because the term *sustainable* has been affixed to a wide range of at times conflicting activities. It is hard to cohere social transformation around contradictory applications and unclear definitions.

Despite vagueness, the word *sustainability* has traveled widely in Seattle's urban governance since its formal emergence in city documents in 1994. For instance, after the wto debacle (discussed in chapter 1), former mayor Paul Schell created the Office of Sustainability & Environment in 2000 and tasked this office with developing and overseeing the move to a sustainability emphasis throughout city government. Schell explained that city government has "numerous opportunities, each day, to adopt more sustainable practices ourselves, and to influence choices made by others" (Office of Sustainability & Environment 2001, 4). These choices range from regulatory power to service provision to purchasing practices. Catalyzing these choices would make Seattle, as Schell stated, "the 'greenest' City government in the world—the most water-efficient, the most energy-efficient, the least polluting, in short, the most 'sustainable'" (Office of Sustainability & Environment 2001, 1). Schell further noted in the same report, titled *Sustaining Seattle: Our Defining Challenge,* that sustainability contributes to the competitive advantage of the city, especially if there is a well-cultivated association between Seattle and greenness, and provides a successful strategy for businesses. He described the natural fit, in his view, of economic goals and environmental ones, saying, "Our best economic development strategy is to build an environmentally sustainable city" (Office of Sustainability & Environment 2001, 1). Schell's zealous commitment to sustainability echoes the persistent drive for status and recognition within Seattle's urban governance. This time, though, it was not world-class status in the form of attracting the wto. Instead, Schell yearned for global affirmation of Seattle as a leader in green, a designation that reflects both environmental stewardship and economic growth.

Within the context of implementing sustainability efforts throughout city government, Schell asked the ose to develop ways for the city government to reduce its environmental impact, generate awareness about the city government's triple bottom line sustainability approach, and partner with community and regional organizations to extend the reach of sustainability projects (Office of Sustainability & Environment 2001, 5). This work constituted in many ways "Office sustainability . . . [a] sort of practical sustain-ability," as Derek explained in his depiction of the OSE's purview. Derek continued to note that "rather than defining sustainability, we define the actions and activities we think will get us there" and the partners who can help reach that destination. The OSE now oversees Seattle's climate protection programs, the urban refor-estation endeavors, the urban agricultural policies and activities, and the green facilities management and construction plans, all efforts that contribute to a generalized sense of a sustainable city. These endeavors also underpin prominent themes evident in the *We're So Green* video. As such, these actions demonstrate the rela-tional and context-specific underpinnings of *"imaginative geogra-phies of green"* (Harris 2014, 801, emphasis in the original), which discursively establish Seattle as a leader in urban environmental governance and as uniformly committed to a specific set of pre-determined green and sustainable practices.

Many of OSE's current projects focus on reductions in citywide carbon emissions as a central strategy for realizing sustainability. Resolution 31312 of 2011 demonstrates this concentration as it dis-cusses specific carbon reduction practices related to the OSE's work and defines net zero greenhouse gas (GHG) emissions by 2050 as the number one climate protection and adaptation goal for Seat-tle. The resolution includes 2020 and 2030 targets for GHG reduc-tions in three sectors—transportation, buildings, and waste—as crucial for reaching this net zero emissions target (City of Seat-tle 2011c, 2–3). With this laser-sharp focus on carbon neutrality by 2050, the municipal government has added incentive for crafting reductions throughout Seattle and further gaining national atten-tion for such changes. Producing residents who partake in daily carbon conscious activities that advance the overarching goals of local government is therefore key (Rice 2010). Professor of social policy Liisa Häikiö (2007, 2148) contends that urban governance practices have increasingly shifted from a more direct exertion of power and authority to one where the local government is a facil-itator and cooperative partner. To this point, as the carbon reduc-tion programs such as Way to Go show, the OSE strives to facilitate behavior change among Seattleites so as to generate sustainability outcomes through individual and institutional choices, even though proposed options are not available to all residents. The actions and outcomes of the OSE help constitute the sustainability imagination and translate the social value of sustainability into practice.

Way to Go, a Sustainable Transportation Initiative

The Way to Go transportation initiative, initially started by OSE in 2000 and managed by the Seattle Department of Transportation (SDOT) until it concluded in the end of 2017, centered upon reducing individual carbon emissions through changes in transportation patterns. About 66 percent of measured GHG emissions in the city come from road transportation, and the CAP for the city aims to reduce emissions dramatically over the next few decades, hence the focus on transportation choices in this program (Office of Sustainability & Environment 2016a, 9). As city employee Sarah stated, the tenets of a sustainable urban transportation system include the following: "Provide better transportation choices. More transit, bike, walk, and then engage people in the solution [to] think about their behavior." Until the advent of Mayor Jenny Durkan's tenure in January 2018, the Way to Go program followed this approach and was one of the longer-standing and continuously supported sustainability initiatives in Seattle. The Way to Go homepage included information about bus, streetcar, and light rail routes, car sharing and carpools, and tips for urban biking and walking. It had a host of maps and apps to help individuals navigate the city in a less carbon-intensive fashion. In other words, Way to Go offered insight into various transportation options within Seattle, a city that has struggled with providing comprehensive public transportation due to the topography of the area and the shifting tides of urban transportation policy prescriptions. Currently, the city's public transit includes light rail, ferries, streetcars, buses, and a monorail (a vestige of the World's Fair). Washington State Department of Transportation, Sound Transit, King County Metro, and SDOT manage different aspects of the transportation infrastructure.

Focusing on the reduction of carbon emissions through transportation choices helps build what geographer Jennifer Rice (2010, 929) terms "a new type of carbon-relevant citizen." Individuals take responsibility for climate change through their own personal actions and choices. This is a satisfying model for policy makers because it revolves around clearly articulated carbon reduction benchmark targets, which are then either concretely met or missed (Holden 2006). Benchmark metrics are often opt-in kinds of endeavors in that a municipal government does not mandate compliance but celebrates those who participate and help meet specific goals. The practice of municipal governments encouraging residents to change behaviors in the name of sustainability is a strategy used by many cities (Cidell 2017). As an example of how the Seattle municipal government facilitates these behavior choices, city employee Amiko mentioned, "If you've noticed in Seattle, one of the hugest [advancements] in the last few years is all the bike lanes that we've been adding everywhere to, again, encourage people to ride the bike. The City Hall actually put in new showers to encourage the employees to bike." With such inducements, Seattle city government hopes to incentivize people to change their personal modes of transportation and to report these carbon-reduction actions. Such data enable the municipal government to calculate that a certain percentage of the urban population now bikes to work half the time, for example, and to estimate the decrease in carbon emissions as a result. Analyzing self-reported transportation choices affords a quantifiable response to climate change, yet arguably does not challenge systemic factors, such as capitalism, that drive climate disturbance (Heynen and Robbins 2005).

Over time, Way to Go had a fairly extensive application in Seattle's transportation sector. The initial form Way to Go assumed, however, was as a sporadic transportation challenge. Specifically, the program asked families with two or more cars to reduce auto trips by giving up one car for six weeks and relying more on public transit, walking, biking, and carpooling. The goal as OSE explained, was to have families "track the choices they make and the miles of driving they reduce by using one less car. Participants walked more, rode their bikes, used the bus and better planned the car trips they did make. As a result they reduced air pollution, traffic congestion, and stress, and saved money" (Office of Sustainability & Environment 2001, 6). This was a way for individuals and families to become more intimately involved in understanding their own contributions to carbon emissions and to make choices to alter such patterns.

Sarah, who works on sustainability issues and has a deep love for mass transit, bikes, and the transportation infrastructure of Copenhagen, outlined some additional benefits of Way to Go. She noted: "We have a Way to Go program where people try getting around without their second car for a while. And one of the things we really heard from them was that they're getting to know their neighbors more. Because as opposed to like getting in their car and driving away, they're walking by their neighbors on the way to the bus stop or on the way to the neighborhood store and feeling more of a sense of community and connection as a result." Sarah expressed a commitment in our interview to place making and community building, so the Way to Go program resonated with her. While experiencing a greater sense of connection is a laudable outcome of this initiative, a key shortcoming in this challenge was that it presumed families owned at least two cars and lived in neighborhoods with certain characteristics, such as adequate street lighting, general public safety, availability of goods within a walkable distance, and bus schedules and routes that aligned with job and other life obligations.

The ability to live in a well-resourced neighborhood with multiple transportation options is not the reality for all Seattle residents, especially people living in poverty, many of whom live in Southeast Seattle (see the introduction). Makela, a longstanding resident of Southeast Seattle and self-identified black woman, explained in a conversation about transit-oriented development that in her neighborhood "people are too busy keeping a roof over their head and food on the table.... There is not a lot of discretionary money and there is not a lot of discretionary time" for considering alternative transportation practices or other sustainability measures. Rick, another longstanding Southeast Seattle resident, concurred as he discussed the relationship between sustainability and social justice efforts: "A lot of the poor people just focus on what they know day-to-day, and so traditionally, they've viewed sustainability as something that's maybe more of a white thing that doesn't quite impact them. Their issues are more bread and butter. Do I have a job? A bus pass? This kind of thing." As Makela and Rick's comments suggest, the planning time required and the opportunity to choose between a car and public transit is not a choice that every resident in Seattle can make. Yet Way to Go as a program relied upon such choices. As a result, class stratification and differentiation became part and parcel of Way to Go. Riding the bus was not framed as a usual necessity. Instead, it was a choice mobilized to show environmental consciousness. Only the people who publicly opted for riding the bus rather than driving received recognition for their greenness through Way to Go. People who rode the bus out of circumstance did not generate accolades, so the benefits of this program were not shared throughout Seattle. Such an application contributed to the exclusive inclusion of the initiative.

Several bus routes in Southeast Seattle were cut due to the costs associated with the construction of the light rail line, further limiting access to participation in Way to Go. Eliminating bus routes was especially problematic because a high portion of Southeast Seattle residents relied on buses to get to work in parts of the city not serviced by light rail (Cohen 2009; Lloyd 2011). This meant that many people had to figure out alternative transportation—often by individual car—or different work. Thus while certain residents and communities in Seattle were congratulated for reducing their carbon footprint through Way to Go, others had to expand theirs in order to make do given the changes in public transportation routes. Such paradoxes indicate that the initial iteration of Way to Go produced a sustainability initiative that sat comfortably within class privilege and amassed positive status to the publicly recognized environmentally conscious participants. Residents who did not partake in the program were further positioned as outsiders. Such discrepancies bear out city employee and Southeast Seattle resident Melanie's assertion that her colleagues use the phrase sustainability "in terms of environmental or ecological sustainability and there are too few moments thinking about economic and social sustainability." In the context of Way to Go, Melanie's critique serves as a reminder of how the program focused on assumed choices available to reduce GHG emissions and therefore exhibited a fairly narrow application of environmental sustainability. Crafting a program that accrues positive and public status to certain privileged individuals and relegates others to the margins exhibits exclusive inclusion.

The classed assumptions of Way to Go emerged in other settings as well. For instance, the September 2010 edition of the Way to Go newsletter, the WALK BIKE RIDEr, suggests that giving up a spare car can add simplicity and whimsy to life and that becoming a "Walk, Bike, Rider" makes one a healthier, happier, and wealthier person. This edition of the newsletter included the added bonus of a joke: "What costs less than $100 per month and makes the average car use less gas than a Prius? Answer: A transit pass. Take transit, drive less and you will use less gas than someone driving twice as much in a Prius" (Allen 2010). The July 2012 edition of the newsletter offered a summer transportation incentive and the possibility of winning an electric bike, a gift certificate for REI, or a zipcar membership if the daily car trips replaced by biking, walking, or riding were thoroughly tracked online (Way to Go, Seattle! Team 2012). The packaging and representation of Way to Go in the newsletters suggest an expected and targeted classed audience. Consequently, Way to Go bore out the value of sustainability in a constrained fashion. The reliance on choice helped reproduce classed patterns of privilege and exclusive inclusion, thereby reducing sustained transformation throughout the city.

A classed ethos permeated much of the city sustainability discourse as well. For example, city employee Derek, who focused on sustainability in Seattle in his personal and professional lives, illustrated latent class privilege as he outlined a prominent thread of resistance associated with the transportation choice emphasis in Way to Go. He commented:

> The problem with transportation is it's the most personal thing of all the choices, of all the choices that we make, and turning down your thermostat is pretty personal, but moving your body around from one place to the other, and moving the bodies of all these people around is intensely personal because it's moving your own little body. And you've got your house, place of work, your kid's school, your kid's daycare, your kid's soccer field, the grocery store, the dry cleaner. You have all those things you need to do, and I can't do all these because the bus takes you from here to here. So, is there a way for me to go from here to here to here to here without using my own personal car? There's not. Will there ever be? Probably not. Probably not.

As Derek reflected on the sense of autonomy afforded by individual transportation he illuminated some of the tacit classed assumptions that wove through city government sustainability work. There are Seattleites who have to use public transportation to get to numerous places to fulfill everyday obligations. Such practices are overlooked, however, in Derek's discussion. Instead, he mused about the impossibility of getting groceries, picking up a child, and making it to work via public transportation. While this could be his critique of the complex multi-jurisdictional and multi-modal public transportation system in Seattle and its lack of user friendliness, I also read this comment as evidence of latent class privilege framing and underpinning ose's sustainability activities. The presumed sacrifices families with multiple cars would make to participate in Way to Go were deemed significant given the seeming impossibility of accomplishing daily tasks via public transportation. Yet the daily sacrifices many Seattleites make to survive did not overtly register in the construction and application of this initiative.

The perpetuation of classed differentiation and exclusive inclusion through sustainability efforts in Seattle mirrors the specific U.S. social movements that birthed sustainability coalitions. To this point, Beth, who works in the for-profit sector and has also spent time as a community organizer and city employee, described the racialized and classed aspects of the early environmental movement. She said, "I think historically, environmentalists were considered upper- and middle-class people who could afford to be environmentalists. They were, and poorer communities or people of color felt like environmentalists would come and tell them how bad they were because they weren't doing the right things. And would tell you you'd have to buy a refrigerator that costs $100 more, and how could I buy a refrigerator when I don't even have enough to buy what I want? . . . The environmental movement was a pretty white movement." Being an environmentalist was a choice, a decision made, according to Beth, by mostly upper- and middle-class white people. The assumption of options and disposable income to make "better" decisions for the planet and future generations led to a practice of public moralizing and shaming, which, as Beth intimates, did not contribute to a multi-class and multiracial environmental movement.

Patty, an employee in a non-profit with sustainability and social justice foci, concurred with this assessment as she outlined the development of the contemporary sustainability movement. She noted, "I think you have to go back in part to the origins of the environmental movement and how that has evolved and become institutionalized. It has a lot to do with leadership. It has a lot to do with money. It has a lot to do with people who had the relative luxury of being able to choose to be activists around issues that, if you will, were more of the head than of the heart." Patty describes how an affluent, liberal whiteness became connected to environmental and then sustainability movements (Alkon and McCullen 2011; see also Finney 2009). The focus on choosing to be an activist and having the money to make such choices in particular secured this privilege. This perspective on the history of the environmental and sustainability movements echoes reflections from Beth. Acknowledging this history helps explain why and how classed assumptions shaped Way to Go.

Daniel, a born and raised Seattleite who self-identified as African American, gave a longer explanation for the mix of racial and class milieus that inform environmental and associated sustainability work. In response to my question about the traction sustainability efforts have in Seattle, Daniel replied:

> I think when you take initiatives that tap into the environment, folks of color and white people have completely different orientations to how we interact with the world and how the world is interacting with us. So, although I don't want to say that environmental impacts are a white thing, if a little kid would come up here and say, "I don't give a damn about the environment, that's for white people" ... there's a reason why that child may have that lens and they may not even be aware of that.... It connects to the same historical realities that are facing today's society, that certain initiatives get more traction. And why certain movements and initiatives, particularly environmental movements, may get more political visibility, so on and so forth.

Daniel's comments revolve around a perspective that white people and people of color, as he said, "navigate the world differently," and that social movements started by certain groups of people persistently reproduce dominant perspectives for those groups. He also indicates that particular issues and groups have greater pull in political circles because of historical legacies of classed whiteness. The privileging of certain people and experiences and the invisibilizing of others was evident with the exclusive inclusion of Way to Go too. Daniel outlines how the accretion of such practices over time has contributed to a bifurcation between the mostly white and wealthier people engaged in sustainability and the people of color and people living in poverty excluded from such endeavors.

James, who has spent much of his professional life in city government and has deep roots in the sustainability field, suggested a different take on the history of the environmental movement. In response to my question about the whiteness and classed components of the movement, he responded: "I wouldn't say that's incorrect but it's a little bit misleading. The fact is that the chief victims of environmental impact are low income and poor communities." He also noted that every major environmental issue brought through Congress has had the support of the black caucus. "The primary focus of the environmental movement over time has been clean air, clean water, toxic waste sites ... the face of the environmental community has been white. The face doesn't necessarily match the foot soldiers," he said. From James's perspective, the narrative of the environmental movement as predominantly white and upper- and middle-class is not accurate and renders invisible the environmental justice coalitions, often comprising people of color, and work undertaken in the name of clean air and water and the cessation of toxic waste dumping.

The comments from Beth, Patty, James, and Daniel collectively speak to the racialized and classed aspects of the environmental movement in its nascent years and in related contemporary sustainability work. Lyrics from the *We're So Green* video reiterate these associations. For example, the line "It feels so good to be clean" (Office of Sustainability & Environment 2013a) is accompanied in the video by images of wind generators and solar panels, suggesting a tie with "clean" "green" energy. This emphasis makes sense due to the broader focus on GHG emissions within Seattle. Yet given the racialized and classed histories of the environmental movement, as just discussed, the language of "clean" also draws forth associations with whiteness. The trope of whiteness and cleanliness and blackness and dirtiness has long been part of racist discourse. Witnessing this frame emerge in this city outreach video indicates how embedded whiteness is within sustainability efforts, such that this lyric passed through pre-production scrutiny. The following lyric of "you know who you are and we're talking to you" further locates the intended audience of the video—the ones who are asked to give feedback on the *Climate Action Plan*—as predominantly white. The racialized and classed affinities evident in the *We're So Green* video mimic the ones in Way to Go and collectively indicate how exclusive inclusion informs the translation of sustainability into practice.

In summary, the central premise in the initial Way to Go program of shifting transportation choices for a short period of time pivoted on assumptions of access and amenities. The choices it asked people to make were not equally possible for all Seattleites because of their class underpinnings. As a result, Way to Go tacitly affirmed class differentiation. Moreover, the exclusive inclusion set in motion by this initiative located Way to Go within a well-worn racialized and classed enactment of sustainability. The development of the environmental movement helps explain how these systems of separation initially solidified. I suggest that the Seattle city government furthered such associations—intentionally or not—by forming a transportation initiative focused on choice and framed within exclusive inclusion. Teasing out these dynamics in Way to Go is necessary because such attention might help de-emphasize the logic of choice in other programs and make possible the implementation of equitable sustainability initiatives instead.

The Contested Green Fee

Accenting the importance of individual choice as a way to produce sustainability in Seattle emerged in sites beyond the transportation sector. In this next example, the routine consumer choice of paper, plastic, cloth or no bag surfaces as a controversial aspect of the municipal government's translation of sustainability as a value into practice. The story begins in 2008 when a study conducted by Herrera Environmental Consultants and commissioned by Seattle Public Utilities (spu) found that the environmental impact of disposable paper and plastic shopping bags was significant and that voluntary programs to encourage shoppers to choose reusable bags have minimal impact on the reduction of disposable bags (Herrera Environmental Consultants 2008). Based on this study, then mayor Greg Nickels and the City Council concluded that in the name of the greater good a fee-based regulation was needed to encourage Seattleites to choose reusable rather than disposable bags. The City Council subsequently passed solid waste management Ordinance 122752 in July 2008, which proposed instituting a twenty-cent advance recovery fee, the "Green Fee," for disposable paper and plastic bags. All grocery, drug, and convenience stores would collect this fee for each bag provided to customers (City of Seattle 2008a). Much like Way to Go, the policy development of the Green Fee ordinance centered on the choice to pay a fee for a particular type of bag or bring a reusable one. A summer 2009 SPU pamphlet delivered to all addresses in the city foregrounded this assumption of choice: "'Choose reusable.' It's as simple as that. When you remember to shop for groceries with a reusable bag and don't need to get disposable bags from the store, you'll be helping make Seattle a more sustainable city" (Seattle Public Utilities 2009, 2). Citing the environmental impacts engendered by the production and discarding of disposable bags and motivated by the recognition that "Seattle has become a national leader among cities in green house gas reduction and seeks to further that effort through waste reduction and increased recycling" (City of Seattle 2008a, 2), the Council voted 6–1 in favor of this ordinance.

A core premise with the Green Fee ordinance, one of the first of its kind in the nation (Mulady 2008; Grygiel 2009a), was that by encouraging certain consumption choices and charging for choices that do not align with such plans, the city government could facilitate a shift in resource use, which would subsequently help future generations within and beyond Seattle to thrive. As the penultimate whereas statement in the ordinance proclaims, "it is in the best interest of the health, safety and welfare of the people that regulation include the imposition of a fee to discourage the use of disposable shopping bags, to reduce the cost of solid waste disposal by the city, to protect the environment, and to recover the costs of regulation" (City of Seattle 2008a, 2). The rationale here is that resolving some of the short-term solid waste management challenges and litter issues offers long-term benefits for Seattle and the planet. Such a perspective resonates with understandings of sustainability that stem from the Brundtland report and signal efforts to govern for a specified future.

The 2008 Green Fee ordinance extended a resolution passed in 2007 that sought to phase out Styrofoam containers and shift to compostable packaging. According to the Green Fee ordinance, the revenue from the Green Fee itself would help support the distribution of free bags to Seattleites, the two proposed additional government positions, and the costs of solid waste management more generally. Stores with under one million dollars in annual gross sales would keep all the Green Fee earnings, while stores with over one million annual gross sales would give 75 percent of the total collected to the city coffers (City of Seattle 2008a). Providing free reusable bags to low-income customers, shoring up support for food pantries and food banks that often rely on donations in disposable bags, and working with non-profits to distribute reusable bags to low-income Seattleites were also parts of the ordinance (City of Seattle 2008a, attachment A). City officials publicly heralded this fee as another example of Seattle's forward-thinking mentality with sustainability. For example, Lila, a career employee in city government, when I asked her about examples of significant sustainability endeavors, answered that Seattle is "trying to do the bag fee thing, making sure all restaurants are using compostable products for take-out." The Green Fee ordinance commanded attention locally and nationally as an important sustainability measure, one that highlighted Seattle as a place willing to put a cost on polluting behaviors and not just incentivize, as with Way to Go, but also regulate consumption practices to achieve sustainability benchmarks. This ordinance fit within the popular imaginative geographies of a green Seattle and helped substantiate the sustainability imagination. As the subsequent voter rejection of the Green Fee elucidates, however, this ordinance did not resonate with the majority of the electorate. I suggest that the reliance on choice and the tacit exclusive inclusion underlying the Green Fee contributed to Seattleites voting down this ordinance prior to implementation.

Before Ordinance 122752 could go into effect, a coalition funded by the American Chemistry Council gathered enough signatures to prompt a voter referendum. In August 2009 the voters of Seattle defeated the Green Fee with a 58 percent majority and caused its repeal (Grygiel 2009b). The American Chemistry Council, which has a vested business interest in the perpetual use of plastic bags, spent over $1.4 million on the campaign, largely fronted by the

Coalition to Stop the Seattle Bag Tax (Seattle City Council 2012). Opponents noted that the Green Fee, described as a tax even though the legislation itself does not use this word, would not accomplish much since littering is a relatively small issue in Seattle compared, for example, to GHG emissions from vehicles (Nickerson 2008). The 2008 designation by *Forbes* magazine of Seattle as the second cleanest city in the country further supported this view that litter is a general non-issue (Van Riper 2008). The sentiment that this ordinance was mostly a "feel good" approach and could not exact significant change was another critique (Rucker et al. 2008, 4).

The contentious debate about a bag fee revealed some stark divides in Seattle and signaled some divergences between the City and the city. On the one hand, the majority of City Council members and other supporters felt the Green Fee was a reasonable mechanism for reducing trash in the city and for enacting the value of sustainability embedded within planning objectives and the city's frequently expressed green identity. Opponents, many of whom were small business owners or identified as immigrants, in addition to the older, conservative, and Republican voters who supported the repeal of the ordinance, voiced concern about the added cost to business owners of providing alternative bag options to consumers. The likelihood of reduced sales since people would shop less to avoid the bag fee was another point of contention. Some opponents also stated that the City Council leaned on their class privilege in this ordinance so as to effect environmental change.

Joanna, an employee in a for-profit family business in Southeast Seattle, for example, emphatically opposed the proposed Green Fee of twenty cents per disposable bag and voiced frustration with the existing ban on Styrofoam. Born and raised in Seattle, during our interview Joanna expressed both a deep commitment to her home city and concern about current policy developments. As we chatted about how the Seattle Vietnamese community thinks about and engages with the city's sustainability efforts, Joanna turned the conversation to the Green Fee and associated actions. She began with the following assertion: "Honestly, some of the city laws . . . they just don't work." Underlying this comment is an implicit assessment about for whom the laws do and do not work. Joanna hinted that the city laws are not working for the Vietnamese business owners who make up her community. She continued, "If you're going to ban Styrofoam, then you've got to think of an alternative . . . way to help business owners save money because the alternatives to Styrofoam are quite expensive. . . . Before you implement this, . . . can the city, I don't know, have some buying power where they buy alternatives and then sell it back to the business owners? Because otherwise it's like— okay, this is how much the fine costs . . . and this is the alternative products. I'm going to go with the fine." Joanna talks through the decision-making process her colleagues and friends used when determining whether to switch away from Styrofoam containers. Ultimately, as she explained, many people opted for the financial imposition of a fine rather than the financial burden of different eco-oriented products. This outcome is contrary to what the city government hoped for when it passed the Styrofoam ban, which suggests that lawmakers may not have consulted with a wide range of Seattleites on the legislation.

Joanna then shifted her attention to the defeated Green Fee, which she terms the bag tax:

> It's great to be a "green" city, but you also have to be practical, too. And you have to have practical alternatives before you can try to push people to be "green." . . . I mean, the Vietnamese definitely would not have supported that bag tax. . . . I think it was an ill-conceived law, too—or bill. . . . What that really means is that people would go shopping less. There would be less traffic. . . . "oh, I could swing by Vine Market . . . , but I don't have any bags with me. That's fine. I'll wait until the weekend, right?" . . . Frivolous buying goes down.

From Joanna's perspective, the Green Fee would have hurt small businesses directly by reducing foot traffic. As a result, she confidently reported that the Vietnamese community was against the Green Fee ordinance. She next noted, "The City Council is all white, all kind of . . . very liberal," which informed the policy making in detrimental ways, in her view, and overshadowed the heterogeneity of the city. Joanna bristled at the suggestion that the voter repeal of the Green Fee was due entirely to the funding from the American Chemistry Council and instead emphasized how this sustainability policy did little to connect with immigrant and low-income communities and instead unduly burdened them. Overall, Joanna felt that the Green Fee and Styrofoam ban were evidence of the city government trying to be green without thinking through the implications and without helping businesses make a change to alternative products or attract more customers.

The Green Fee also brought to light an interesting tension about the meaning of bags. For some Seattleites, using a disposable bag indicated some achievement of wealth. One had enough resources to just throw away a bag if so desired. The idea of bringing a bag to the store undermined this experience of status. For others, plastic bags indicated a lack of environmental awareness and caring among city residents. The relative homogeneity of the City Council at this time might have contributed to no councillor reflecting upon the varied meanings of a disposable bag for the diverse constituents of Seattle. The ordinance also presumes that single-use bags are predominantly used just once, which overlooks how many people reuse these bags for other purposes within the home. This assumption hints at another class overlay within the ordinance. For some, plastic bags are trash and symbols of environmentally bad practices. For others, these bags are storage bins, tools of transportation, trash receptacles, and more. The idea of paying to pollute, in a sense, invisibilizes the costs of shifting to a different system and some of the ways in which bags circulate within communities and families. If someone needs a bag for a use beyond carrying items out of a store, that future use and need is unacknowledged in the Green Fee ordinance.

Overall, what Ordinance 122752 failed to consider is how latent class privilege frames this "solution" to environmental concerns about disposable bags. For some residents, the fee did not pose much financial burden, while the possibility for gaining positive public status grew tremendously. Indeed, as the lyrics in *We're So Green* affirm, "We're so green, we bring our bags to the store" (Office of Sustainability & Environment 2013a). Put differently, to reuse bags means to bear out the identity of the sustainable and green Seattleite. Inclusion in the ranks of the exclusive sustainable Seattleites becomes more visible with the personal agreement to pay a fee or pack groceries in a variety of cloth bags. For other Seattleites, the real and perceived costs of the Green Fee from both the consumer and business sides were deemed prohibitive. The desire for an option of a disposable bag became coded as a bad choice and regulated as such. People who contested the fee or carried plastic bags did not fit within the exclusivity of the sustainability imagination in Seattle. While the usual contestations about regulation and government interventions played a role in this debate, I suggest that the class privilege underlying the Green Fee indicates how consumer choices and tastes (and class reproduction more generally) became intricately involved with legislation, thereby furthering the exclusive inclusion of this sustainability effort.

Moreover, the foregrounding of immediate choices for longer-term benefits as expressed in the regulation of bags does not necessarily acknowledge the immediacy of poverty. As several interviewees noted, many Southeast Seattle residents, among other Seattleites, do not have abundant extra money or time. The Green Fee potentially ate into discretionary money someone might have. If people shifted their consumption practices to minimize exposure to the fee, this could also possibly consume extra time. Giving out cloth bags to low-income residents alleviates aspects of these concerns, but it does not fundamentally resolve the systemic factors that underpinned some of the opposition to the Green Fee. Residents who chose to reuse bags or did not contest the fee for a disposable one entered into the exclusive inclusion of the green and sustainable Seattleite status, a designation reserved for people who purportedly make choices for the betterment of present and future inhabitants. All others were implicitly consigned to the edge of the normative urban identity and positioned as not making choices in the best interest of themselves, the city, or the planet.

Voices in favor of the Green Fee bear out exclusive inclusion as well. For example, Val, a county employee in the health field who was just starting out her career in local government, offered the following passing comment on the bag fee, situated here as a proxy for sustainability endeavors in the city. In talking about what makes Seattle unique, she noted, "In the work I've been doing, I've realized that we do have a pretty good understanding, relatively, of sustainability and climate change and social duty. That being said, stuff like the bag fee still aren't passing." Val's casual comment holds some incredulity about the people who voted against a regulation on disposable bags. She states that a "pretty good understanding" of sustainability and social duty is evident within the city, but the defeat of the Green Fee ordinance dampened this assessment of Seattleites. The perceived disconnect voiced by Val between opposition to the Green Fee and the city identity as green and sustainable signals the specific, and in many ways narrow, application of sustainability in urban governance. From her vantage point within local government, it is inconceivable to counter the Green Fee because of the deep premise that self-determining individuals choose to care for the planet and future generations by making environmentally sound choices now. The way Val's comment overlooks how such a fee could have negative financial implications for individuals and businesses serves as a reminder that local governments and their actions are constituted through and by people, who carry personal perspectives and socialization to their work. Keeping in mind the positionalities of policy makers helps demonstrate how latent class privilege can infuse sustainability efforts and propel the exclusive inclusion that emerges alongside the premise of choice. The Green Fee is an example of how seemingly progressive values, when translated into practice in urban governance, can weave inequities into the fabric of the city rather than resolve them.

Despite the repeal of the Green Fee ordinance in 2009 due to the voter rejection, City Council continued to consider ways to reduce the amount of environmental impact produced by disposable bags. Noted success emerged on December 19, 2011, when the Council unanimously passed Ordinance 123775, the centerpiece of which is a ban on single-use plastic bags from all retail establishments in the city. The ordinance also implemented a five-cent fee for any new recyclable paper bag used by customers. These changes went into effect in July 2012. Several of the rationales for this ordinance are the same as the ones for the earlier Green Fee ordinance, namely the waste reductions mandated by the Washington State Legislature and the negative environmental impacts of both plastic and paper disposable shopping bags. Ordinance 123775, however, disentangles paper and plastic bags from each other and offers different solutions to the stated problems posed by each. Now, rather than a fee for a single use plastic bag, they are banned from the retail sector of the city entirely. Paper bags must be recyclable and have at least a 40 percent post-consumer content. The use of a paper bag incurs a five-cent pass-through charge, except for anyone purchasing items with a voucher or electronic benefits card. Retailers retain the revenue from the pass-through charge. The $500 maximum fee for violating this ordinance is higher than the $250 one proposed in the Green Fee ordinance (City of Seattle 2011d).

The passage and implementation of this ordinance suggests a reduction in the logic of choice in this sustainability effort. With the banning of single-use plastic and biodegradable bags, all residents have the same experience in retail establishments. There is no incentive or fee for a single-use plastic or biodegradable bag. They are simply unavailable in all stores. As the SPU public information sheet about the bag ban states, "Single-use bags are wasteful. They also often end up blocking storm drains, littering our streets, polluting our waterways, contaminating compost, and creating more trash" (Seattle Public Utilities 2016). The elimination of bags helps to equalize experiences throughout the city, especially as compared to the focus on grocery stores, drug stores, and convenience stores in the Green Fee ordinance. The five-cent charge for paper bags is not as onerous for consumers financially, although purchasing bags with a certain post-consumer waste content can be more expensive for stores to stock. The minimal compliance structure in place suggests that there could be variability in the application of this five-cent charge. This too reduces the emphasis on the choice between using reusable bags to carry purchases (and secure public status) and paying the fee associated with disposable bags. While this ordinance does not generate funds for city services and departments and may not reduce the litter and GHG emissions associated with disposable bags as quickly as the Green Fee ordinance would have, it seems like an approach that begins to distance sustainability from a classed project embedded in logics of choice and exclusive inclusion. Perhaps this approach to the solid waste management of bags signals some new pathways for the urban governance of sustainability in Seattle.

Environment Washington, a citizen-based environmental advocacy group, conducted an external review of the plastic bag regulations implemented by Ordinance 123775 in 2012. They found that of the nearly 900 people surveyed around the city, just over half of the participants agreed with the ban. They also found that white people supported the ban in greater numbers than people of color, women more than men, and people in the 21–40 age cohort more than the 41–60 age cohort (Jornlin 2013, 5). Employees in supermarkets registered much higher support for the ban than small business owners (78 percent compared to 52 percent; Jornlin 2013, 9). Both types of retailers noted an obvious increase in the use of reusable bags by consumers. An internal 2013 SPU evaluation of the plastic bag ban found mixed reviews among the 169 respondents. The vast majority noted that carryout bag use stayed the same or went down after the ban went into effect. Some said that bag use dropped overall, whereas others reported a rise. Most retailers polled did not start selling reusable bags after the ban, and many reported increases in the cost of purchasing bags given the recyclable content requirement for paper bags. Several respondents noted that the bag ban was a bad idea and discouraged customers while also burdening retailers (Seattle Public Utilities 2013).

SPU reported a significant drop in the presence of single-use plastic bags in the solid waste streams, but a rise in the contamination of city compost due to confusion about what constitutes a biodegradable bag. Consequently, in October 2016 the City Council passed and then mayor Ed Murray signed Ordinance 125165 to extend the bag ban and pass-through fee, to add provisions for what constitutes a compostable bag, and to mandate that only fully compostable bags be tinted green (City of Seattle 2016). These new regulations are meant to reduce contamination in city compost and further encourage the use of reusable bags. The regulation of consumer bag usage and the current framing of bags indicates how a particular issue can become a centerpiece in policy making within Seattle's urban governance. The continued legislation and debate about bags in the city shows that such waste management practices will remain a key part of sustainability efforts and, therefore, will serve as illustrative sites for examining class privilege as exercised through logics of choice and the production of exclusive inclusion.

Conclusions

The final stanza of the song in the *We're So Green* video deletes the usual internal reference "you know who you are," which signals an in-group affiliation, utilized throughout the song, and replaces it with a broader enjoinder, "we're talking to you," as a reminder of the normative Seattle identity "we're so green" (Office of Sustainability & Environment 2013a). This slight discursive shift enables the cartoon to end on a note of calling out the work that lies ahead, all of which presumably builds on the noted successes depicted in the video, and of affirming a collective green and sustainable urban identity. In many ways the general push to associate Seattle with sustainability and greenness has worked (Saha 2008). There is less overt focus now within the city on seeking recognition as a green leader because of the tacit acknowledgement that Seattle is widely considered at the forefront of sustainability efforts. For example, political science professor Kent Portney (2013, 250) describes Seattle as "exemplary" when it comes to sustainability. Similarly, Seattle City Council Resolution 31312 about climate protection and adaptation measures begins, "Whereas, the City of Seattle is a nationally and internationally recognized leader in climate protection and environmental sustainability work" (City of Seattle 2011c, 1). The resolution goes on to explain the many advances Seattle has already made in the field of sustainability and the ones yet to come, particularly in the arena of carbon neutrality. This list recapitulates the promotion of activities deemed sustainable in *We're So Green* but also emphasizes policy endeavors at the broader city scale—such as urban forest protection and affordable housing—rather than primarily focusing on individual actions. Being seen as a leader in this field is a fundamental part of Seattle's sustainability imagination. Yet, as I discussed with Way to Go and the Green Fee, it is time to elevate the representational status of Seattle so that it emerges as a place guided by the ethos of equity. Such a transition would give more depth of credit to the frequently mentioned designation of Seattle as a leader in sustainability.

The phrasing "We're so green" from the video reminds Seattleites to see themselves as green and to make choices accordingly. This discourse fits well with the Climate Action Plan (CAP), which was initially released in 2006 and then updated in 2013.[2] For example, the "What you can do" chapter of the 96-page CAP stresses, "your choices + your neighbors' choices = a big difference for the climate" (Office of Sustainability & Environment 2013b, 66). The chapter details why and how it matters what transportation someone uses, what someone buys and how long commodities stay in one's home, and what a person or family eats. Specifying a fascinatingly prescriptive set of recommended individual and household actions, the chapter states: "Because most emissions are emitted during driving, our best opportunity to reduce its lifecycle emissions is by buying a fuel-efficient car"; and "Because most emissions are emitted during production, our best opportunity to reduce our carbon footprint through food choices is by eating more fruits and vegetables and less meat and dairy" (Office of Sustainability & Environment 2013b, 68). The underlying message here is that individual choices about food and transportation help curtail GHG emissions and therefore lower the carbon footprint of the city as a whole. All these practices help bear out the sustainability imagination of Seattle.

On the one hand, a close reading of this section of the CAP could indicate the primary strategy used by the municipal government to curb overconsumption and to encourage predominantly wealthier Seattleites to rein in their habits and associated resource consumption through a forum that celebrates changes in behavior patterns. On the other, this section exudes assumptions of choice and material life circumstances, such as owning a house and more than one car, having wide-ranging options for transportation, and having the time to make the normatively "appropriate" carbon-sensitive decisions. As my interviewees revealed, this is not always the case. Yet the language and ethos that underpin the CAP carry such class overtones, thereby demonstrating again the presence of this perspective within sustainability efforts. I read statements such as "Going green is not just something Seattleites talk about; it is a core value that guides choices" (Office of Sustainability & Environment 2013b, 87) as evidence of the persistent logic of choice and the exclusive inclusion of sustainability in Seattle. The silence on equity is loud and bears out Portney's (2013, 204) claim that "if equity issues are important conceptual components of sustainability, then sustainable cities initiatives in the United States do not seem to take it very seriously." This is striking because the value of sustainability cannot be realized in practice if equity is not present in the construction, implementation, and outcomes of sustainability initiatives (Agyeman 2013).

Rice (2010, 935, emphasis in the original) effectively explains how the encouragement and mandate to *Be a good carbon citizen*" in Seattle emerged through the carbonization of urban governance and the re-territorialization of the jurisdictional power of local governments. Civic participation in the enactment of sustainability is crucial to this approach to urban governance (Portney 2005). My analysis of the Green Fee debate and the Way to Go transportation initiative illustrates how the assumptions of choice underpinning the construct of being a good carbon citizen and upholding the green identity of Seattle actually truncate the execution of sustainability activities. Through the frame of exclusive inclusion, I demonstrate that practicing urban governance in this fashion results in the amassing of positive status and the possibility for obvious group inclusion for some and the exclusion of others. Making visible the exclusions wrought by privilege and choice, such as those instantiated in the Way to Go program and the Green Fee, is important for changing systems.[3] Indeed, taking note of the unexamined assumptions guiding contemporary policy and program development and implementation is crucial for altering such processes and bringing values and practices into closer alignment.

A more holistic approach to sustainability and urban governance could help reduce the disparities between social value and practice within sustainability efforts. On this point, professor of globalization and cultural diversity Paul James (2015, xv) calls for a recasting of "prosperity" to signal something other than the aspiration toward unmitigated economic growth, with all the concomitant environmental consequences, to something more life sustaining.[4] To aid with such recasting, James (2015) offers the frame of circles of sustainability to emphasize the integration of politics, ecology, culture, and economics. He accents social processes in circles of sustainability because, as he notes: "If positive sustainability is defined as practices and meanings of human engagement that project an ongoing lifeworld of natural and social flourishing, then sustainability is a *social* phenomenon long before it is an economic or even just an ecological phenomenon" (James 2015, 51–52, emphasis in the original; see also Davidson 2010). The author suggests that this approach is more robust than the triple bottom line or three E's concepts (environment, economy, and equity) because in his view these other models mostly focus on economic growth. The entry point into sustainability through the social connects with his general premise that urban challenges have arisen principally due to human actions: "Why are our cities in crisis? Because our cities *are us*" (James 2015, 11, emphasis in the original). Circles of sustainability as a methodology and assessment tool, therefore, emphasizes the social as it considers the intersections of economic, political, and ecological activities. Adopting such an approach to sustainability could mitigate the reproduction of exclusive inclusion and assumptions of choice.

Another prominent alternative to standard sustainability practices within municipal government is "just sustainabilities" (Agyeman et al. 2003). The concept of just sustainabilities connects the environmental conservation model of many sustainability efforts with the core principles of the environmental justice movement, which foregrounds community-level grassroots activism and broader scale policy reformation aimed at ameliorating the environmental, social, and economic injustices that frequently go hand in hand (First National People of Color Environmental Leadership Summit 1991). This approach stresses "the need to ensure a better quality of life for all, now, and into the future, in a just and equitable manner, whilst living within the limits of supporting ecosystems" (Agyeman et al. 2003, 5). As such, the just sustainabilities paradigm recognizes the limits of systems and seeks to manifest inter- and intra-generational equity, all the while emphasizing that more equal societies are better for everyone (Agyeman 2013). This framework addresses the relationships between ecological devastation, power, and inequity and offers alternative ways forward. Underscoring plurality is important because such a stance recognizes the salience of place, history, and community. There is not just one approach to sustainability that works in the same way with the same outcomes everywhere. The concept of just sustainabilities highlights multiplicity and, therefore, attends to the interweaving of local and globalized processes (Agyeman 2013).

Such an approach is crucial for many reasons, not the least being the linkages noted between racism and environmental degradation. For example, as policy analysts J. Andrew Hoerner and Nia Robinson (2008) state, climate change exacerbates existing inequalities as the impacts of global warming disproportionately affect those who are food insecure, have health challenges, live in insecure housing situations, and exist within economic precarity. These individuals and communities generally have much lower carbon footprints than wealthier people and communities, and yet they bear the most intense burden of economic variability, natural disasters, and health disparities. As a local case in point, environmental studies professor Troy Abel and geographer Jonah White

(2011, S252) found that although Seattle has deindustrialized since 2007, the "burdens of its remaining industrial facilities fall disproportionately on some of the city's most socially vulnerable populations." Their examination of air toxin exposure illustrated yet again the confluence of systemic racism, classism, and environmental degradation. Hoerner and Robinson (2008, 2) remind that "Climate Justice is Common Justice" and that trying to address environmental challenges without considering systemic racism, including the history of the environmental movement itself and the promulgation of intense discrimination, will neither resolve environmental problems nor remediate structural inequalities. Moving the discourse away from a sole focus on the vague entity known as the future (and future generations) to a simultaneous consideration of present realities can enhance the application and realization of just sustainabilities.

The prevailing practices in the Way to Go program and the Green Fee ordinance sat comfortably within a classed milieu and revealed little evidence of just sustainabilities. The tides are possibly changing, however. After a decade of concerted focus on dismantling institutional racism within city government (as discussed in chapter 4), Seattle city government finally publicly recognized the shortcomings of its sustainability efforts and sought to remedy the persistent programmatic silences on equity. To this point, in April 2015 then mayor Murray launched the Equity and Environment Initiative (EEI), which aims to ensure that environmental policies benefit all residents, that people bearing the brunt of environmental degradation are key collaborators in establishing environmental priorities, and that a more racially, ethnically, linguistically, and class diverse group of people become involved in environmental work (Murray 2015).[5] This retooling of city sustainability efforts includes centering equity in all decision making, program development, and policy implementation. The recognition that reaching a goal in one area is not a success if it produces negative consequences in another marks a significant transition in thought and outcome measurements for the city.

The inclusion of a more systems-based and relational approach to urban governance through the EEI indicates a different way of enacting the social value of sustainability and the sustainability imagination. How these changes manifest in tangible and ongoing actions remains to be seen, as significant and lasting impact usually relies on shifting socio-environmental practices and revamping institutional infrastructure and discourse (Cidell 2017, 138).[6] Still, as Seattle repeatedly secures positive appraisals as a leader of green, it is vitally important to examine how the value of sustainability has translated into practice alongside the furthering of exclusive inclusion and latent class privilege. The bar for engaging with and bringing forth sustainability needs to be set much higher to consider holistically the relational entanglements of humans and non-humans, living and nonliving beings in Seattle. Manifesting equity within sustainability endeavors is both necessary and worthwhile as urbanization continues apace, stark disparities persist, and the realities of climate change are ever more obvious.

3

People, Products, and Processes

Creativity as Economic Development

As one of my first interviewees, Marta took it upon herself to teach me about how initiatives evolve in city government and how decision making unfolds. She did not rely on political platitudes for this task, though. Instead, drawing on her decade or so of employment in policy analysis and development in city government, with forthright and honest language she described specific trainings, strategic interventions, and particular actions undertaken to create institutional change. Marta outlined the challenges facing such work as she simultaneously rendered transparent the often intangible power structures underpinning urban governance. She pointedly reflected upon the need for nuance within urban issues. Through this discussion, Marta invited me to take in fully the complexity of institutionalizing transformation within Seattle.

While the themes of systemic change wove through the interview with Marta, she also emphasized the need for Seattle to push persistently its competitive edge, which was bound up with imaginative geographies about the city's distinctiveness. For instance, when I asked her what makes Seattle unique, she stated: "We have this regional culture that people here are not your usual folks. People that end up here usually are folks that like to push the envelope. And they're not very happy with just things as they are, that's why they end up here, far away from everything. . . . People are always talking about being in the cutting edge, like being counter-culture, cutting edge, innovative, creative." As Marta suggests, Seattle is frequently described as being ahead of the curve, a place that gains recognition and status for its originality. As if to confirm this point, while I was doing fieldwork the progressive business magazine *Fast Company* designated Seattle its City of the Year based on the city's creativity, as expressed in the development of businesses like Boeing and Microsoft, the "green" mentality of residents, the extensive cultural and arts scenes, and the renowned medical establishments (Stein 2009). The perceived ties between Seattle and creativity, innovation, and entrepreneurialism are reiterated in advertisements on buses, in the offices and corridors of City Hall, and within city documents. As city employee Henry pithily declared, "Innovation's been in our blood," a nod to the spirit of entrepreneurialism associated with this city, as discussed in chapter 1. Creativity, innovation, and entrepreneurialism are crucial facets of Seattle's imaginative geographies and shape urban governance in consequential ways.

The primary public definition of creativity in Seattle stems from urban writer Richard Florida's (2002) concept of the "creative class," an economic class of people described by Florida as catalysts in urban economic transformation because they purportedly intensify economic value through their creativity, their lifestyle choices, and their participation in the knowledge economy (Florida 2001; 2002; see also Peck 2005, 740; Krueger and Buckingham 2009). People employed in fields like the arts, entertainment, education, and architecture comprise the creative class core. A set of creative professionals, those who are employed in finance, health care, and law, round out the members of the creative class, according to Florida (2002, 8). The three T's of talent, tolerance, and technology are central components of Florida's typology of the creative class (Florida 2002, 249), this group of generally young, college-educated professionals who are purportedly drawn to places with high-tech industry, innovation, and openness to diversity, as measured by Richard Florida's "Gay Index" (Florida 2001).

In his widely read books on the subject, Florida applauds Seattle's efforts toward becoming a broadly creative community and notes how the amenities of Seattle appeal to the creative class (Florida 2002, 7, 288–89). He further identifies Seattle as one of the elite few urban areas in the United States that has attracted a disproportionate share of talented workers, who ostensibly expand the economic robustness and social liveliness of the city. Given such praise from this popular writer and prominent urban consultant, it is unsurprising that, according to local lore, former Seattle mayor Greg Nickels was a charter member of the Richard Florida Fan Club; or that when I asked long-time city employee Geneva what draws people to the city now, she replied, "Seattle is one of those Richard Florida cities." Literal and figurative investment in the creative class concept helps reposition the dominant narrative of Seattle as a company town to Seattle as a creative innovator.

Despite this hype, my analysis of the translation of creativity as a social value into practice in Seattle's urban governance shows that relying on the creative class theory contributes to a narrow application of creativity and likely produces a deepening of racialized and classed inequities. To bear out these points, I examine how the ethos of the creative class and its focus on specific people deemed creative underpinned the development of a cultural overlay district in the neighborhood of Capitol Hill (see map 1). I illustrate how this constrained focus on creativity as linked to certain people can both produce some economic stability and render "non-creative" residents disposable and hindrances to the new brand of the neighborhood. Such discursive reorganizing of a place around this kind of creativity-based economic development can therefore contribute to gentrification, the classed and often racialized transition of a neighborhood from one generally occupied by residents with lower socioeconomic status to one with residents of higher socioeconomic status (Lees et al. 2008). Accentuating displacement—the "pattern of change" in a neighborhood that leads to businesses and residents involuntarily moving out due to price increases, the shuttering of culturally relevant stores, and the disintegrating of social networks (Greenwich and Wykowski 2012, 6–7)—is another possible negative outcome from creative class, people-based creativity policy approaches.

The translation of creativity as a value into practice emerged within economic development proposals based on certain products as well. To think through some implications of this approach to creativity and economic development, I next turn to a proposed retail revitalization plan for Rainier Valley to show how the proposed public-private partnership aimed to leverage racial and ethnic diversity as a commodity. In this case the ostensible creativity and innovation stem from packaging diversity as a product. The commodification of ethnic businesses and racialized people in this way reveals how providing ethnic and racial diversity as lifestyle amenities for the creative class propels unequal power dynamics and othering. The Rainier Valley retail revitalization proposal also represents one more venue wherein the perspectives and values of the creative class theory, and associated notions of creativity as principally linked to certain people and products, contour Seattle's urban governance.

Conceptualizing creativity as a process, however, can produce different results. My third case for analyzing the social value of creativity as translated into practice is the recent equitable transit-oriented development (ETOD) plans for Southeast Seattle. These plans outline a sustained process for producing equity through different kinds of urban development approaches, thereby demonstrating the linkage of creativity with a specific process. In total, the three policy proposals and approaches under discussion in this chapter, the first two of which were significant action areas during my fieldwork, underscore how different facets of creativity, namely as something tied to a person, a product, or a process, guide economic development policy conceptualization and implementation within Seattle's urban governance (Simonton 2011, 73). In examining the translation of creativity into practice through these three examples, I argue that engagement with creativity as a process provides and encourages a fuller expression of equity and instantiates greater opportunities for urban justice. In contrast, working to actualize creativity through tying it principally to certain people, as in the creative class, or to products, can contribute to a greater commodification of difference, which can augment racialized and classed disparities in the built environment, economic development, and everyday life in the city.

Cultivating Seattle as Home to the Creative Class

Even though I expand the application of creativity within urban governance to examine policies linked to people, products, and processes, the overwhelming assumption in Seattle is that creativity equals the creative class. The stated ties between Seattle and the creative class are significant because the people in this group have come to be heralded as the centerpieces of urban economic development within and beyond Seattle city government. The lauded entrepreneurs and innovators of the creative class purportedly draw in businesses and revitalize slumped economies and neighborhoods. Lance, who strives to increase the number of people of color involved in business in Seattle, explained that his organization focused on people-oriented strategies for economic development because "sharp people wanna be around other sharp people, and they wanna be around people who can tickle their imagination to take them to places they have never been before." A people-centered approach to economic development made sense to him.

Lance was not alone in his assessments. On the contrary, the creative class premise of economic development cropped up in conversations throughout city government. For example, Sebastian, a city employee who works in the arts field, described how the creative economy played a significant role in helping Seattle weather the 2008 recession and then commented, "You can do all you want to bring business there. If you don't have people, it's not going to matter. So, the new question is: . . . what do people want, rather than what do businesses want?" Drawing directly upon Richard Florida's work, Sebastian suggests that future economic success is contingent upon enticing the right people and cultivating the right urban features. Offering the amenities desired by the creative class and promoting the livability of a place is, therefore, a long-awaited urban fix, one that Seattle city government eagerly adopts. Sebastian continued, "Embracing creativity, embracing folks that think a little bit differently, and then letting them just go to work is the best economic development we can do." In line with Florida's portrayal of the creative class, he outlined a people-oriented tactic for economic development. This approach promulgates an imaginative geography of Seattle as a place that meshes "think outside the box" people with a "think outside the box" city.

The promotion of Seattle as an unusual and creative place soared during my interview with Henry, a city employee in the arts field. Within moments of the interview starting, Henry waxed rhapsodic about the commitment Seattle city government has had to arts and culture:

> I think there's recognition that arts and culture is one of our strengths, ... over the past fifteen, maybe twenty years now, we've made substantial investment in cultural facilities. Looking around the landscape, McCaw Hall, Benaroya Hall, and the Experience Music Project and Central Library and all of these kinds of facilities. ... I think it's in our DNA. ... the writings of Richard Florida sort of helped underscore that. And I think also because we're one of the best-educated cities and one of the most literate cities in the nation. ... Historically, our doors have been open to the world. ... So, I think it's that combination of being a magnet for an intelligent, well-educated workforce and the connection to being a magnet for artists and for arts and culture.

Henry touches upon several themes in this passage as he describes the commitment to the arts and culture evident in the built landscape, the impact of Florida's ideas, and the literal embodiment of creativity within Seattleites. He also notes how Seattle attracts and produces well-educated people, so there is an assumption of embedded talent within the current pool of residents. He references the ethnic and cultural diversity of the city, which could be read as evidence of the livability metrics required by the creative class, according to Florida (2002). Importantly, Henry's portrayal of Seattle also conveys much of the language of the creative class concept, thereby indicating how Floridian perspectives have seeped into urban governance. Put plainly, Henry and colleagues repeatedly suggested that Seattle is a natural home for the creative class.

True believers in the power of the creative class abound, and associated development plans are evident in places as diverse as

Singapore, Rotterdam, Austin, and Toronto. The infatuation with the creative class is fairly ubiquitous within municipal governments. Critics voice concerns, though, about the unquestioned adoption of this template for economic development and the overarching implications of this theory (Gibson 2003; Ley 2003; Gibson and Klocker 2004; Hackworth and Rekers 2005; Peck 2005; Markusen 2006; Hoyman and Faricy 2009). Florida himself worries about the class divides produced by the headlong rush for talent and recognizes that the "list of unequal metros [in terms of wage inequality] reads like a who's who of Creative Class centers" (Florida 2012, 359). Yet he suggests that an easy solution to such disparity is to designate service industry jobs as creative too (Florida 2012, xiv). He adds that creativity is a "limitless resource" (Florida 2012, xi) that we all share. Thus Florida opines that we just need to unleash our creative potentials—ushering forth "the *creatification* of everyone" (Florida 2012, 385, emphasis in the original) —to produce greater prosperity, happiness, and well-being. This fairly glib response to the widening gap between the richest and the poorest and the off-hand suggestion that a designation as creative would diminish inequality elicits critique. Furthermore, it is never entirely clear what Florida calls creative. His "creative compact" seems to suggest that basically any work is nominally creative (Florida 2012, 384). If this is the case, why highlight the creative class?

Paradoxically, Florida offers the same template for economic development to every place, so it is questionable what kinds of comparative advantage and capital influx the creative class model can actually produce (Zimmerman 2008; Hoyman and Faricy 2009). After all, if many cities now boast a legion of creative workers, many new urbanist neighborhoods that evince the ideals of "live/work/play," and have a tangible "buzz," what makes any place stand out? How exactly do the lifestyle amenities enjoyed by the creative class produce benefits for all urban residents? Despite such questions, the creative class concept has garnered the attention of city boosters and policy makers around the world and become the basis of "how-to manuals for anxious city leaders and opportunistic policymakers" (Peck 2007, 1). Geographer Jeffrey Zimmerman (2008) describes this rush toward the creative class urban development policy as a hallmark of the latest chapter of the entrepreneurial city and evidence of a new economy, one that weds cultural capital with human capital.

In line with this assessment, the discourse of entrepreneurialism frequently emerges in tandem with calls for and acknowledgment of the creative class in Seattle. The underlying assumption is that members of the creative class are inherently entrepreneurial. While there is not one shared definition for entrepreneurs or entrepreneurialism, there are some commonly held attributes. For instance, entrepreneurs are frequently involved in innovative projects that rub up against the edges of current imagination. They notice gaps, take advantage of possibilities, are heterogeneous as a group, and generally strive to reap financial rewards. Translating such appraisals into urban landscapes, as much of the literature on entrepreneurial cities and urban entrepreneurialism does, demonstrates how municipal governments adopt the stated characteristics of entrepreneurs as economically successful innovators and mavericks (Hubbard and Hall 1998; Ward 2003). Places jostle for top ten ratings and vociferously declare themselves the "first," the "most," or the "leading" on any number of indicators as they participate in the race for high ranking. In the case of Seattle, this expression of being on the cutting edge and entrepreneurial often translates into discourses of "world-class" status, as I reviewed in chapter 1.

Entrepreneurs cannot risk being anywhere but at the forefront, and that mentality permeates much of city policy development. As an extension of such perspectives, translating creativity into practice within Seattle frequently means drawing upon the legendary entrepreneurial spirit and "can do" attitude of Seattleites and meshing such narratives with the work of the creative class. For example, Janice, who has lived in Seattle for a few decades and always worked in the arts sector, stated, "Because of the technological entrepreneurship that's in the area, there's kind of a nice fusion there of a willingness to look for new forms and embrace them. . . . Whether that's your own little iPhone application or gallery that's a restaurant, you know, I just think that spirit is alive and well." From Janice's perspective, a particular confluence of people, economic processes, and an innovative streak contribute to what she names as the "creative community" in Seattle. She shares the popular sentiment that an entrepreneurial spirit is thriving in Seattle as evidenced in everything from app development to art shows. The emphasis on entrepreneurialism is not new in Seattle, as the discussion in chapter 1 makes plain, but it is a powerful focal point in the imaginative geographies of Seattle as a city full of and attracting the creative class. As interviewee after interviewee mentioned the role of the creative class in fostering economic development and urban vitality and noted the longstanding role of arts and culture in Seattle, it became intensely obvious that creativity was a shared social value within municipal government and that the translation of this value into practice principally drew upon the creative class theory. Harnessing the purported economic productivity of the creative class therefore requires urban policy focused explicitly on this group, which brings me to the development of cultural district designations.

CODAC: Districts of Culture and Creativity or Staging More Gentrification?

The 2008 economic recession left many Seattle arts organizations and artists feeling especially squeezed in their efforts to find suitable and affordable work and living spaces. The concurrent purchase and retrofit of the iconic Odd Fellows' Hall in the Seattle neighborhood of Capitol Hill left numerous arts organizations unable to afford their previous home in the historic building (CODAC 2009, ii–1). This specific event, along with the broader trends of increasing real estate prices within the city, prompted focused consideration during my period of fieldwork on the preservation and expansion of the arts in Seattle. To this point, in 2008 the Seattle City Council created the Cultural Overlay District Advisory Committee (CODAC), a voluntary advisory group of business owners, artists, and housing developers, to establish a set of recommendations for City Council about possible ways to leverage economic benefits through the designation of cultural districts.[1] The twin goals of developing long-term strategies for maintaining studio and performance spaces in Capitol Hill and bolstering the economic profile of the city through the arts and associated lifestyle amenities underpinned this economic development approach.

The CODAC met from July 2008 to April 2009 in order to draft recommendations for City Council. The initial emphasis was on assessing the feasibility of creating a cultural district within Capitol Hill, replete with development incentives for preserving or creating affordable art and cultural spaces, to see what could be possible in other neighborhoods throughout the city.[2] The committee focused on Capitol Hill because, as a City Council member rationalized in a CODAC meeting, it is "the liveliest part of the city" (fieldnotes June 2009) and the "density of artists living and working on Capitol Hill is essential to the Zeitgeist of the neighborhood" (CODAC 2009, 2). Furthermore, Capitol Hill is known "as a neighborhood that is fierce about its identity—box stores? No! Artists? Yes!" (fieldnotes June 2009; see also Brown et al. 2011). Capitol Hill is also described as the primary locus for the LGBTQ community. According to the 2010 Census, the demographics of Capitol Hill were 77 percent of the residents identified as white, nearly 6 percent as black, 9 percent as Asian, and 5 percent as two or more races (City of Seattle 2011a). Given histories of systemic residential segregation, as discussed in chapter 1, Capitol Hill has a higher portion of residents who identify as white compared to neighborhoods in Southeast Seattle.

On August 17, 2009, the City Council passed Resolution 31155, thereby formally accepting the CODAC's final recommendations and lending support to the eventual creation of cultural districts in Seattle's comprehensive plan (City of Seattle 2009a). The resolution also states that the City Council will explore implementation plans for the six primary recommendations from the CODAC: (1) create cultural districts; (2) designate a district cultural manager; (3) build a cultural space "brand"; (4) provide technical assistance to arts and culture organizations to help with the neighborhood branding; (5) engage with neighborhood residents to raise awareness about how arts and cultural space can contribute to environmental sustainability, community cohesion, and overall quality of life; and (6) develop public and private partnerships to make cultural neighborhood designations financial and social successes (City of Seattle 2009a; CODAC 2009, 7).

The creative class concept guided much of the CODAC's work. For example, as the final report of the CODAC committee states, "Latest theories in urban planning strongly suggest a correlation between livability and a city's ability to maintain healthy commercial cores and attract work force, businesses, and residents" (CODAC 2009, ii). In other words, sound economic development revolves around investing in people and the lifestyle amenities they desire. This Floridian frame for economic development centers livability as tied to creativity. Cultivating creativity through a cultural district designation signaled to the CODAC committee a wise investment with high potential for robust economic returns (Rantisi et al. 2006). Furthering this point, the CODAC report notes that entrepreneurs and innovators, presumed key drivers of economic growth, are drawn to "creative and sophisticated markets" (CODAC 2009, 4), so a cultural district designation is good for current artists and future creative class members, like LGBTQ people, who could move to Capitol Hill or at least spend money in the neighborhood. This rationale for the cultural district designation draws directly from Florida's playbook on the creative class.

The implementation plan for an arts and cultural district program and the first designation of a neighborhood as an arts and cultural district came to fruition in November 2014 with Resolution 31555.[3] This resolution designated the area around and between the intersections of Pike and Pine Streets and 12th Avenue in Capitol Hill as an officially recognized arts district and stated that the citywide arts and cultural district programming would be a part of the Office of Arts & Culture (City of Seattle 2014; see map 4). This area of Capitol Hill is described as "the densest arts neighborhood in the State of Washington" (Office of Arts & Culture 2019). Put differently, this is a place where the cultural district designation makes sense, as it is already an informally recognized hotbed for artistic activity. Resolution 31555 encourages all Seattleites, and especially those within the cultural district, to support and promote artistic and cultural activities in the area (City of Seattle 2014, 2). The resolution further acknowledges the economic importance of arts and cultural activities within the city and expresses a desire to assist existing and future arts businesses through the cultural district designation (City of Seattle 2014, 1).

The widespread belief that the arts exert a positive economic influence on urban landscapes was repeatedly stated with regard to cultural districts, even though the authors of the CODAC report acknowledge that it is hard to quantify the economic value of such activities (CODAC 2009, 3). This is where Florida's ideas about the creative class are especially crucial to the CODAC policy proposals. Florida blithely and repeatedly argues that the creative class undoubtedly boosts the economic growth and viability of a place. Although various scholars have challenged the causality that Florida outlines between particular professions and economic output, his invocation of creativity as embodied in certain people is so appealing that many policy proposals do not necessarily look for other concrete evidence (Peck 2005; Markusen 2006; Russo and van der Borg 2010). Enacting urban governance in the absence of data that bear out the assumptions of the policy can undermine public trust in policy makers and can produce negative unintended consequences. For instance, geographer David Ley (2003, 2540) finds that within the four largest Canadian cities the presence of artists in a census tract remains one of the strongest statistical predictors of subsequent gentrification. Indeed, the aestheticization that often emerges in places where artists live and work can lend cultural capital to a neighborhood that over time becomes commodified economic capital. Therefore the valorization of cultural capital within a city, Ley illustrates, further enables the close ties between artistic activity and ensuing gentrification.

Related to Ley's findings, in our conversation about the tension between preserving space for arts and managing the pressures of gentrification, Janice described the classic cycle of neighborhood change: "If they [artists] come in and the real estate market is depressed and they're able to rent, and they hold those spaces and make that a lively environment, then when the real estate market refreshes, they once again have nowhere to go. It's this sort of vicious circle of gentrification, settlement, gentrification, expulsion, essentially." Janice's pithy summary reflects trends noticed in urban spaces over the past several decades. This pattern raises questions about how the cultural designation in Capitol Hill could inadvertently spark such neighborhood transitions. Leslie, a county employee, identified the dissonance for her with individuals "talking about the negative impacts of gentrification as they pack up and move in." Housing trends echo what Leslie had noticed on the street. The August 2009 median home value in Capitol Hill was $348,000. The median home value in the same neighborhood in August 2018 was $705,000 (Zillow 2018b). The overall median home value in Seattle in September 2018 was $739,600 (Zillow 2018a). Rental prices have also assumed an upward trend, with October 2018 apartment rents running from $1,150 to $5,600 in the cultural district of Capitol Hill (Apartments.com 2018). While the housing prices have risen dramatically throughout Seattle over the past few years, the changes in Capitol Hill are notable.

To be clear, gentrification and the entrenchment of disparities are not the fault of artists (Ley 2003). In response to my question about any ties between gentrification and the creative economy, city employee Amiko explained, "People always point to . . . creativity is what led to that [gentrification], but that's . . . not really the cause of the gentrification. It might be a consequence . . . but the creativity is not the cause of the gentrification." To elaborate further, creativity in and of itself does not necessarily produce stark disparities and upend the collective success of urban residents. However, creativity that has been co-opted and folded into people-only economic strategies that focus on a specific group and presumed lifestyle amenities, such as policy development based on the creative class, can lead to gentrification because artistic undertakings often revalorize a neighborhood and make it ripe for reinvestment. Geographer Jamie Peck (2005, 751) reveals how the implementation of creative-class-conceptualized enterprises exacerbates processes of gentrification already in motion because the amenities allegedly desired by the creative class are those found more readily in gentrified spaces. Hence if cities want to attract members of the creative class, they need to renovate their neighborhoods. Through such work, gentrification acquires a rosier portrayal as creative urban revitalization (see also Ley 2003). To this point, the driving premise behind the implementation of a cultural district in Seattle was that the arts and other creative enterprises both improve the quality of life in Seattle and bolster the city's economic situation (CODAC 2009).

The potential use of transferable development rights (TDR) within cultural districts is a particularly interesting forum for thinking through gentrification and the ways in which land use decisions carry benefits and burdens. Specifically, the recommendation from CODAC is to enable the sale of development rights from lots that include permanent affordable arts and cultural space and as such are not developed to the zoned maximum (CODAC 2009, 21). The "receiving site" for these development rights could then be upzoned, which means changing zoning regulations to allow more intensive development, so as to construct bigger buildings with the addition of these purchased development rights. While this plan could increase the likelihood of more affordable spaces for artists and cultural workers in Capitol Hill and other cultural districts, it also means that density and development pressures relocate to other parts of Seattle. Shifting development pressures out of Capitol Hill and other cultural districts could disproportionately burden lower-income neighborhoods and communities of color that become the receiving sites for the TDR. Such a practice is especially complicated in the presence of this underlying belief expressed in the CODAC report: "One of the main roles of government is to intervene for the greater good of the public, for reasons of social equity and also to optimize economic outcomes over the long term" (CODAC 2009, 2). The relationship between social equity and economic imperatives is a tricky one, as my analysis of sustainability, creativity, and social justice policies routinely shows. The tight link forged between arts and economic development in the CODAC recommendations and the subsequent cultural district designation with incentives like TDR has significant implications for enacting equity throughout the city.

Despite the close ties between the potential furtherance of gentrification and the cultural district designation, the term *gentrification* is not commonly heard in city offices in Seattle. City employees recognize the negative connotation of the word and work to distance city projects from possible linkages with gentrification. In response to my query about the word and its absence in city discourse, Liz, a newer city employee who has spent her career conducting economic development in U.S. cities, said, "Yeah, because no one wants to say it! [*Laughter*] Because it's a dirty word. . . . We talk about displacement here. . . . It's not a substitute for gentrification, but I think it more narrowly addresses what the concern is, because having a cleaner neighborhood that's safer and has better retail options and better transportation options, that is not a bad thing, and that's sometimes what gentrification means. And so I think what we're worried about is, you know, wholesale displacement of communities." Liz's comments demonstrate a useful specificity as she focuses on displacement. She notes that the neighborhood changes often ushered in through gentrification are not necessarily negative, so she cautions against the complete disavowal of this process of neighborhood transition. The widespread displacement of current residents, on the other hand, generates concern for her and her colleagues as they engage in economic development.

The assumptions about what makes a neighborhood better reflect a particular point of view. The commitment within city government to the merits of the cultural district designation suggests that the marginalization of people who are not part of the creative class and of enterprises that do not contribute to lifestyle amenities may not be significant concerns for city employees. This means that the displacement of certain businesses and people could happen largely unnoticed because the attendant changes in Capitol Hill may be seen as ones that augment the production of a normatively "cleaner" and "safer" neighborhood. Such a silence largely stems, I suggest, from the overarching commitment to the creative class theory, which pushes forward economic development without much attention to social impacts, within the cultural district designation. Since the creative class ethos shapes the translation of creativity into a set of specific people-centered policy recommendations within the district designation, the invisibilizing of gentrification potentials emerges too. Focusing on displacement is important, as Liz rightly points out. Shying away from the real possibilities for class conversion within a cultural district, as has been shown in art neighborhoods in other cities, could mean that both gentrification and displacement unintentionally accompany the rollout of the cultural district designations.

Furthermore, the cultural district designation functions as a neighborhood brand, which indicates that people and places not associated with this brand could recede into the shadows (Gibson 2003; Atkinson and Easthope 2009). What lines of racialized and classed exclusion and marginalization could emerge as Capitol Hill undergoes the necessary transformations to become a cultural district? And what happens to the enterprises and built forms that do not promote the "right" character? Are they simply ignored, overlooked, or removed? While answers to these questions will take some time to surface, since the cultural district designation in Capitol Hill happened in 2014 and the other two more recently, they are points worthy of consideration. The inculcation of creativity as linked to the creative class within the cultural district designation conveys the distinct possibility of diminishing the heterogeneity of residents and organizations in a neighborhood and overemphasizing the activities of those who fit the new cultural brand. Establishing a widely absorbed "message" about a cultural district is deemed necessary for economic success (CODAC 2009, 37). This means that some uniformity in the public presentation of the district will arise. Such work can efface the presence of difference in the neighborhood, a paradoxical outcome as Capitol Hill circulates as a hub of difference within imaginative geographies of Seattle neighborhoods.

In his writings about the creative class Florida advises seeking out and encouraging talent—as embodied by people who work in various professions—to enhance the overall economic performance of a neighborhood and city. These very same perspectives underpin much of Seattle's cultural district designation. The cultural district policy proposal conceptualizes creativity as defined by a specific group of people engaged in various artistic and cultural professions. Yet focusing principally on the so-called creative class within a policy proposal can set the stage for displacement and gentrification, both classed and often racialized processes, because of the emphasis on the economic impacts of the arts, the lifestyle amenities afforded by cultural activities, and the overshadowing of "non-creative others." While the aspiration of maintaining affordable living and work spaces aligns with considerations of justice, equity, and social sustainability, the actual form of the cultural district policy recommendations carries the potential for displacement and gentrification. Such urban outcomes are familiar and arguably not very creative or innovative.

Revitalizing Retail: Commodifying Diversity in Rainier Valley

The fifty or so attendees at the Rainier Chamber of Commerce's September 2009 meeting filled the conference room at the Rainier Community Center for the unveiling of the proposed *Retail Development Strategy for Rainier Valley*, a highly anticipated and eagerly accepted proposal for economic development in Rainier Valley. Conceptualized by the Virginia-based Community Land Use and Economics (CLUE) group, retained by the City of Seattle's Office of Economic Development (OED) to craft strategies for strengthening and growing the retail sector of Rainier Valley, the revitalization plan focused on the near-term and longer-term possibilities for expanding measurable economic activity in the Valley, an area of the city made up of several neighborhoods within Southeast Seattle (see map 1). As the lead author and founder of the company rattled through the report in her presentation, sitting in rapt attention was a mostly white audience, consisting of members of city government, representatives from service organizations in Southeast Seattle, and a few business owners. The presenter's quick list for how to expand a business rapidly appeared to resonate with the crowd—"1. Create website; 2. Add new product lines; 3. Change storefront window displays; 4. Sell things in other stores, use pop up stores; 5. Offer deliveries" (fieldnotes September 2009). Such solutions indicate that image, speed, and technology are the primary drivers of retail success and that the small business owners in Rainier Valley should have access to these business development tools. Overall, it seemed that the audience felt persuaded by the assessment that there is an oversupply of undeveloped retail space along the new at-grade light rail line (which opened in the summer of 2009); that the lack of property ownership by businesses and the increases in commercial rent are significant issues; and that Rainier Valley needs an "aggressive marketing program" (CLUE 2009, 2). The suggestions for this marketing program centered upon the possibilities afforded through capitalizing on the racial and ethnic diversity of the Valley.[4] It is the suggestions for this marketing program that I unpack here as an example of linking creativity to products in the translation of a social value from concept to practice in urban governance.

Given the described economically underperforming nature of Rainier Valley and the associated external desire for rebranding, the CLUE report proposes a wide range of retail development and marketing strategies, many of which pivot upon racial and ethnic diversity. Within Rainier Valley, in 2010 Columbia City residents self-identified as about one third white, one third Asian, and a quarter black or African American. People of two or more races and some other race comprise the last 10 percent. In Rainier Beach the group of people choosing two or more races and some other race is just over 10 percent. About a third of this neighborhood identified as Asian and a third as black or African American. A quarter identified as white. The neighborhood of Mount Baker, on the other hand, reported numbers of just over half white, 17 percent black, and 16 percent Asian. Taken together, over half of the residents in Rainier Valley self-identified on the 2010 Census as people of color (City of Seattle 2011a). Within the context of this diversity, the CLUE retail economic revitalization proposal presents people and small businesses in Rainier Valley as entities that need access to a wider range of goods and services (CLUE 2009, 6–7). The report also identifies the cultural diversity of the Rainier Valley business community as "one of the community's greatest—and largely untapped—assets" (CLUE 2009, 12). Describing businesses and people as untapped resources labels them as items, products of sorts, and can create distance between the embodied realities of people living and working in the Valley and an abstracted economic bottom line. As a result, diversity—or at least a certain version of it, measured and meted out in a specific formation to beget a particular outcome—emerges as an intriguing feature and marketable product of Rainier Valley.

Positioning diversity as a thing to be marketed in this way contributes to the othering and exoticization of racialized and ethnic communities. Such othering can further entrench disparities within Seattle's urban landscape and governance. Edward Said's (1978) concept of Orientalism, the politicized and situated knowledge production of the "Oriental" "other" that sought to legitimize and advance European and U.S. imperial conquest, matched with scholarship on racism, underscores the negative consequences of the commodification of ethnic businesses and racialized people as products within the proposed marketing plan for Rainier Valley. As Said elucidates, the particular idioms deployed in Orientialist writing, such as the exotic and weak female who needs rescuing and the violent and barbaric man who must be subdued, cohere into a system of truths that shape relationships between people and place in latent and manifest ways. I submit that similar processes underpin many of the retail revitalization actions that the CLUE report recommends.

By way of example, the CLUE report states that the international businesses of Rainier Valley have loyal customer bases and that such enterprises offer an "authentic cultural experience" for visitors (CLUE 2009, 88). Consequently, the authors emphasize the need to preserve and promote "the community's international flavor" (CLUE 2009, 15), largely because of the deemed growth opportunities associated with this diversity. To this point, CLUE recommends developing an image-building campaign with taglines such as "I slipped away to Mumbai for lunch today," "Every Saturday morning, I go to Vietnam," and "Last night, I went shopping in Mogadishu" (CLUE 2009, 38). The logic is that such representations highlight the internationalism of the Valley and draw people into the local businesses. At the same time, such taglines reduce local Rainier Valley restaurants to exotic stops along a global culinary and consumption tour and implicitly rely upon assumptions of foreignness. The conflation of one business in Seattle with an entire city or country in the taglines also contributes to reified representations of place.

Furthering notions of exoticism and foreignness, the CLUE report also advocates for passing out free "passports" to Valley restaurants so that diners can record the key stops on their global tour. Handing out prizes for people who travel the world through their Rainier Valley eating forays is another suggestion (CLUE 2009, 38). Such theme-park type approaches to urban redevelopment disregard the dynamics of the place and situate ethnic restaurants and people of various ethnic backgrounds as commodities. In these recommendations, there is no room for business owners and Valley residents to promote their neighborhoods in the ways they see fit. Instead, a stereotyped and essentialized approach to the neighborhoods and residents underpins the economic development proposals. The suggestions pivot on an assumption that marketing businesses is all about dollars spent. Meaningful cultural exchange does not maximize profit in a short time frame. In contrast, enticing interest in "foreign food" holds the potential for greater immediate economic results and thus economic development. The linkage of this supposedly innovative and creative retail revitalization plan with the commodification of people and businesses as products demonstrates how such an inculcation of creativity can further existing separations between the racial and class majority residents of Seattle and the people who live in the Valley.

Not only do the CLUE marketing suggestions feed on Orientalist stereotypes of the exotic "other," but also they point to the goal of providing avenues for external funds to flow into Rainier Valley (Said 1978). The underlying rationale is that "to truly transform Rainier Valley's retail environment into a significantly more successful one, it will need to attract visitors from outside the community" (CLUE 2009, 36). Accordingly, CLUE (2009, 38) promotes providing information "that explains what to expect when visiting the business or taking part in the festival, translating the cultural experience for a broad audience." Such translation overtures, CLUE maintains, would help "people feel comfortable, like insiders, when visiting Rainier Valley businesses, restaurants, and events" (CLUE 2009, 38). Clearly this marketing is not meant to encourage local residents or people of shared ethnicity to come shop or eat in these Rainier Valley businesses. The focus is on bringing outside people in. After all, Rainier Valley competes with other neighborhoods, where immigrants and people of color also live, so economic development in the Valley depends on quickly capturing mobile capital. Packaging diversity in an easily consumable and sanitized way is one avenue to realize such capital accumulation.

As a city employee focused on economic development, Liz described the key assets in Rainier Valley that the city government hoped to build on with help from the CLUE report. She exclaimed, "What people love about ... Rainier Valley is that you can go there and you can buy all kinds of crazy, very specific, ethnic goods, and for me, it's crazy, because ... it's not from my ethnicity. . . . I can buy really interesting, what is it? Filipino food? ... So for me, it's a really interesting shopping experience outside my own culture." Liz's enthusiasm for providing pathways for a greater number of people to experience the richness of Rainier Valley as she has was present throughout her interview. Her comments, though, convey a persistent othering and exoticizing of the people and businesses in the Valley neighborhoods. Describing foods and goods as "crazy" suggests a normative position as something seemingly non-ethnic. This kind of language usually emerges in settings where whiteness is the benchmark to which everything else is tacitly compared. Remembering that the city government is made up of individuals and all their individual socializations and that policy generation comes from these very people helps explain how the CLUE proposal with its commodification of ethnic businesses and people of color was generally well-received by city officials. Indeed, the sensationalized taglines and passports for Rainier Valley proposed by CLUE correspond with Liz's perspective of cultivating adventure in the Valley. This translation of the value of creativity as a measure of innovation into practice, however, recapitulates unequal systems of power as it recommends commodifying brown and black bodies to entice capital reinvestment. The CLUE retail development suggestions largely position diversity as a profit-making product that can be manipulated, managed, and controlled to provide economic success.

Infusing the area with outside capital is not inherently a negative goal. Yet the recommendations for how to accomplish such a project and the ways in which local residents are commodified, at least in the report, suggest a pathway for economic development that relies on caricatures and stereotypes of the ethnic and racial diversity of the Valley. Rather than discussing strategies for helping forge economic viability through partnerships with people already in the Valley, the CLUE retail revitalization plan focuses on how to use individuals wearing traditional garb, businesses with signs in languages other than English, and restaurants with cuisines from all over the world as items within an economic development toolbox. In line with geographer David Harvey's (1989) depiction of urban entrepreneurialism, the CLUE proposal advocates for more public-private partnerships and an influx of private capital to realize the Rainier Valley retail revitalization aspirations (CLUE 2009, 13). Focusing on external sources to generate "solutions" and revitalization plans precludes local residents from weighing in on and helping shape strategies for the Valley. If displacement occurs due to these policies and development approaches, the CLUE report does not register significant concern, perhaps because gentrified neighborhoods usually augment a city's coffers positively.

The CLUE report's emphasis on economic development arising from capital flowing into the Valley and the need for leveraging local assets to maximize such capital influxes was echoed

PEOPLE, PRODUCTS, AND PROCESSES

within city government. For example, Liz, in an extended monologue about economic changes and possibilities in Southeast Seattle, explained:

> We also know that there's gonna be a lot of newcomers in the neighborhood who, maybe, are people who moved from different parts of the city, maybe, who aren't part of the ethnic groups that are there now who might be interested in shopping in some of those stores, but really don't know exactly how to go about doing that. It's a little intimidating. I don't know if it's been intimidating for you, but it is for me, sometimes, to even go into the International District (ID), and I see a lot of posters on the windows. I'm not sure, exactly, what's in there. I don't know if they're gonna speak my language, or what exactly do they sell, and so how do we create opportunities for new customers to be introduced to those businesses? And how do we help those business owners learn how to be more welcoming to people that maybe aren't part of their ethnic group, if they're interested in doing that? That's certainly not to say that people have to do that, but I think they will if they want to survive.

This passage speaks volumes about prominent perceptions of Southeast Seattle, and Rainier Valley as part of this broader area of the city, as a place that will experience tremendous residential change and economic transitions due to post–light rail economic development. It also reveals how one's positionality and life experiences shape racialized perspectives. Liz's comment about feeling intimidated when she encounters unfamiliar storefronts and signs in languages other than English within the International District probably reflects a relatively common white fear of—and intrigue with—the foreign non-white "other," a dynamic that mirrors the simultaneous allure and revulsion of people in the "Orient" by people from the "Occident," as discussed by Said (1978). The impulse to educate store owners about "how to be more welcoming to people" who may be their new customers signals an underlying aspiration to make store owners preserve their foreignness enough to be exotic while simultaneously becoming familiar enough linguistically to be legible to non-co-ethnics (a large share of whom would presumably be white people, given the general demographics of Seattle). Liz concludes that store owners do not have to undertake this kind of assimilative behavior, but she hinges their success on such adaptation. This observation suggests an underlying assumption that economic development plans in the Valley will bring in more white residents and consumers (as the CLUE report tacitly advocates), so current businesses need to change accordingly. Such a premise, and related retail economic development approach, relies upon maximizing opportunities for capital attached to white people to enter predominantly brown and black neighborhoods rather than enacting economic plans that strengthen and sustain existing networks and infrastructure.

The ethnic and racial diversity of the Valley is not just something that the CLUE consultants noticed. Jill, a relatively new Southeast Seattle resident who moved to the area explicitly for the ethnic and racial diversity, raved about her neighborhood. She enthused, "I love the diversity in every sense of the word." She mentioned the tremendous assets and challenges of the place and the noticeable changes happening on the ground. She explained that in the Valley there are "newcomers and folks who have been here for fifty years, and evolving businesses, and [questions about] how you save businesses . . . it is absolutely fascinating. It's sitting in the middle of a social experiment." Jill has gotten involved in local neighborhood groups and actively embedded herself in her new community. The energy she feels from living in such a dynamic and diverse place was evident throughout the interview. Makela, a self-identified black woman, "rabble rouser," and long-term Southeast Seattle resident, also centered diversity in her description of the Valley. She commented, "We value the diversity out here. It's just a joy to go out here and see people in different clothing. . . . This place is very welcoming to immigrants." Makela's extensive involvement in community activism in the Valley has brought her into collaboration and friendship with people from many different backgrounds. The diversity of the residents in the Valley is a treasured part of her daily life. Sal, a city employee who works in

PEOPLE, PRODUCTS, AND PROCESSES

community outreach, when asked about the greatest attributes of Southeast Seattle, affirmed the prominent imaginative geographies of the area by saying, "People always equate Southeast with diversity and that we have the broadest community here in Southeast." The CLUE report recognizes this community sentiment. Yet the ways in which these residents value diversity and how the CLUE report advocated for marketing diversity noticeably depart from each other.

Furthermore, the diversity depicted in taglines and passports is reductionist and has little resonance with the complexities of lived diversity. For instance, Rick, another Southeast Seattle resident who expressed deep affinity for his home of the last twenty years, stated, "You have all these different communities, and I think that's the strength." Yet Rick carries on to outline some of the challenges associated with this diversity: "The problem is that they don't always communicate well among themselves. There's been some tension, usually . . . white-black tension, but there's been some tension between some of the people of Asian heritage and African Americans." For Rick, the variety of people from different racial, ethnic, and class backgrounds living in the area marks a positive and unique characteristic of his neighborhood. At the same time, these differences offer challenges and call into question the degree of interaction between groups. Sal described the "in-fighting" between different ethnic and racial communities in Southeast Seattle as well and discussed the issue of having many different people all struggling to make ends meet while sharing the same space and limited resources. These features of life in Rainier Valley do not emerge as context or factors to consider in the CLUE report.

The CLUE report does not explicitly mention that cultivating interest in and excitement about retail in Rainier Valley while also advertising inexpensive housing stock could lead to gentrification and displacement as well. Yet this is an important subtext to the incorporation of diversity as a product within economic development strategies (Hackworth and Rekers 2005). A 2012 report, *Transit Oriented Development That's Healthy, Green & Just: Ensur-*

ing Transit Investment in Seattle's Rainier Valley Builds Communities Where All Families Thrive, put out by the organization Puget Sound Sage, found evidence of displacement in the shifting racial composition of Valley residents between 2000 and 2010 (Greenwich and Wykowski 2012). During this decade (the time when the light rail was built), the population of people of color grew by only 5 percent whereas the share of white people grew by 17 percent. To put these numbers in some context, during the same time period the population of people of color within King County (the county of which Seattle is a part; see map 3) grew by 47 percent and the population of white people shrank by 2 percent (Greenwich and Wykowski 2012, iv). It seems that people of color are moving out of the Valley. Makela, a long time Southeast Seattle resident, spoke to these trends. In the midst of our conversation about gentrification in Seattle, she remarked, "There are more different people moving in here," indicating that changes in her daily experiences of her neighborhood mirror what the demographic trends suggest. She continued, "I'm not opposed to people with more discretionary income moving in because this area is poor, but I will not stand for people being pushed out to have that happen." The CLUE report pays scant attention to such concerns, which raises questions about the priorities driving the retail revitalization proposal.

Matched with the demographic shifts in Southeast Seattle are the changes in land values. Land values around the Southeast Seattle light rail stations have increased by over 50 percent from 2005 to 2012 (Greenwich and Wykowski 2012, 10; Saldaña and Wykowski 2012, 14). Such patterns echo a common trend in the United States, which is that transit investments often propel gentrification processes (Welch 2013). The class transitions of gentrifying neighborhoods and the related displacement can certainly lead to greater racial, ethnic, and class homogeneity, as the demographic numbers already indicate. CLUE's recommendations to leverage diversity as a commodity and the focus on external consumers could further propel class transitions and contribute to a decrease in the celebrated heterogeneity of Rainier Valley. Consequently, I suggest that this kind of application of creativity as linked to the product of diversity is not an equitable way forward. The potential for amplifying social differentiation and stratification—thereby reducing urban justice and social sustainability—is real.

Trying to get ahead of the rising land use values and rents and changes in the built environment is especially hard for small ethnic businesses. Julian, who immigrated to the United States as a child and works now in the field of economic development for ethnic businesses in Southeast Seattle, commented on this point in response to my question about on-the-ground conversations regarding gentrification in the Valley: "I think that, you know, to be honest, a lot of businesses they sort of, they don't see the longer-term picture of what might happen to the neighborhood mostly because they're so caught up with trying to make it month to month. So, the question of will this neighborhood be gentrified five years from now, ten years from now, doesn't necessarily enter their consciousness on a regular basis." These realities are not primary concerns in the CLUE report either. As few provisions are offered for how to maintain the internationality of the Valley, it seems that the diversity is desired primarily for initial economic growth opportunities. Yet the very businesses and people who expand the capital growth in Southeast Seattle could become displaced through associated neighborhood changes.

Despite such concerns, some of CLUE's ideas have taken hold, if only because people realize that self-commodification is the most obviously supported pathway to greater economic security offered by the city government. For example, the MLK Business Association (2018), a business association founded in 2008 to promote businesses along Valley thoroughfare Martin Luther King Jr. Way, echoes the CLUE's phrasing as it describes itself as "your local, global market." Similarly, the Rainier Chamber of Commerce (2018) expresses, "We welcome visitors to an area so steeped in cultural diversity that according to national media sources, we are the most diverse neighborhood in the United States with over 60 languages spoken here.[5] You can stay local and feel global in our neighborhoods!" These descriptions echo the taglines CLUE recommended.

The ways in which the CLUE retail revitalization proposal packages diversity signal how the demographics and ethnic businesses of Rainier Valley were cast as products. Residents and businesses gained value through their representational status—could businesses be foreign enough and still approachable enough to make a "passport" program work? Could the presence of residents engaging in daily life evoke an authentic "cultural" experience? The CLUE report, the much anticipated and vaunted economic policy focus for Southeast Seattle when I conducted fieldwork in 2009, tacitly assumes yes. My analysis of the CLUE marketing recommendations for retail revitalization shows a case where a superficial invocation of diversity positions racial and ethnic diversity as a commodity, a product that can be sold, for economic development. This kind of action is framed as innovative and creative urban economic policy. Such a narrow interpretative slice elucidates, though, how the translation of the value of creativity into such a policy prescription can propel systems of racialized and classed inequities rather than craft plans for greater justice.

Equitable Transit-Oriented Development (eTOD): A Process for Equity in Southeast Seattle

Since 2012 a new focus on equitable transit-oriented development (eTOD), which offers a framework for including a plurality of local residents in economic development plans around transit nodes in order to produce greater equity, has emerged within Seattle city government (Office of Housing 2013). Significantly, eTOD marks a departure from the classic transit-oriented development model that "emphasizes walkability, density, and transit access" where "racial and social equity are not its cornerstones" (Saldaña and Wykowski 2012, 13). The intentional changes to standard practices are particularly important for Southeast Seattle given the racial, ethnic, and class diversity of the area, the legacy of underinvestment in the neighborhoods, and the expected development around light rail line stations. In Southeast Seattle, eTOD efforts connect with regional scale planning endeavors to integrate housing and transportation changes across spatial scales so as to create places of opportunity for everyone.[6] ETOD therefore represents a forum to link environmental sustainability with social sustainability, which has been largely overlooked within Seattle's urban governance, as discussed in chapter 2.

Significantly, unlike the CODAC policy, the creativity invoked within ETOD does not connect with certain people, such as the purported creative class. It does not focus on particular products, such as commodified ethnic businesses, as in the CLUE marketing proposal. Instead, the ETOD initiatives in Southeast Seattle draw upon creativity as a process. I contend that this shift to a process-oriented approach moderates displacement pressures and offers the most equitable instantiation of creativity in Seattle's urban governance. Even though the ETOD focus emerged after my fieldwork, I examine it here to demonstrate how translating the value of creativity into practice as a process of urban governance amplifies possibilities for equitable—and arguably more creative and sustainable—outcomes. Indeed, if all policy proposals related to creativity (as expressed through entrepreneurialism, innovation, and general creativity) foregrounded processes and relationships, policy generation and implementation would likely be more in line with the progressive social values stated by both city employees and residents. Furthermore, such an approach could offer a forum for flexible, creative evolution so that the relevance of policy approaches would remain and neighborhoods would have the adaptive capacities to weather urban transitions.

Standard transit-oriented development (TOD) and associated economic development strategies frequently stimulate gentrification and contribute to displacement (Greenwich and Wykowski 2012; Saldaña and Wykowski 2012; Dierwechter 2013; Office of Housing 2013). ETOD, therefore, strives to diminish such outcomes by foregrounding equity from the outset of any development project. Offering a different model for the process of economic development, under ETOD the residents in areas planned for redevelopment participate fully in the decision making—in more than an advisory way—in order to effect more inclusive and responsive on-the-ground transformations. Most important, racial and class equity and the ability to thrive in place are guiding principles at all stages of the economic development process. This kind of methodology can help disrupt patterns of disenfranchisement and displacement that often accompany urban redevelopment projects (Saldaña and Wykowski 2012).

How did ETOD become a focal point within Southeast Seattle? Following three years of neighborhood planning efforts (which I discuss in chapter 4), in 2011 the City of Seattle received a $3 million Community Challenge grant from the U.S. Department of Housing and Urban Development to work on implementing aspects of the neighborhood plans in Southeast Seattle. In particular, this funding centered upon actualizing the goals of building a wider range of housing types, providing greater housing affordability, supporting the existing commercial districts and expanding ones around light rail stations, and constructing multicultural community centers. Community Cornerstones was the grant-funded program coordinating this work. The commitment to equitable development outcomes in Southeast Seattle resulted in Community Cornerstones focusing on three main strategies for enacting change: (1) an equitable transit-oriented development (ETOD) loan program; (2) a commercial stability program; and (3) capacity building for a multicultural community center (Office of Housing 2013, 1–2). The implementation of these three strategies reveals creative, processual approaches to economic development and neighborhood revitalization and a dedication to the advancement of "prospering in place" (Gardheere and Craig 2015, 7) for current residents and businesses, a commitment that in concept is more equitable than suggested tactics from CLUE, for instance, to bring in outside capital and residents to Rainier Valley.

The ETOD loan program focuses on generating privately developed and funded residential and employment opportunities near transit, a core idea of TOD. What makes this loan program different, though, is that it advocates for securing real estate near transit hubs for equitable development rather than building up an area with at-market housing and more expensive commercial usages to raise funds for subsequent equity work. This latter strategy produces displacement in the short term and does little to ensure that equity projects will occur in the long term. In contrast, incorporating equity in the form of an ETOD loan program at the beginning of neighborhood redevelopment means that desirable locations within transit-rich neighborhoods, where many low-wage earning individuals rely heavily on public transportation, can be preserved for local businesses and current residents (Greenwich and Wykowski 2012, 8). Thus the best aspects of living and working near transit arise for the people who are often displaced through TOD. In the context of Rainier Valley, rather than have real estate prices continue to grow quickly and lead to further displacement, the local ETOD loan program offers residents and local businesses alike a chance to secure capital so that they can participate in— and benefit from—the transformations that could accompany development along the light rail (Saldaña and Wykowski 2012). The process of heading off displacement through intentional and upfront capital investments in existing businesses and residents illustrates the novel approach underpinning this loan program.

Although the initial Community Cornerstones grant was for a finite amount and the ETOD loan program needs long-term investment in order to sustain success, the commitment to equitable development was not conceptualized as a one-off in Southeast Seattle. On the contrary, Southeast Seattle coalitions have pursued a variety of avenues to sustain this crucial loan program after the Community Cornerstones grant funding concluded at the end of 2014 (Gardheere and Craig 2015). For instance, in December 2016 the public-private Regional Equitable Development Initiative launched to "help finance the acquisition of property along transit corridors to preserve the affordability of future housing and community facilities" (Enterprise 2018; see also Abello 2016). This initiative follows the same protocol for securing property and sustaining the ability to thrive in place as the initial ETOD loan program. Such a process marks a creative engagement with TOD and lays the foundation for more equitable outcomes than usual to emerge.

The second strategy of Community Cornerstones, the commercial stability scheme, indicates another inculcation of creativity as a process (Office of Housing 2013, 2). This strand of the grant program focused on (1) providing technical assistance to current building owners and ethnic businesses so as to help them prosper in the changing economic climate, and (2) creating more job opportunities in the area. Offering small grants for façade improvements helped business owners attract customers to their shops. Suggesting ways to populate vacant commercial space and providing tools to make that happen was a crucial aspect of the commercial stability focus as well (Office of Housing 2013, 2). Overall, the goal was to support existing businesses and residents with community-supported job creation and economic activity (Gardheere and Craig 2015). This tactic for safeguarding and enhancing the existing diversity of the area stands in marked contrast to the recommendations put forward in the CLUE report. Both proposals name racial and ethnic diversity as an asset in Southeast Seattle, but they adopt divergent approaches to maintaining and assisting the livelihoods of diverse individuals. CLUE emphasized commodifying ethnic businesses and the cultural dynamism of the Valley. Community Cornerstones, on the other hand, partnered with local businesses to offer support amid the shared vision of success for current enterprises. Such a practice and outcome signal a different application of creativity in considerations of retail and overall commercial economic development in Southeast Seattle.

The third branch of the Community Cornerstones program was the planning and fund-raising for a Multicultural Center. Conceived of as an explicitly multicultural gathering space, the Multicultural Center endeavors to reduce separations between different racial and ethnic groups in Southeast Seattle because the neighborhood planning process (discussed in chapter 4) revealed that many people had analogous visions and goals for their neighborhoods and did not realize these commonalities (Office of Housing 2013, 2). Another core premise for the project was that strengthening local community relationships and networks through a community-owned and managed center could help residents and organizations withstand economic transitions that often lead to property and price increases (Race to Democracy 2018). The center aims to help hold organizations and communities intact during neighborhood changes and serve as a concrete place for awareness raising, capacity building, community events, and networking. The process used to develop the steering committee that formulated these plans for the Multicultural Center centered upon equity as well. Specifically, rather than ask for volunteers for the center steering committee, which could have brought forth the same people who self-identify as leaders of different groups within Southeast Seattle, city employees surveyed residents and asked who people turn to for advice and guidance within their communities. These individuals were then asked to join the steering committee that crafted plans for the center (Stephens 2015).

Over the past few years and through many community meetings, aspirations for the Multicultural Center coalesced into plans for the Southeast Economic Opportunity Center, now called Othello Square. Described as a "creative, community-driven response to the pressures of extraordinary growth in Seattle" (Weber Thompson 2018, 1), Othello Square will be located adjacent to the Othello light rail station, in the New Holly neighborhood (see map 1). The multi-building complex is designed to include an early learning center, a health clinic, ground-level retail stores and restaurants, job training opportunities, a charter public high school, affordable housing for rent and purchase, small business incubators, and a community-owned and operated multi-purpose Multicultural Center, which aims to be an anchor point for eight distinct ethnic and cultural groups in Southeast Seattle (Nafziger et al. 2014; Barnett 2017; Southeast Economic Opportunity Center 2017; HomeSight 2018a; 2018b). The long-term management of Othello Square will be done by HomeSight, "a community development corporation and longstanding member and representative for the Southeast Seattle community" (HomeSight 2018a, 2), so as to ensure community control. Much of the necessary $203 million in funding has been accounted for. This project signifies "the most ambitious equitable development ever attempted in Seattle" (Barnett 2017). Importantly, the master plan for Othello Square describes the eighteen months of collaboration that underpinned the project development and acknowledges, "The process is as important as the outcomes" (HomeSight 2018b, 2), illuminating how crucial a processual approach has been to this substantial equitable development project. The eventual use of Othello Square as a forum for enacting neighborhood, city, and regional racial justice signals that the project will be an evolving and process-based place as well. Centering equity within and as a process in the development of Othello Square certainly sets the stage for the benefits of eTOD to impact the residents of Southeast Seattle positively and enable people to thrive in place over the long term.

Although an external evaluation of the Community Cornerstones program found some aspects of the approach did not work as well as anticipated (for instance, not as many businesses as expected wanted technical advice, and no one responded to the initial eTOD land acquisition request for proposals), the evaluators outlined several dimensions of the eTOD policy proposals that succeeded. In particular, evaluators commended the cross-cultural and cross-disciplinary nature of work teams. The more sustained and deeper inclusion of a variety of stakeholders within the planning and implementation processes and the multi-scalar facets of the work, particularly with regard to regional planning efforts, were also applauded. The focus on long-term goals and outcomes with Community Cornerstones and the tangible advances being made to actualize more equitable economic development were other noted accomplishments (Carlson et al. 2014, 12). Pertinent to my analysis of creativity, all of these observations acknowledge an effective process-based approach rather than principally a people- or product-oriented one. This demonstrates how the translation of creativity as a social value into policy conceptualization and implementation processes can help produce the context for greater equity.

Community Cornerstones provided funding to set up a process for articulating, designing, and implementing equitable development plans that will carry Seattle forward for many years to come (see City of Seattle 2018a). Even though the funding for the Community Cornerstones work has ended, coalitions and organizations (both new and longstanding) continue advancing equitable development aspirations in Southeast Seattle (Gardheere and Craig 2015). For instance, the Mercy Othello Plaza apartments, 108 affordable apartments with different bedroom configurations, opened in summer 2017 next to the Othello light rail station (Daily Journal of Commerce 2017; Mercy Housing 2017). The process of eTOD offers the most hopeful, and arguably politically progressive, translation of the value of creativity into practice in Seattle's urban governance.

Conclusions

In the early 2000s Richard Florida named Seattle as the fifth most creative city in the United States (Florida 2002, 251). Despite such appraisals, I contend that Seattle's urban governance has been relatively uncreative in the ways in which it incorporates and utilizes creativity as part of economic development strategies. The cultural district designation put forth by the CODAC, for example, demonstrates how creativity as linked to the creative class can further gentrification and displacement as such outcomes have often followed artists in other North American cities. Indeed, commodifying artists and cultural organizations through economic development plans can set the stage for the translation of cultural capital into greater economic capital, usually to the long-term detriment of artists and other current residents in a neighborhood.

The recommendations for retail revitalization in Rainier Valley outlined in the CLUE report indicate how creativity can assume material form through a policy proposal that relies on making a product—in this case, consumable ethnic and racial diversity—and then economically gaining from that commodity. This application of creativity is problematic as it reduces people and businesses to things and relies on discourses of foreignness and exoticism. The marketing suggestions for the Valley were not co-produced with residents and local stakeholders. As such, this imposition of an economic development plan illuminates how creativity as a product can exacerbate already evident classed and racialized inequities in the urban landscape.

The ETOD plans in Southeast Seattle, on the other hand, show a departure from "business as usual." Through collaboration, partnership, and a keen focus on equity, the ETOD works to actualize a different process for economic development. Spending resources on building local capacity and forging relationships does not produce tangible outcomes as readily as funders and politicians may like. Yet such work sets the stage for meaningful engagement in and a commitment to thriving in place for current and future residents and businesses. The ETOD process demonstrates how using creativity to lay a different economic development foundation and decision-making structure can ultimately produce greater social, environmental, political, and economic returns. It may also offer a powerful forum for cultivating healing from potent legacies of disenfranchisement and exclusion.

ETOD indicates one forum where city government, private and public partners, and residents alike are striving to manifest their vision for equity through a creative process. Plans that revolve around creativity as it pertains only to people or products are corollaries to linear planning; they are not as effective from a justice standpoint. Planning and creative endeavors that draw upon and vitalize relationships, consider multiplicity, and evolve through a dynamic process, on the other hand, have salience and can become written into the built environment in profound ways. The economic benefits of such work may not surface immediately, but over time such emphases achieve more equitable, sustainable, and just results. These are the truly innovative ways forward for creating transformational social change.

4

Unsettling Whiteness

The Race and Social Justice Initiative and Institutional Change

I was still figuring out my way through the Seattle Municipal Tower (SMT) when I interviewed Geneva, a self-identified person of color who moved to Seattle as a young adult and spent her career in city government. Her warm smile and "Come on in!" invitation elicited audible relief as I exited the web of carpeted hallways and stepped into her office. We sat at a small, white, round table and quickly found common ground in shared interests and passions. Our interview traversed assorted topics from her experiences working on social justice issues within city government to the impacts of light rail on neighborhoods to the comparison of Seattle to other places. Throughout the conversation, we clapped the table in laughter and clasped our heads with despair. When I asked about her initial impressions of Seattle when she moved to the city, she paused and then offered a crystallization of the place that stuck with me. She noted: "The racial politics are much gentler here and it's a very simple reason. There aren't enough people of color for the white people to feel threatened.... I guess I've always just thought of Seattle as urban race-light. And even now, its people, politicians, and white activists, they've learned how to say the right things." Gentler racial politics, saying the right thing, an urban race-light context (just as a point of reference, Seattle in 2010 registered at 69.5 percent white [City of Seattle 2011a]). These words brilliantly encapsulated much of what I had noticed through, for instance, my examinations of segregation patterns, my experiences riding public transit through different neighborhoods, and my forays into the Seattle Municipal Archives. Geneva's assessment of Seattle found reverberations in other interviews as well. For example, Hilary, who self-identified as white and worked in the for-profit sector, explained, "We could have an interesting conversation ... about the city and social justice and racial equality and all of that. And I've often thought, you know, it's really easy in a pretty white community to talk about that stuff. And Seattle is great about inclusiveness, as long as you're like them." Such depictions offered crucial insight into the calls for racial equity within the city and the frameworks mobilized for such social transformation.

After my interview with Geneva I began to question more pointedly, how does a race-light place enact social justice? Although there are different possible venues through which to respond to such a query, in this chapter I wrestle with it primarily in terms of Seattle's Race and Social Justice Initiative (RSJI), a citywide effort managed by the Seattle Office for Civil Rights (SOCR) and started in 2004. The RSJI provides a venue through which to examine the formalization of anti-racist social justice work within a specific institutional apparatus. Many municipalities throughout the United States have held dialogues about race and racism (Walsh 2006), but according to the RSJI, Seattle is the first city government to tackle directly the systemic reproduction of racialized inequities and institutional racism through citywide capacity building, policy changes, shifts in departmental practices and expectations, and the implementation of equity filters (Seattle Office for Civil Rights 2008). The RSJI has focused its work throughout urban governance on five primary areas: workforce equity; purchasing and contracts equity; greater immigration and refugee services; enhanced outreach and public engagement; and capacity building (Seattle Office for Civil Rights 2008, 8). A sense that the Seattle city government needed to "get our own house in order" before working on social change within the broader urban landscape prompted the initial internal focus for the RSJI (Seattle Office for Civil Rights 2008, 3). Now, community engagement throughout Seattle parallels continued internal work on eliminating institutional racism and producing racial equity within city government.

In the context of the RSJI, institutional racism means, "Organizational programs, policies or procedures that work to the benefit of white people and to the detriment of people of color, usually unintentionally or inadvertently" (Seattle Office for Civil Rights 2008, 3). The RSJI focuses on racism, while also acknowledging other hierarchies of power that systematically marginalize people, such as class, gender, sexuality, and ableism, because of the stark racialized divides in Seattle in the past and present and the barriers racism presents for the pursuit of equity (Seattle Office for Civil Rights 2008). Moreover, the RSJI leads with race because of the shared assumption that racism is "a learned behavior that can be unlearned through analysis, strategic organizing, and intentional changes in policies, practices, and procedures" (Bronstein et al. 2011, 159). Consequently, the RSJI aims to transform systems, structures, and actions such that race is no longer the most salient predictor of health, employment, and educational outcomes within Seattle. The Seattle City Attorney's office initially balked at the use of the term *institutional racism* within the RSJI because the phrase acknowledged the presence of racism within city government, which the attorney's office deemed a legal liability (Gooden 2014, 85). The founders of the RSJI did not compromise on this point, though, so the primary focus on dismantling institutional racism and race-based disparities remains. The RSJI has persisted through different mayoral administrations and become ever more embedded within Seattle's urban governance. As such the RSJI is an instructive site to examine where and how a municipal government chooses to notice race and racism and for what purposes.

As the fulcrum for social justice work in Seattle municipal government, the RSJI offers the most compelling forum for examining the translation of the value of social justice, as articulated through racial justice and equity work, into practice. Of the three social values I researched in Seattle, the programs, policies, and protocols associated with social justice implemented through or because of the RSJI marked the ones that most closely aligned concept and practice. The struggles undertaken in the name of addressing race-based inequities, the roadblocks associated with actualizing such efforts, and the labor intensiveness associated with policy alterations exemplify the difficulties of translating social justice as a value into practice through the RSJI. Still, despite the shortcomings and setbacks, the RSJI provides reason to believe in the possibility of substantive social change. Consequently, I round out my analysis of sustainability, creativity, and social justice in Seattle by discussing the development of the RSJI, analyzing examples of the RSJI in practice, and describing how the RSJI has emerged as a model initiative and informed county and national social justice and equity work.

Within the urban race-light context of Seattle, I argue that unsettling whiteness has been fundamental to the institutional transformations brought about by the RSJI.[1] Unsettling whiteness refers here to intentionally disrupting the normative power of whiteness to reproduce racial hierarchies and craft systems, structures, and stances that principally benefit white people. The word *unsettling* further invokes the personal discomfort that many white people felt as their implicit power and privilege were identified and challenged by the RSJI and recognition of their individual complicity in systemic racism emerged. I further use the term *unsettling* to capture the emotional responses Seattleites had as they realized the popular imaginative geographies of Seattle as a progressive City did not fully match the lived realities of the city. Indeed, the impacts of racism are as profound and familiar in Seattle as in any other U.S. city (Bronstein et al. 2011). Altogether, the phrase *unsettling whiteness* encapsulates both the structural practices undertaken to upend the centrality of whiteness within Seattle's urban governance and the challenges advanced by the RSJI to white fragility, meaning the assumption of racial comfort in all settings and the minimal tolerance for racial discomfort (DiAngelo 2011).

Given how whiteness is built into the normative practices, policies, and procedures of daily life in the United States, and often even more secure in race-light places like Seattle, unsettling whiteness has been crucial for actualizing the goals of the RSJI. The RSJI in concept and practice does not blame current white individuals for the historical establishment of systemic racialized advantages;

yet it also does not allow white people to opt out of recognizing contemporary personal responsibility for and involvement in such systems. As Malcolm, a community leader and organizer in Southeast Seattle, stated, "There's no illusion about how systems work, and that systems, as we all know it, are designed to perpetuate themselves." Knowing that systems frequently work to reproduce themselves, the RSJI requires through its format and structure that people confront racism. The initiative also illustrates the benefits evident in evolving personal perceptions and actions to generate a more equitable city. Statements by white people of feeling threatened by discussions about race and racism is one of the key ways in which whiteness persists in institutions (Ahmed 2012, 67, 147–53). The RSJI did not leave much room for this excuse and consequently ushered in authentic and sustained inter- and cross-racial conversations about individual, institutional, and systemic racism. Employing racial equity toolkits, intentionally extending capacity building for employees, focusing on cross-sector and cross-rank involvement, and foregrounding a systematic and systemic focus on racial equity are guiding principles for the RSJI. As a result, Seattle city employees have become more educated about anti-racism, white privilege, and structures of power and have been motivated and required to re-craft urban governance through a racial justice and equity lens. Creativity and sustainability, particularly in terms of innovative approaches and a focus on social sustainability, have threaded through the RSJI, indicating the power of interdependent engagement with social values in urban governance. Through unsettling whiteness, the RSJI demonstrates how social transformation can occur.

Developing the RSJI

A series of discussions about race preceded the development of the RSJI in Seattle. In the early 1990s the Urban Enterprise Center (UEC), a historically black economic development group affiliated with the Seattle Chamber of Commerce, instigated an "It's Time to Talk" plenary series as a way to think through and reframe race relations in the city. The UEC partnered with other organizations and institutions of higher education to lend stability and longevity to the series. Speakers such as Wilma Mankiller, Bill Bradley, Lani Guinier, Edward James Olmos, and Anna Deavere Smith came to discuss race relations and facilitate conversations. This series was meant to forge ties among different constituents within the city and to deepen the overall understanding of race and racism.

Taking inspiration from discussions happening in other sectors and the UEC series, in the late 1990s Germaine Covington, then head of the SOCR, conceived of CityTalks!, forums for talking about race and racism within city government. The central premise of CityTalks! was that learning how to dialogue was a crucial precursor to engaging in conversations about race. CityTalks! therefore strove first to educate city employees in the art of dialogue and then to facilitate conversations about racism and race. Initially a hand-selected group of people from positions of power throughout city government met to conceptualize and engage in CityTalks! The conversations next extended to include participants from all levels of government. Marta, a city employee focused on policy analysis, explained that the monthly CityTalks! conversations always began with the questions: What is race? And what is racism? Participants then considered how they perceived race and noticed race in the news and in the city landscape. Marta noted that people at first "thought that if government were to have those conversations, the whole system would collapse. That was the fear." This fear speaks to how white fragility often curtails people's ability to engage meaningfully in substantive conversations about race and racism. Marta continued, "Then when people started sharing their stories, they realized . . . that white folks didn't really know the extent of the impact [of racism]. But also, people of color realized that there was some impact on white people, and that they really didn't know that either." As Marta described, the CityTalks! format enabled participants to gain racial literacy and fluency so they became more confident about unpacking the many facets of racism and recognizing the detrimental role racism plays in everyone's lives. The conversations also generated possibilities for mutual learning and the consideration of racial jus-

UNSETTLING WHITENESS

tice work within the city government. After five years of monthly meetings, participants in CityTalks! wanted action beyond conversation. This impulse helped set the institutional stage for the emergence of the RSJI.

A simultaneous lived experience within the political sphere of Seattle pushed forward the generation of the RSJI as well. Marta recounted this moment.

> [Greg] Nickels, when he was campaigning [for mayor], he noticed a gap.... He said there's a perception in communities of color that the city doesn't serve them the same.... When he went to Queen Anne, the north end, the eastside of the city, Madison Park, everybody was happy with the city, nobody had complaints [see map 1]. They thought the city was great, great services, it couldn't be better. When he went to Southeast, that was a whole different story, everybody was angry, a lot of tensions.... He said, "Well, you know, I understand that if we create more services, it's like throwing money in a black hole. It's never enough. There's always more need, so I want to really look at how we can change as a city, how can we change the way we do business to be better, so everybody has equal access. So we want to get the response that this guy had [in North Seattle]; I want to see it in communities of color."

This personal conviction and policy focal point proved instrumental for the creation of the RSJI as Greg Nickels won the 2001 mayoral election. Having campaigned on a platform of building inclusivity within the city, Nickels quickly called for the development of the RSJI, and it was officially launched in 2004 through the Seattle Office for Civil Rights.

The architects of the RSJI drew upon ideas from several organizations, such as Crossroads Institute, the People's Institute for Survival and Beyond, PolicyLink, and Western States Center, and from individuals, such as Peggy McIntosh and Tim Wise. Ideas from critical race theory, which grew out of legal studies to demonstrate how legal systems perpetuate hierarchies of power that create conditions of marginalization for people of color, also informed the creation of the RSJI. In particular, critical race theorists, just like the work of the RSJI, mobilize around an ethos of race-consciousness that produces equity instead of oppression and focus attention on current structural injustices and the need for a radical revamping of racist systems (Crenshaw 1995; Price 2010; Delgado and Stefancic 2017). Many people hired into city departments under then mayor Nickels were former community organizers, so strategies and tactics from this work and an attitude that change is possible entered urban governance practices as well. Educator and philosopher Paulo Freire's (2000 [1970]) *Pedagogy of the Oppressed* was an especially significant inspiration and guide for many city employees who became involved with the RSJI.

The primary organizing theory of action for the RSJI was institutional transformation to address the structural production and individual recapitulation of institutional racism and race-based disparities. RSJI organizers recognized that working toward equity did not necessarily mean destroying the hierarchies of government. Instead, drawing upon experience as community organizers, key members of the RSJI sought to use power, an inevitable part of systems, to advance change and produce racial and social justice (Bronstein et al. 2011, 173). Examining root causes and generating solutions, rather than offering more services that principally assuage the impacts of racism, was central to this work. Although some of the implicit motivation for the RSJI may have been gaining voters or broader branding recognition for the city, the intentional and explicit focus on sustained and systemic work, informed by strategies of unsettling whiteness through self-education, equity analyses, and policy shifts, has contributed to substantive institutional change.

"Together We Can Achieve Racial Justice in Seattle": The RSJI in Practice

When I conducted fieldwork on the RSJI in 2009, a strategy team within the SOCR managed the initiative and provided citywide support.[2] Additionally, a forty-person-strong core team, made up of employees from throughout city government, met monthly, as they had since the inception of the RSJI, to plan and conduct capacity building exercises and to share notes about new developments within city government (Bronstein et al. 2011, 160). Participants in the core team rotated over time. Department supervisors constituted a subcabinet for the RSJI and offered leadership within departments, an important role since city departments submit annual work plans to illustrate how they are implementing the RSJI (Nelson et al. 2015, 29). A network of department level change teams further coordinated the development and realization of the RSJI. The framework of a strategy team, core team, subcabinet, and change teams helped facilitate the diffusion of the RSJI throughout Seattle city government, an institution that comprises nearly ten thousand employees (Bronstein et al. 2011, 162).

While the core team consisted of members from the entire city government, the department-based change teams were located within, and focused specifically on, particular departments. Change teams worked fairly independently of each other. They had their own meeting schedules and individualized approaches to raising consciousness about institutional racism and the need to change departmental practices. Sierra, a city employee in the social justice and equity fields and a self-identified person of color who grew up in Seattle, described the decentralization of the RSJI through change teams as "kind of a franchise operation." She added that there were some parameters around the ways departments took up the central objectives of the RSJI, such as employees had to have training on privilege, power, and individual and systemic racism, "but there's a lot of flexibility inside. As a result, all departments are not in the same place" in terms of the collective goal of eliminating institutional racism. Some departments had crafted extensive workshops and exercises for fundamentally revamping how they do business and conceptualize policy. Other departments lacked such activity. Although the range of RSJI work in different departments posed some communication and collaboration challenges, Sierra suggested that offering a variety of ways for departments to develop buy-in was important for the longevity of the RSJI. She and her colleagues involved in this social justice work realized that unsettling whiteness takes time and that some employees may express sustained resistance to such efforts due to white fragility. Therefore they facilitated various pathways for involvement and divergent time frames for participation. This approach helped the initiative gain traction throughout city government and ensured widespread uptake of the initiative's overarching priorities over time.

To get a glimpse of change and core teams in action, I attended a professional development training on interracial work groups held for these city employees in July 2009. A self-identified person of color and a self-identified white person co-facilitated the workshop. These leaders first reviewed common dynamics within interracial teams that reproduce inequities and the triggers that can silence or marginalize participants. The leaders next asked the group of about thirty to discuss internalized oppression and internalized domination in small groups. The multiracial group of colleagues dove into conversation and reflected honestly and seriously on their positionalities and socializations. The participants then used these insights to strategize about how they could craft collaborative interracial work groups within Seattle's urban governance given systemic and individual factors. The level of discourse and racial fluency in the workshop ruptured my assumptions about staid city bureaucrats. Significantly, trainings such as this one also help unsettle whiteness through building understanding and relationships, reflexively acknowledging blindnesses and internalized and systemic racism, and envisioning a different practice for work. As just one of many capacity building exercises organized by the RSJI strategy team and attended by members of the core and change teams, in this training I witnessed how transformation can begin within smaller groups and extend out through networks to the entirety of an institution. This model for creating institutional transformation seemed successful and powerful.

Although there are some parallels between corporate diversity management programs and the RSJI—such as education to change perspectives and behaviors, inclusion and competency as crucial facets of a globalized marketplace, and the integration of diversity and inclusion principles throughout an organization—overall the RSJI departs in several notable ways from diversity management strategies commonly employed by institutions (Anand and Winters 2008). First, the RSJI was generated internally and conveyed intrinsic motivation rather than emerging as a response to external pressures and forces, such as legal compliance mandates. Embodying more intrinsic motivation helps position the RSJI as a catalyst for social transformation. Part and parcel of this internal development was the consistent leadership of former mayor Nickels. His bully-pulpit style of leadership in this circumstance proved to be quite useful as he repeatedly returned conversations and actions to questions of equity and institutional racism. He did not allow people, particularly white employees, to shy away from this important work. His focused leadership—and extensive institutionalization of the initiative so that it could outlast his tenure as mayor, as I discuss later in this chapter—situates the RSJI as distinctive from usual diversity management approaches.

Much of institutional diversity management centers on the language of diversity rather than institutional racism or equity because such phrasing is deemed more amenable and accessible to the status quo (Ahmed 2012, 61). The notion is that social change requires buy-in and should not turn people away. Consequently, most diversity management seeks to create a new institutional image through the phrase of diversity. The RSJI subscribes to a different theory of social change in that it highlights institutional racism and does not gloss over the stark racialized inequities in Seattle and the United States more generally. The original conveners of the RSJI recognized that city employees needed to learn about race, racism, whiteness, privilege, and oppression before they could substantively actualize the RSJI. They also acknowledged that sanitizing racism and giving white people a free pass, if you will, for not seriously engaging with their own positionalities and responsibilities would not bear out the goals of the RSJI. Thus, rather than allow employees to deflect concerns about racism by hearing the term as an attack, the RSJI created space to process such responses and delved into racist practices (Ahmed 2012, 146–50). Directly naming and confronting racism is a signif-

icant distinction between the RSJI and many diversity management programs.

A further difference between the RSJI and standard institutional
diversity management is the function and role of mainstreaming. As
feminist scholar Sara Ahmed (2012, 135–40) illustrates, many diversity management approaches within institutions of higher education decentralize equity efforts from a central office to the entire
institution to suggest that "everyone" is involved in and committed
to diversity. She suggests that such decentralization often results
in minimal engagement and change because an assumption arises
that if everyone is involved then each individual does not need
to do much. Although the RSJI has extensive reach throughout
Seattle city government, as the core and change teams attest, the
impact of diffusing the RSJI has not seemingly produced the outcome where people opt out of involvement because they assume
that other people are doing the work. Instead, the institutionalization of the RSJI requires individuals and departments throughout city government to work continually and persistently toward
eliminating institutional racism and race-based disparities. This
divergence from classic mainstreaming approaches results in an
influential initiative that has wide reach and substantial impact.

Rather than tolerating an assertion that discussing racism injures
an institution and poses an assault on the self-identity of white
people, particularly those who self-identify as anti-racist, the conveners of the RSJI created forums for people to understand systemic racism and their complicity within systems. City employees
were not held responsible for the creation of these patterns of
inequity; it was widely and routinely acknowledged that systemic
injustices have deep and historic reach. Yet city employees were
held accountable to all residents of Seattle and were expected to
undertake meaningful efforts toward dismantling institutional
racism through their public service work. To this end, since 2005,
the vast majority of city employees have undergone at least the
basic RSJI capacity building training, which includes a one-hour
orientation and an eight-hour training centered on the PBS series
Race: The Power of an Illusion (Pounder et al. 2003; Seattle Office

for Civil Rights 2012; n.d.). Managers and employees engaged in outreach activities also complete the inclusive outreach and public engagement training, which ranges from four to eight hours in length. Department managers, supervisors, and change team members receive an additional four- to eight-hour training session in anti-racism. Management teams, leadership groups, and change team members participate in a tools for organizational change training for a couple hours as well, while project managers, planners, supervisors, and department managers receive the three-hour racial equity toolkit training. Supplementary training opportunities in cross-racial dynamics, cultural competence, structural racism, and using a racial equity lens in communication round out the capacity building opportunities for city employees within the RSJI (Seattle Office for Civil Rights n.d.). The performance contracts for managers and supervisors throughout city government include a section on facilitating the RSJI training of staff and implementing the initiative within daily work as an accountability measure, which helps guarantee that city employees throughout city government participate in the trainings. Even the city employees who are not interested in attending several capacity building trainings are required to learn something about the negative impacts of institutional racism and the benefits reaped from remaking urban governance with social justice and equity in mind. Consequently, nearly all city employees have gained some common vocabulary and understandings about race and racism (Gooden 2014). Additionally, more than half of city employees state that they are actively involved in implementing the RSJI in their work (Seattle Office for Civil Rights 2012, 9). The mandatory participation in capacity building and the understanding that the RSJI was a mayoral initiative that demanded accountability and results provided the leverage and legitimacy to get the resistant and undecided city employees at least nominally involved in the initiative.

Yet even with this institutional structure for promulgating the RSJI, securing the necessary initial commitment to address racialized disparities in urban governance, change systems and policy processes, and examine biases, all facets of unsettling whiteness, was not an easy task. As city employee Amiko stressed, Seattleites are "still so PC about stuff that until we get past that, it's actually going to be hard to get to the real root of some of those [social justice] issues." Dave, who works on integrating equity and racial justice analyses within fiscal practices and policy development in city government, concurred that at first his colleagues found it difficult to talk about race and racism: "When you deal with race issues they ... tend to be very passionate, very emotional topics, and so [*pause*] for Seattle that was very difficult to get people comfortable with that and on board." Both Amiko and Dave tacitly refer to the white fragility and internalized biases that surfaced in potent ways once the concerted focus on institutional racism and race-based disparities emerged in city government. Amiko further stated that confronting white privilege in Seattle vis-à-vis the RSJI meant that city employees "have to kind of lay it out on the table and deal with it. It's going to feel very uncomfortable, and that's the one thing that Seattleites don't like to face is being uncomfortable, or thinking that you're offensive, so they'd rather not say anything than say something and say the wrong thing." Indeed, interviewees recounted moments when colleagues refrained from speaking so as to avoid saying the "wrong thing" and resisted being called in as participants of racist systems. The desire for the easy geographical imagination of Seattle as politically progressive to stay intact produced little room for serious interrogation of racism and racialized disparities. Consequently, providing capacity building to help employees gain fluency in discussing race and racism and moving through their personal aversions to these topics was crucial for unsettling whiteness and advancing the RSJI. Educating city employees in whiteness, privilege, internalized and externalized oppression, and racial disparities was not with the intention of cultivating a colorblind kind of mentality; on the contrary, the capacity building of the RSJI enabled reflexive and thoughtful disruptions of whiteness.

In addition to this compulsory capacity building curriculum, department change teams routinely organize voluntary ongoing professional development and capacity building trainings to illuminate how the RSJI can and should inform daily work in a department. For instance, the Department of Planning and Development (DPD), a department with one of the most active capacity building programs in the city at the time of my fieldwork, ran a DPD Talks! series.[3] Modeled on the Citytalks! program, past DPD Talks! had focused on the power of words, white privilege, and dominant interpretations of culture. I joined the DPD Talks! session about environmental justice in June 2009. The event lasted about one and a half hours and took place in the fortieth floor conference center of the SMT. The placards about energy efficiency, the muted earth-toned furniture, carpets, and walls, and the suite of uniform meeting rooms imbued this floor with an air of professionalism. We sat in one of the brightly lit conference rooms around a central table flanked by smaller breakout spaces. It was easy to imagine the shuffle of feet in and out, the adjustment of chairs as occupants found comfortable positions, and the array of presentations filling this room day in and day out.

About twenty employees primarily from DPD came to the talk. The format of the event included an introduction given by a member of the RSJI strategy team about equity, neighborhood planning, and the meaning of environmental justice, a screening of the film *Place Matters* (Adelman and Smith 2008), and small group discussions about the film. During the introduction the strategy team member mentioned how the city uses the RSJI to think about public policies that have racial inequality written into their structure. She explained that identifying such patterns makes it easier to see how to enact social change. Although she discussed particular work within Seattle, she also described how the RSJI joins a societal shift in consciousness about what levels of inequity are "acceptable." She expressed the long road to change, the need to address histories of inequality, and the responsibility of recognizing one's collusion in the current production of systemic inequities. Equity work in city government is often an add-on or afterthought; the strategy team member emphasized how different outcomes can be achieved if city employees begin, rather than conclude, with an equity perspective. Blending information on the broader picture of racial disparities within the United States and motivational speaking about the relevance of equity to planning and development work, the strategy team member effectively set the tone for the gathering as she outlined the utility of this professional development workshop to people's daily work and to social movements unfolding at the broader scale.

After the introduction we watched *Place Matters*, a twenty-nine-minute documentary that adopts a public health perspective to understand the massive health disparities between different communities and neighborhoods. The film features High Point in West Seattle as an example of a mixed-income housing development that included an equity perspective in the planning and development of the neighborhood (see map 1). This differently conceived project has contributed to better health outcomes for residents as compared to other places profiled in the film, such as Richmond, California (Adelman and Smith 2008). The post-film breakout group discussions revealed that the majority of attendees thought seriously about racial justice and reflected upon their roles and responsibilities as city employees in the provision of safe and healthy affordable housing. Many participants remained deep in dialogue about the concrete practices of enacting equity and addressing poverty and unequal access to housing well after the event ended. Although it was clear in people's comments that participants held differing levels of interest and commitment to the RSJI, it was also striking that many city employees thoughtfully and thoroughly incorporated the initiative into their daily work. Capacity building exercises, such as this one, constitute a vital tool for unsettling whiteness as city employees gained skills and knowledge to identify and address institutional racism in a host of different settings. In the process, many white employees, in particular, evolved from a guilty self-consciousness about race to the positionality of an engaged participant in collective social transformation.

It is hard to quantify the impacts of capacity building trainings, such as the DPD one, as change in individual perspectives is not necessarily immediately apparent. Yet as I talked about training city staff on institutionalized racism and social justice with Adi, a former community organizer who worked for the city in community outreach, she described notable shifts over the course of the previous decade. In the past, white city government officials would shut down when she mentioned race. She recounted that at the time of my fieldwork when she started to talk about race and racism, white city employees would "wait for the next word," rather than get defensive or dismissive. This is not an inconsequential change in the practice and culture of Seattle urban governance. To have the majority of city employees equipped to discuss racism thoughtfully and work to dismantle it institutionally within a matter of years shows how unsettling whiteness can lay the foundation for real change.

Unsettling whiteness and challenging racial complacency happens in other governmental practices as well, such as the budget and policy proposal systems. The first attempts to have city departments consider race-based disparities in budget requests got "shelved" because the format offered to reimagine budgeting included "racial questions ... that kind of dove right to the heart of the matter and that made a lot of people uncomfortable" (Dave). After more capacity building and a few years of the RSJI, in 2007 then mayor Nickels asked a group of people to craft a procedure that could produce greater equity within the city budget. There was a noted need to understand department requests, resource allocation, and the overall equity of the financing of the city (Bronstein et al. 2011, 169). As Nickels explained, "All of us who work in city government have a role to play in achieving race and social justice for everyone, and the budget process is central to this effort" (City of Seattle 2008b, 18).

In response, an RSJI team created a budget filter, a set of two questions that must be answered for each line item, to ensure that city employees consider how financial decisions further or alleviate race-based disparities and institutional racism. The filter asked: "1. How does this action accomplish the Mayor's Race and Social Justice Initiative? How did you determine the reasoning for your response? 2. Please identify any unintended consequences from this proposal" (City of Seattle 2008b, 4). The RSJI core team then developed a toolkit to help people understand how to use and respond to the budget filter. The filter was first used in the 2008 budget rounds and continues to guide budget decisions. The process for implementing the budget filter has not been seamless. Lila, another city employee involved in this effort, shared that "some of the budget analysts weren't as diligent. They were just, you know, 'whatever'" in the first round of the budgeting. But people paid attention when budgets were rejected and resources were not allocated as desired when the filter questions were not addressed. Having worked in city government in a variety of departments for three decades, Lila knew the legwork needed to get the budget filter inculcated into the budget process. Therefore, she and colleagues did significant outreach and training with fellow city employees. Then, as she noted, once analysts made the connection between their decisions about budgets, the likelihood of receiving line items, and the impacts of budgeting on different Seattleites, people completed the budget filter. Importantly, budget analysts also began to recognize more broadly the need to ameliorate the impacts of skewed resource distributions through Seattle's urban governance.

As a result of the broader incorporation of the budget filter, "what happens is as departments ask for more money than the base budget or as they're trying to cut the budget, for all the adds or the cuts they have to ... answer those questions [on] the budget filter," stated Whitney, a city employee also involved in the implementation of the RSJI. This intentional engagement with the distribution of resources and the associated acknowledgement of how such spending or cutting influences various residents of Seattle helps interrupt the flow of "business as usual" by calling into question financial allocations and producing different resource distribution patterns. As city employee Sierra explained, "Part of not being business as usual is going to be paying attention to racial impacts and class impacts." Shifting budgeting constitutes a venue to unsettle whiteness because resources no longer are principally allocated to constituencies that advocate the most vocally or campaign the most actively on their own behalf. Instead, resources are spent in ways that bring about greater equity in experiences and opportunities for all residents of Seattle. This is a notable way to bear out the value of social justice.

The structure of the budget filter extended to other contexts as well, such as the mayoral briefing memos. Briefing memos are key sites through which people present policy ideas to the mayor. Applying an equity filter to the briefing memo process meant that each policy consideration had to articulate how it would diminish or further race-based disparities in the city. This specific attention to equity in policy generation helps unsettle whiteness through creating opportunities to question underlying and normative assumptions embedded within policy proposals. Both the budget and mayor briefing filters built upon the racial equity impact analysis worksheets, developed by the RSJI core team in 2002. Akin to an environmental impact or assessment report, the racial equity impact analysis offered a methodical line-by-line process for evaluating the impacts of practices and policies on different racialized groups (City of Seattle 2008b, 7–10). By 2010 departments throughout city government were using the racial equity toolkit, a synthesized form of the equity analysis, budget filter, and briefing memo filter, to assess decision making and resource allocation (Bronstein et al. 2011, 169). In 2015 then mayor Ed Murray mandated that city departments complete the analysis enabled by the racial equity toolkit for at least four different departmental projects and initiatives a year. The completion of the racial equity toolkit, which now requires some primary research into the impacts of policies or programs, must be done by a multiracial work team (Seattle Office for Civil Rights 2016).

Emphasizing equity within the budget and briefing memos through the racial equity toolkit has led to measurable changes. For instance, from 2004 to 2012 the City of Seattle grew contracts with women- and minority-owned business enterprises (WMBES) in non-construction goods and services from $11 million to $34 million (Seattle Office for Civil Rights 2012, 8). The Department of Finance and Administrative Services has hosted reverse trade shows to introduce small businesses and WMBES to city departments (Seattle Office for Civil Rights 2012, 8). By 2011 the Department of Neighborhoods (DON) awarded more than $6 million to over two hundred projects geared toward underserved and immigrant and refugee communities (Seattle Office for Civil Rights 2012, 6). The Department of Information Technology focused funding on boosting opportunities for underserved communities to achieve reliable online access. This department also used the toolkit to help ensure that new technology projects maintain an equity focus (Seattle Office for Civil Rights 2012, 7). Also aided by the toolkit, the Office of Housing and the Human Services Department altered their shelter and housing policies to address the racialized inequities of homelessness (Seattle Office for Civil Rights 2012, 6).

The Seattle Department of Transportation's (SDOT) pedestrian master plan included equity as one of the evaluation tools used to determine which projects would move forward and which would not (Seattle Office for Civil Rights 2012, 6). Thinking through priorities within the department along these lines bears out the intentions of the racial equity toolkit and illustrates how considering equity throughout decision-making processes can alter outcomes. Seattle city government has "historically been a complaint-driven city for things like potholes or streetlights or graffiti or clean up, … or code violations. They're all you call, you complain and then we go out and do something" (Whitney, Southeast Seattle resident and city employee focused on equity work). But largely informed by the RSJI, city employees have increasingly realized that the "whole process of picking up the phone and calling is something that's much more comfortable for some parts of our population and not so comfortable for a large portion of our population" (Whitney). Consequently, the SDOT is working to change from a largely complaint-based structure to one that is more pro-active and considers equity and social justice in all its practices. Such procedural and priority shifts make it possible to begin enacting a different kind of urban governance and institutionalizing a more just experience of the city.

Seattle Public Utilities' (SPU) policies, projects, and budget decisions have also "been profoundly influenced because somebody said, 'Hey, wait a minute, aren't we supposed to be doing an equity analysis?'" (Sierra, a self-identified person of color and city employee who focuses on social justice and equity). As a result, SPU has reduced the number of jobs requiring a college degree after analysts showed that this requirement influenced workforce equity (Seattle Office for Civil Rights 2012). Related, in the Office of Arts & Culture, "We no longer require a bachelor's degree to work here. All a bachelor's degree says is that you've completed an academic program. Doesn't say what you've accomplished" (Henry, city employee in the arts). Considering more than educational credentials for positions and only mandating background checks for jobs that absolutely necessitate such knowledge are powerful mechanisms for shifting hiring practices. Departments within Seattle's city government have successfully blended capacity building and revised hiring practices to the extent that by 2012 the racial demographics of city employees more or less mirrored patterns in the city as a whole (Seattle Office for Civil Rights 2013). At that time, 63 percent of city employees self-identified as white, 14 percent as Asian, 12 percent as black or African American, 5 percent as Hispanic or Latino, 3 percent as multiracial, 2 percent as American Indian, Alaska Native, or First Nations, and 1 percent as Pacific Islander (Seattle Office for Civil Rights 2013, 11).

Still, despite these revised practices, policies, filters, toolkits, and hiring practices, it is important to note that resource allocations in Seattle are not universally visible or perceived as equitable. As noted by Melanie, a city employee in policy development and a resident of Southeast Seattle, infrastructure projects such as wider sidewalks, the South Lake Union street trolley (affectionately known as the SLUT), and other "vanity projects" are incredibly apparent in the urban landscape and can be easily counted as evidence of city priorities. Funding for after school programs, summer camps, or small business technical assistance are not as obvious and apparent when moving through city spaces. As a result, Melanie voiced frustration about claims that the city generally supports only wealthier and whiter neighborhoods since she sees, for instance, "an astounding amount of city money spent in Rainier Beach," a neighborhood in the Rainier Valley (see map 1). Yet much of this city resource allocation is less materially visible. This circumstance often makes it difficult to "prove" a commitment to more equitable resource distribution. Such situations also highlight the need within social change endeavors for educating people about the concrete and intangible alterations to standard practices.

Moreover, when considering metrics of inequities within Seattle, it is clear that equitable resource allocation and access require further effort. At the time of my fieldwork, nearly a third of the indigenous community in the city lived in poverty, and high school graduation rates for Seattle public schools revealed that less than half of enrolled African American, Latino or Latina, and Native American students graduated, compared to 67 percent of white students and 70 percent of Asian American students (Seattle Office for Civil Rights 2008, 6). Even though the city government aimed to end homelessness within Seattle by 2015, the "One Night Count" in January 2015 documented over 2,800 unsheltered people in Seattle (Seattle–King County Coalition on Homelessness 2015). Accounting for people living in transitional housing and shelters brought the count of homelessness up by thousands more. In 2015 the Seattle metropolitan area had the fourth-largest homeless population in the nation, following New York, Los Angeles, and Las Vegas (Bernard 2015). The point-in-time 2017 count of people experiencing homelessness in Seattle and King County registered 11,643 individuals, about half of whom were unsheltered (All Home 2017). These statistical renderings of inequities and lopsided resource distribution and access within Seattle illustrate the time lag often evident between reprioritizing budget decisions and lived experiences in the city. They also demonstrate that revamping urban governance policies cannot single-handedly dismantle histories of systemic racism and oppression and that hierarchies of power are often slow to change.

Although alterations to budgeting practices and the use of the equity toolkit may have been more hidden in their impact on the daily lives of all Seattleites, other institutional modifications imple-mented through the unsettling of whiteness in the RSJI have been more immediately obvious. For example, in January 2007, then mayor Nickels wrote an executive order, titled the Translation and Interpretation Policy, that mandated the translation of many city documents into first- and second-tier language groups and granted residents access to translators and language-appropriate help lines (Office of the Mayor 2007). The first-tier translation languages are ones spoken by large shares of Seattle residents and include Span-ish, Vietnamese, Cantonese, Mandarin, Somali, Tagalog, and Korean. The second-tier languages are Cambodian, Amharic, Oromo, Tigrinya, Laotian, Thai, and Russian. These are languages spo-ken by more than two thousand Seattle residents (City of Seattle 2018b). The implementation of the Translation and Interpretation Policy has manifested in changes throughout city government. For example, the SPU "Go Live!" campaign promotes recycling through translated materials and community trainings with language inter-preters (Seattle Office for Civil Rights 2012, 5). The DON now offers translation and interpretation services within the P-Patch Commu-nity Gardening Program to provide greater access for all Seattleites to these local resources. In the DPD, boiler inspectors carry trans-lation cards to ensure that everyone understands the results of an inspection (Seattle Office for Civil Rights 2012, 5). The provision of RSJI information in multiple languages on city websites also helps improve communication between residents and city employees. The implicit English-only approach of urban governance that pre-ceded the Translation and Interpretation Policy demonstrates the power of whiteness to obscure dominant group privilege and main-tain systems that benefit those already in power. Broadening the linguistic practices of city government both ensures more effective and inclusive urban governance and helps unsettle whiteness. All of these changes have strengthened overall relationships between immigrants, refugees, and city government and indicate how mar-shaling the values of creativity and sustainability, particularly social sustainability, in policy development alongside the pursuit of social justice can have tangible positive impacts.[4]

Providing numerous ways for Seattle residents of many linguistic and citizenship backgrounds to feel welcomed, access information, register concerns, forge connections, and voice ideas characterizes much of the ongoing immigrant and refugee services work within the RSJI. This emphasis also illustrates how the implementation of the RSJI has expanded beyond internal transformation and getting the city government's "house in order." Indeed, by 2009, even though institutional racism certainly remained, the RSJI shifted toward a partnership model wherein city government wrestled with race-based disparities internally and with community counterparts working throughout the city of Seattle. For example, the RSJI Community Roundtable convened twenty-five community organizations and public institutions working to achieve racial equity in Seattle. To focus their collective efforts and enhance their impact, the roundtable focused on educational disparities within Seattle, particularly in terms of discipline policies and support for on-time graduation from high school, and advocated at the state level for broader educational reforms. Disrupting the school to prison pipeline and expanding restorative justice practices within Seattle schools are crucial facets of this ongoing work. The community partners in the roundtable not only address these issues collaboratively; they also commit to using equity tools in their daily practices to minimize the reproduction of structural inequities within their organizations (Seattle Office for Civil Rights 2012, 2). Unsettling whiteness in the education and criminal justice sectors in Seattle sets the stage for greater equity for the next generation.

The addition of community work to the RSJI represents enhanced capacity for actualizing social justice within urban governance. These shifts also reflect an opportunity to extend trainings and partnerships to a broader sphere of influence. Lila, a longstanding city employee who has played a significant role in the RSJI, spoke proudly about these transitions: "The beauty about taking it [the RSJI] out into the community now is to say to agencies that have been doing this work far longer than the city has done it, 'Now we can partner with you because we understand that there's a race and social justice issue. We understand institutionalized racism. We understand how poverty links with disproportionality in schools and blah, blah, blah.'" Lila expresses that city employees can now partner more effectively with community groups because of capacity building trainings and changes in institutional structures. She acknowledges that many city employees have learned about how poverty connects with disparities in educational achievement, for instance, so they are more capable of connecting with community partners on such issues. At the same time, the "blah, blah, blah" part of Lila's comment raises some questions. Is it merely a phrase to signal the many factors shaping educational achievement? Perhaps simply a conversational transition to the point she next made about city employees gaining the skills needed to guide white middle-class homeowners, who are accustomed to influencing urban governance in their favor, to understandings of equity? Or maybe "blah, blah, blah" reflects some sense of fatigue or exhaustion associated with the extensive list of social justice concerns that need to be addressed by city government? It is hard to know what Lila intended with that phrase and what, if anything, such a passing comment might signify about community partnerships or the RSJI.

The neighborhood plan updates of 2009 exemplified how shifts in community engagement around institutional racism and race-based disparities unfolded within urban governance. In the 1990s Seattle gained recognition for its participatory neighborhood planning process (Diers 2004; Sirianni 2007). At that time, over 30,000 people in 24 neighborhoods collectively produced 38 neighborhood plans. These plans were originally conceived of in a twenty-year time frame, but by 2008 concerns had emerged about the relevance of the plans given demographic shifts and evident changes in the built environment, primarily due to the construction of an at grade light rail line in Rainier Valley. Thus the city government chose three neighborhoods in Southeast Seattle for plan updates: North Beacon Hill, New Holly–Othello, and North Rainier Valley (see map 1).[5] The neighborhood plans are all part of Seattle's Comprehensive Plan (City of Seattle 2015a), which dictates how neighborhoods and the city as a whole will bear out the mandates articulated in the 1990 Washington State Growth Management Act (Municipal Research and Services Center 2018). This act guides planning and development for the state and stipulates that dense and rapidly growing population centers must develop comprehensive plans. The plans should address the following aspects: land use, housing, capital facilities, utilities, transportation, economic development, parks and recreation, and, for counties, rural landscapes (Municipal Research and Services Center 2018).

Although the Growth Management Act did not include an explicit equity approach, as the current comprehensive plan for Seattle does, city employees keen on executing the RSJI centered social justice practices in the neighborhood planning process in 2009. Roger, a city employee involved in planning and outreach and well established in his career, explained: "There's been a really specific focus [now] on making sure voices are heard. And not just the traditional ones, which are often white, are often homeowners, and that's a challenge because those are people that we don't connect with [so that] takes a special level of outreach." English language learners, the disabled, the elderly, and the African American community were particularly sought out for participation in the neighborhood updates. Rather than unintentionally reproduce white privilege and classed and linguistic exclusion, as the planning process in the 1990s did, this new approach reconceptualized neighborhood planning to help unsettle whiteness and advance social justice (Hou and Kinoshita 2007).

Although the DPD and the DON—the two city offices tasked with leading the neighborhood planning process—still held the traditional community meetings with the usual white home-owning residents in attendance, these departments focused the majority of their time and staff resources on more grassroots type community outreach and engagement for the three neighborhood plan updates. There was widespread recognition that for a plan to be relevant, sustainable, and supported, it needed to include insights gleaned from a wide range of neighborhood residents, not just home and business owners. For this expanded approach to neighborhood planning, the DPD and DON modified the "trusted advocate" model designed by the Annie E. Casey Foundation and created what they called the "planning outreach liaison" (POL) to elicit community input. The POLS, in 2009 a group of thirteen individuals, worked as bilingual, bicultural bridges between communities and city government and facilitated the neighborhood plan update outreach and engagement process in the three neighborhoods (Seattle Office for Civil Rights 2012, 5). Nine of the POLS were language and cultural translators. Four worked as liaisons with Asian, Native American, and African American communities and people with disabilities in the neighborhoods. City employees did not want to "make more enemies in this [planning] process than friends because of cultural faux pas," so they thought that the POLS could keep the city government "from doing the kind of obvious blunders" (Roger).

The POLS collectively held eighty workshops about the plans and over 1,650 people attended these gatherings. Additionally, POLS did substantial outreach to and held informal meetings with over 2,700 residents to educate people about the planning process and neighborhood plan specifics (Clark et al. 2010). The POL approach takes seriously the notion that people are the experts on their own lives. Hence if city government wanted to understand what worked well and what needed changing in the neighborhoods, it made sense to engage the people who spend significant time in these places. The actual financial cost of the POL approach was lower than that of the neighborhood planning strategy used in the 1990s, although the extensive face time for city employees at all the meetings was higher. Through this POL-led participatory planning process, the city strove to cultivate collective investment in the neighborhoods, a significant task since "every individual around a table could all live on the same block, and their sense of place could be very different" (Anna, city employee in planning). Although POLS were initially hired for the neighborhood planning update process, they continue to help with civic projects as community engagement coordinators under the auspices of the DON (Seattle Department of Neighborhoods 2018).

In addition to having POLS lead the conversations and set the tone for planning meetings, DPD and DON recognized the value and importance of having discussions about the neighborhood plan updates in familiar places. Roger recounted how city employees realized that asking residents to come to City Hall to voice their views in a large meeting room could be incredibly intimidating, especially since government offices in Seattle historically have been majority white spaces. Holding the planning meetings in community centers, places of worship, schools, and other community gathering places, on the other hand, could make the meetings more accessible and inclusive. Roger stressed that people are "much more forthcoming, much more engaged, much more involved when we're the minority in their majority community rather than the other way around. . . . And of course, it's much more comfortable where you're conducting a meeting in their language as opposed to in English." The visual transformation in planning meetings from city employees standing at the front of the room and presenting information in English in a city-maintained conference room to city employees sitting and taking notes in the back of the room, wearing headphones for instant translation, and sharing food and ideas with constituents in a community space was striking. The patterns of who mostly spoke and who listened, the spatial arrangement of seating, and the ambiance of the rooms were all different than the traditional format at City Hall and the SMT. Such changes illustrated the unsettling of whiteness in practice and signaled how social justice materialized as a value in concrete ways through the reimagining of planning processes.

Linguistic and literacy factors certainly shaped the neighborhood planning. As Roger explained, "The Filipino community has been in this country, for the most part, for one or two generations. They don't need a lot of material translated in Tagalog. In fact, [they] may be insulted if you did that. . . . But having a Tagalog speaker is probably not a bad idea, and it also shows a cultural sensitivity. But, other cultures, they don't even have, say, literacy in their own community. So, that's a challenge. So how do you make sure that you're able to really tease out responses when people can't even

UNSETTLING WHITENESS

write in their own culture?" Roger draws attention to the layers of factors city employees had to address to create more equitable planning in the three neighborhoods. This comment also hints at the ways in which government structures are often built with a certain constituent or audience in mind. In this case the planning structure was not initially conceived primarily to distribute information verbally, to integrate verbal feedback, and to share findings verbally. Expanding the planning practices to be multi-lingual and in different formats stretched the capacity of the municipal government. Roger lamented, "If we were to always translate all of our material into a dozen languages at every part of the planning process, it would kill us." This comment cogently expresses the tension between trying to make the planning process more inclusive and sustaining such efforts in the long term. Questions remain about how to achieve the goals of equity and inclusivity within a highly dynamic and diverse set of neighborhoods when the city government has limited staff time, financial resources, translation services, and personal knowledge of community norms.

While city employees realized that providing culturally relevant meals and childcare for attendees would also make planning meetings more feasible for a wider range of residents, the material questions about budgets persisted. As Roger asked, "How do you make sure that you have the kind of culturally appropriate food in abundance without breaking your bank?" He found himself confronting budgetary limits alongside his understanding of the need for this fundamentally different planning approach. Roger admitted that one way to "undo past inequity [is] through reprioritizing where investments go," so he knew the value of having certain higher expenditures for these neighborhood plan updates. Still, rationalizing costs, in a broad sense of the word, for the anticipated outcomes of this more equity-focused planning surfaced as a significant challenge for city employees. Roger stressed that equity work is "easier to say than always to do." Yet I wonder what further evidence was needed about the negative costs of not utilizing such a participatory planning approach. Clearly the praxis of the last major planning cycle in the 1990s was no longer relevant, so realigning budgetary decisions to accommodate a sustained shift in planning processes was necessary. Unsettling whiteness and addressing the power hierarchies of racism to implement change is difficult *and* crucial so as to align the value of social justice more closely with city policies and practices.

Although the involvement of a wider range of people in the planning process due to the POLs generally earned high praise, some community members suggested that the selection process of the POLs reduced the success of the approach. For example, Joanna, a self-identified person of color who works in the for-profit sector and grew up in Southeast Seattle, outlined the primary concerns: "I've talked to people who were like, 'Oh, yeah—he's a role model for the Vietnamese community' ... that person didn't even know about this organization or that organization that's been helping the Vietnamese community for years! Just because you choose to stand up and say, 'I represent the Vietnamese community,' well, do you really?" Given these apprehensions, Joanna further stated that the most effective POLs would have been people who had longstanding and extensive ties within different ethnic communities and who were not necessarily interested in working with city government but did so to help their communities. These people are harder to find because they generally do not volunteer right away for the job.[6] Moreover, as Roger noted, "Finding POLs who are neutral within their community, who don't have their own political agendas, who aren't wedded to one particular caste or clan ... is a challenge." Furthermore, the best person to be a POL may not necessarily live in the neighborhood but could work, shop, and socialize there. Assumptions about who has the right to speak about a neighborhood and envision its future often get ensnarled with property ownership or residential status. As both Roger and Joanna's comments indicate, evolving government processes and practices with equity in mind does not necessarily mean that everyone agrees with the new system or thinks it works. Even as the POL structure shifted the planning process and unsettled whiteness to produce greater inclusion than before, the approach was not immune to intra-community concerns about who became the key representatives and bridges between residents and city government.

As city employees gathered feedback from residents via the POLS and drafted updated neighborhood plans for review, additional concerns surfaced about the new plans. For example, Makela, a community activist and long-time proud resident of Southeast Seattle, commented, "They [city employees] claim what they have in place now is what they heard from the community." Yet Makela noted that at various meetings she attended, community members said "not only 'no' but 'hell no!'" to significant upzones in New Holly around the Othello light rail station.[7] Much to her chagrin, she found upzones listed in the updated plan. Consequently, she concluded, the "bottom line is that the city is claiming they heard from the community and that it [the plan] is the consensus of what they heard," but that is not true in her mind. Speaking from a vantage point within city government, Roger contextualized such sentiments: "These are people who are participating in the community planning process for the first time. Those of us who are more veteran recognize you don't always get what you ask for every time. Just because you show up and say something's important doesn't mean it will come to fruition." From Roger's perspective, city employees listened carefully to the ideas and concerns of residents and then drafted a neighborhood update plan that reflected the needs and desires of many different groups, including city government. Balancing expectations of what and how community involvement would inform the final updated neighborhood plans emerged as one of the most contested aspects of neighborhood planning during my fieldwork. City priorities for density and significant economic activity often clashed, for instance, with residents' priorities for single-family homes and small businesses, as Makela's comments suggest. The tensions between the City and the city flared in such encounters. The final plans sought to achieve a middle ground but elicited some frustration on all sides.

Extending Makela's point about aspects of the neighborhood plans not reflecting community perspectives, and Roger's take on

the impossibility of meeting everyone's individual interests, Sal, a
city employee who worked in community outreach, described a
central planning challenge that presents barriers for actualizing
social justice outcomes. She said, "I think the mainstream [white]
community or groups are vested in ... the ten-year vision. I think
that people who have recently moved into Southeast [Seattle] from
other countries, I'm not sure if their thinking is there. I think they
are more interested in what is happening now. So, if they have an
issue, how do you deal with that issue now? Not so much ... 'What
do we want Othello to look like in ten years?' I'm not sure if that's
what they actually think about. Even though the city would love
for them to think that way, I'm not sure if that's really realistic."
Sal drew attention to a fundamental tension written into neighborhood plans as products irrespective of the planning process.
She noted that many residents in the neighborhoods undergoing
plan updates were focused on meeting daily needs and thus did
not have the luxury of time and mental and emotional space to
envision what the neighborhood could be like in ten years. The
demographics in this part of the city evolve reasonably quickly—
"when I first got here it was pretty much all Italians, then it was
all Jewish, then it changed over to Vietnamese, then to Hmongs,
and now it's East Africans" (Sal)—which also tests ten-year visions.

As Sal made clear, planning pivots on the assumption of an
extended time frame. This mode of thinking may not resonate
culturally with all residents, especially when there are immediate
concerns that require concerted attention. While city staff tried to
unsettle whiteness and confront racialized hierarchies of power
through the POLs and a new take on participatory planning, the
fundamental premise of a ten-year deliverable may have countered
some of these actions. Such an outcome compels me to ask: What
kinds of flexibility could be built into the neighborhood plans to
accommodate rapid changes and different lengths of residency in
a neighborhood or city? What could a more community-curated
and continually revised plan look like? These questions suggest
that efforts to undo institutional racism must unpack each city
action and policy and hold it up for possible revision. Unsettling

whiteness to produce change in urban governance requires sustained and extensive effort.

As Makela emphasized in our interview, just trying to conduct policies differently and with more justice is not good enough. A wholesale reimagining of urban governance and an enhanced focus on relationships is necessary, in her view. As she explained, in community meetings with city employees, Makela often experienced a "kind of snooty paternalistic approach that is not deliberate. It's just the way they [city employees] are." She stated that city employees have registered offense when she has acknowledged the paternalism. Such responses, fairly common for white people when called in for their racism (DiAngelo 2012), clarified for Makela that "there are people who don't think about what they think. They don't examine themselves. They don't challenge themselves. It's very harmful when you have that attitude because you think you are right." The RSJI is actively confronting the kind of unreflexive approach to one's positionality and work that Makela described. The assumption of being correct and knowing what is best for others is part of how whiteness manifests in Seattle's urban governance. While many city employees may feel well versed in thoughtful engagements with privilege and institutional racism within the confines of the SMT and City Hall, it can become a different story when actually working with community members and adopting different strategies for such collaborations. In these settings, the normative practices of whiteness might more readily become the easy "fallback position." The unintended and unexamined privilege that individuals carry into their work places and manifest in daily interactions is part and parcel of the sustenance of institutional racism. It is crucial, therefore, for city employees to unsettle whiteness persistently in order to construct more equitable structures and systems within urban governance.

While the neighborhood plan update process had some shortcomings, as I have detailed, a significant outcome was that the planning work challenged dominant imaginative geographies of Southeast Seattle as primarily an economically marginalized and disadvantaged area that lacked many resources. City employees began to learn anew about the neighborhoods through listening carefully to residents' concerns and celebrations. Residents' time and experiences were valued, and symbolic compensation emerged through efforts to make meetings accessible and welcoming. City employees began to understand the assets of the neighborhoods in tangible ways and recognized more deeply that while everyone may agree that job creation, for instance, is important for the area, what that actually looks like and the pathways to get there were distinct. This was a process of unsettling whiteness and rehumanizing residents of Southeast Seattle. It is an example of incremental change that engaged with spaces and places in different ways, that challenged aspects of dominant planning paradigms, that recognized authority and expertise within communities, and that sought to be more collaborative and interactive. While much work remains to reach the systemic and structural changes many residents and city employees advocate for, I see reason to hope for sustained evolution over time because a focus on equity and social justice is becoming more widespread.

In the name of understanding community views on the RSJI, the SOCR conducted a community survey to measure residents' attitudes about racial equity in 2013 (Seattle Office for Civil Rights 2014a). The survey unveiled overwhelming support for the city government to prioritize racial equity gaps in key areas, such as jobs, housing, and health. The survey also showed that residents in Seattle see the economy of the city on the rise but the benefits from this economic growth as unequally experienced. Concern about gentrification emerged as the most important issue facing community members. Many respondents perceived Seattle as becoming "a white, wealthy city inaccessible to the diverse populations who helped build it" (Seattle Office for Civil Rights 2014a, 4). Respondents particularly noted how people of color often pay a higher percentage of income for housing and that whites have more economic opportunities than people of color. Additionally, over 70 percent of Seattleites have only some or little confidence in the police treating blacks and whites equally (Seattle Office for Civil Rights 2014a, 2–4). These survey results energized efforts within the RSJI to increase community engagement practices to extend the reach of this social justice work.

Through capacity building exercises, the implementation of tools like the budget filter and briefing papers, the enhancement of translation practices, the evolution in neighborhood planning approaches, tangible changes in daily decision-making processes, and community engagement, the RSJI has ushered in transformations in the enactment of urban governance and translated social justice as a concept into practice. Legislatively institutionalizing the RSJI has allowed the initiative to persist despite different administrations and changes in mayoral leadership. The passage of City Council Resolution 31164 on November 30, 2009, for instance, affirmed the RSJI and structurally embedded it. Then City Council member Bruce Harrell introduced this resolution, which called for continued focus on the elimination of racial and social disparities, particularly in terms of health, education, criminal justice, environmental, employment, and economic outcomes. Addressing these injustices throughout city government, the resolution attests, will promote overall equity and high-quality governance (City of Seattle 2009b, 1). The resolution passed unanimously and helped legitimize the relevance of the RSJI throughout Seattle's governing bodies. Passing this resolution just before Nickels's tenure ended as mayor (he lost the 2009 election) was lauded as a tremendous accomplishment because it further institutionalized—and validated—the initiative within both the municipal government and the City Council. The resolution acknowledged the important changes prompted by the RSJI and noted that institutional racism and racial discrimination persistently impinge upon the opportunities for success for people of color in Seattle (City of Seattle 2009b, 2).[8] Assiduously working to dismantle inequitable structures of power remains critical for the future achievements of the city government and the residents of Seattle.

The RSJI received additional significant support in April 2014 when then mayor Murray signed Executive Order 2014-02, which upholds the central tenets of the RSJI and advocates for extending the reach of the initiative to include more community engagement (Office of the Mayor 2014, 1). This executive order called for expanded incorporation of RSJI toolkits and equity assessment tools throughout city government and the development of new accountability measures to ensure that equity concerns command a central place in all departments. The order also encouraged the expansion of community partnerships, particularly in the fields of education, equitable development, and criminal justice, as these are sites wherein stubborn race-based disparities remain. Acknowledging Seattle's role as the first city in the United States to develop an initiative focused on institutional racism, the order urged city employees to work diligently toward maintaining this status and mentoring other city governments as well.

The priorities of racial and social equity have also informed and served as cornerstones for the 2035 comprehensive city plan, the document that guides long-term development in Seattle. In fact, in May 2015 then mayor Murray forwarded to City Council Resolution 31577 to make race and social equity a foundational and core value for the comprehensive plan. This resolution passed unanimously and calls on the city to develop assessment and accountability on equity measures, use financial and programmatic investments to close racial and social inequities, incorporate racial and social equity goals throughout the entirety of the comprehensive plan, and carefully examine the impacts of proposed development and growth strategies on vulnerable communities (City of Seattle 2015b). This resolution and the inculcation of race and social equity as core values in the comprehensive plan demonstrate additional venues wherein the RSJI has played a significant role and made an impact on urban governance. Importantly, integrating race and social equity within the comprehensive plan helps unsettle the whiteness that was unmarked and normative within past comprehensive planning efforts and documents. All of these and other related actions indicate that the RSJI has become woven into the fabric of Seattle's urban governance. It is part of the institutional makeup of city government, which means that questions of social and racial justice continue to hold a key place in policy generation and implementation.

The RSJI has gained traction through mandatory involvement, individual buy-in and motivation, and legislative institutionalization. As a mechanism for institutional social change and evidence of translating the value of social justice into practice, the RSJI has focused on unsettling whiteness in order to transform urban governance and create a context wherein change becomes possible. The initiative is now in a phase of increasing its accountability to the broader Seattle community to sustain itself for the long term. Although racial inequities persist and there is much more work to do, analyzing the shifts already compelled by the RSJI makes plain that equity *can* become a fundamental part of realizing social justice through urban governance.

The RSJI in Broader Context: County and National Equity Work

Seattle is the largest city within King County (see map 3). As such, the decisions of Seattle's municipal government often carry significant weight for the broader local context. The demographic and political pull of Seattle can create some tensions between city and county governments, especially since the seat of county government is just a block away from City Hall in downtown Seattle, but they can also spark mutual innovation (see map 2). The link between the RSJI and the Equity and Social Justice Initiative (ESJI) of King County is a case in point. Launched in 2008 by then County Executive Ron Sims, the ESJI strives to transform King County into a "place of opportunity, fairness, equity and social justice where all people thrive" (Nelson et al. 2009, 1). Initially conceived of within the Department of Public Health, the ESJI concentrated on upstream causes—the contexts that produce inequity—and endeavored to intervene in such settings to create greater equity downstream. To specify the work, the ESJI outlined fourteen determinants of equity upon which to focus, including common physical, social, and economic conditions where inequities often emerge, such as access to public transportation, quality of public education, and racialized disproportionality in the criminal justice system (King County 2010a). In an effort to change the outcomes for these determinants of equity, department-level ESJI

goals for 2009 included the following: accessing the racial disparities in homelessness; prioritizing improvements in non-motorized
transportation options; and raising recycling rates in communities with high concentrations of English language learners (King
County 2010b). While the RSJI focuses explicitly on racial disparities and institutional racism, the ESJI considers equity issues primarily within low-income communities, communities of color,
and communities with a high proportion of English language
learners. The initial emphasis on determinants of equity meant
that the ESJI was largely outward facing and diffusely engaged
with various forms of discrimination. Accordingly, the focus on
power, privilege, whiteness, racism, and internal capacity building
was less of a concentration in the ESJI as compared to the RSJI.

Even though the ESJI has been explicitly focused on working
within the community, some community partners expressed hesi-
tation about the initiative. Take Eliza, for instance. A self-identified
white program officer in a non-profit organization that frequently
partners with city and county governments, Eliza commented, "I
actually have no idea what the Equity and Social Justice Initiative
is. . . . It seems like it's a meaningful thing to maybe certain people in the county who are part of it, but I don't think it's meaningful to many." She continued, "Where in the county does this
fit in? Is it respected by people who could really help pull some
purse strings or help run it up the chain of command?" Daniel,
a former county employee who works in the non-profit sector,
a born and raised Seattleite, and a self-identified African American, also had some pointed perspectives on the ESJI: "One of my
main criticisms was . . . big mandates like that [ESJI] are public
and they feel good. They're sexy and oh, oh, 'we're progressive.' Yup,
just another notch for Seattle's built up diversity and progressiveness, [laughs] faux diversity, faux progressiveness. I'm sorry. I'm just
gonna call it out." His incisive assessment of the ESJI speaks to the
challenges associated with translating social values into practice.
Daniel's trenchant comments also suggest that the perception of
the ESJI emerging largely due to political machinations and place
promotion rather than a commitment to substantive social change

inhibited collective buy-in. Daniel worked in county government at the time of the ESJI's inception and felt it was another example of capitalizing on the imaginative geographies of Seattle—and King County by extension—as progressive. The external face of the ESJI did little to temper such critiques.

In addition to concerns about the impetus for the ESJI, Raquel, a county employee who works to advance equity in housing, described internal pushback against the ESJI from county employees. She explained, "People heard about this three-and-a-half-hour [ESJI] training [and] it's like 'I've already got a lot of work to do, and now I've got all this.' So it's seen as an add-on." County employees did not see the relevance of the ESJI to their daily work and expressed reluctance about participating in the three-and-a-half-hour equity training (a short mandatory training compared to the nine-hour minimum requirement for city employees). This attitude uncovers a lack of awareness from many employees about institutionalized disparities and how these realities affect service provision. The privilege of blindness about racial disparities afforded through whiteness most likely contributed to the reluctance about the ESJI training as well. Raquel continued, "It's difficult for people to get out of the add-on stage and get in to understand it's about the way you do business. Not about adding something new." This sentiment that equity and social justice considerations are ancillary to the regular obligations of county government, and therefore an added work burden, is something that city employees implementing the RSJI faced to some degree as well. Such a perspective misunderstands the transformative possibilities associated within incorporating an equity lens into projects and processes and reveals the prevalence of whiteness as working to preserve the status quo. Noting, as Raquel does, that the mentality of county employees proved to be one of the greatest challenges for the launch of the ESJI is revealing because it highlights how individual perspectives and priorities can deeply shape the work of local governments. Despite leadership at the level of the county executive, resistance within the ranks of county employees made for a slow roll-out of the ESJI.

The averseness voiced by many county employees to participation in equity training could also stem from a "nervousness"
with examining racial disparities and addressing social equity in
the provision of services and institutional operations, according
to professor of public administration and policy Susan Gooden
(2014, 4). Racial inequities are challenges that many employees
and institutions alike do not want to confront directly. Yet without systemic and intentional involvement in the production of
equity, inequities persist. To this point, Hannah, an established
county employee based in public health and actively involved with
countywide equity initiatives, reflected that even with the ESJI,
inequitable outcomes to policy initiatives persisted in 2009. She
consequently asked, "How do we catch ourselves at not perpetu-
ating those policy decisions that really disadvantage some groups
over others, or burden some groups over others? Where do we put
the solid waste places and ... where do we build things? And where
do we put the third runway [at Sea-Tac airport]? ... We continue
to do those bad calls, from a standpoint of equity, because of the
larger forces." The larger forces that Hannah mentioned included
everything from individual apathy and lack of awareness to under-
funded initiatives and the longstanding impacts of structural racism. These factors, alongside institutional nervousness, certainly
produce barriers to the widespread implementation of the ESJI.
Consequently, Gooden (2014, 18) contends, "Organizational nervousness needs to be effectively managed in order for governmental agencies to proactively address social inequities." The active
unsettling of whiteness in the RSJI suggests that the city government proactively managed nervousness to allow for social justice
ambitions to flourish. The ESJI, on the other hand, demonstrated
minimal efforts exerted to manage organizational nervousness in
the name of creating social justice and equity.

Both the RSJI and ESJI organize around systemic change and
community activism models. Despite some overlaps, initially the
two initiatives mostly ran on parallel tracks. Sophie, a county
employee who had spent her career in public service, explained,
"there is not a lot of coordination between the city on equity and

social justice and King County." She attributed this disconnect to the different origins for the initiatives and tensions between the two local governments. As she noted, "I saw that the county people and the city people didn't trust one another. Therefore, it was hard for them to find a lot of common ground. . . . They have two different perspectives only because the county's [ESJI] came out of the health department. So they're looking at health kinds of things. So they have a health model around equity and social justice, whereas the city's it came out of the race initiatives. They've done a lot of things with regard to race and people of color. So, it's two different things." Although both initiatives strove to address root causes and ameliorate inequities, they emerged in different forms and from disparate institutional settings, as Sophie described. Moreover, there was a stark difference in opinion about whether or not internal capacity building needed to underpin and carry the move toward greater social justice through government policies, practices, and procedures. In municipal government the core belief was that the city needed to address institutional racism internally before looking to transform the broader urban landscape. The county government adopted a different mode and started mostly externally with community partnerships and minimal internal capacity building and training. This could have been due to the nervousness of county leadership about naming and addressing the monumental challenges presented by stalwart and stubborn -isms and about internal concerns regarding unsettling whiteness.

The parallel nature of the RSJI and ESJI shifted when the reformed Equity and Social Justice (ESJ) integrated effort, started in 2010 and further formalized with the opening of the King County Office of Equity and Social Justice in 2015, began to mirror many aspects of the RSJI.[9] For instance, King County, just like the city, now has internal capacity building trainings around the PBS series *Race: The Power of an Illusion* and implicit bias; uses an equity impact review tool; and is translating texts and doing more outreach with immigrant and refugee communities (Pounder et al. 2003; King County 2018). These transitions signal that assumptions about the mechanisms of change have altered at the county.

Greater investment in internal transformations to help facilitate external social change is much more normative now, as is the case with city government. Managing the anxiety often held by county employees when tasked with addressing inequities has resulted in a more formalized and integrated approach to producing social equity. It seems that the county government recognized that trying to wish internal disparities and institutional racism away would not work. Instead, unsettling whiteness by addressing issues directly and educating and training the governmental workforce as a means of confronting systemic disparities constitute much more effective mechanisms for social change. The transitions in the ESJ also indicate that the positive outcomes evidenced through unsettling whiteness in the RSJI encouraged other entities to mimic the work of Seattle city government. Becoming more closely aligned in practice as agents of change may mean that greater collaboration unfolds between the ESJ and the RSJI. Such partnerships would make way for even more integrated, sustaining, and extensive social transformation within the Puget Sound region as both local governments challenge racialized structures of power and unsettle whiteness in the service of greater equity and social justice.

Although collaboration between city and county governments has been piecemeal, the city of Seattle has been an instrumental partner in the formation of national equity networks, such as the Government Alliance on Race and Equity (GARE). Founded in 2015 as a joint project of the Haas Institute for a Fair and Inclusive Society and the Center for Social Inclusion (now joined with the non-profit Race Forward), GARE is a national network of governmental entities collectively striving toward racial equity within their jurisdictions (Chin 2015). GARE provides a forum for technical assistance, capacity building, and networking for local governments embarking on equity work. The Alliance seeks to produce maximum impact by supporting cohorts of jurisdictions working on racial equity, creating infrastructure and plans for government entities to engage in equity, and fostering collaborations between government, academia, policy, and community organizations so as to generate meaningful and lasting social equity (GARE 2018a). GARE has already worked with 109 local and regional governmental jurisdictions throughout the United States and Canada (GARE 2018b).

The ties between GARE and the RSJI are strong. For instance, as of 2018, one of the co-directors of GARE is Julie Nelson, the former director of the SOCR and the person who oversaw the RSJI under mayors Nickels and McGinn. She was replaced during Mayor Murray's tenure (Minard 2013). Glenn Harris, the former manager of the RSJI and now president of Race Forward, is a part of GARE's leadership team, as is Nora Liu, formerly involved with the RSJI and now the project manager for Racial Equity Here (GARE 2018c). These people have crafted an organization that is a national leader in the field of racial equity within government. Much of their professional work and experience, which informs the practices of GARE, stems from the RSJI. In addition to the people who started GARE transferring personal experience and expertise with the RSJI to this new organization, the approaches, tools, and strategies put forward by GARE—all facets of a prevailing theory of change—mirror the RSJI. For example, just like the RSJI, GARE centers race because of the widespread individual and collective damage wrought by systemic racism and persistent discrimination. The racial equity framework promulgated by GARE enables unsettling whiteness as it considers individual, institutional, and structural racism and suggests that achieving racial equity will also enable a reduction of inequities along other axes of identity; this is akin to perspectives shared through the RSJI. Moreover, GARE and the RSJI both assert that greater racial equity benefits everyone, not just people of color (GARE 2018d). In short, the general premises about social change articulated by the RSJI and GARE overlap tremendously.

GARE emphasizes the importance of being data-driven with equity initiatives, partnering with other institutions and communities to realize racial equity more fully within a broader landscape, and recognizing the urgency of the issues and the salience of accountability (GARE 2018a). These three strategies mirror the goals put forward in the RSJI 2015–2017 strategic plan of being more fully involved with community and other partners and increasing measurability and accountability to show that the practices of the initiative make a difference and that city government genuinely cares about the impacts of inequities and actively works to dismantle them (Seattle Office for Civil Rights 2014b, 1). All of this demonstrates not only that national efforts focused on producing racial equity through local government entities emulate the RSJI, but also that key people help translate and extend the theories and mechanisms of social change exercised within Seattle to a broader audience. An underlying assumption in such acts is that the RSJI is working and worthy of replication. Put differently, actively unsettling whiteness facilitates notable social change.

GARE highlights how core tenets and practices of the RSJI get picked up and reconstituted in different sites; this duplication draws attention to the practice of policy transfers.[10] The impulse and practice of distilling multi-faceted initiatives, such as the RSJI, into ubiquitous action plans that travel and purportedly work anywhere is increasingly common. On the one hand, policy transfers reveal the vexing overshadowing of place specificities in the rush to create one-size-fits-all policies. Indeed, as urban and regional planning scholar Joshua Shake (2015) expounds, policy transfers often (ironically) disregard the importance of context and the significance of place. Using the absorption of Jane Jacobs's urban redevelopment ideas in São Paulo, Brazil, as a case in point, Shake demonstrates how translating texts into different languages can facilitate policy transfers with decidedly mixed outcomes. Similarly, the RSJI has found footing in various U.S. cities through the application of its central tenets within new contexts. The question about the relevance of core operating policy assumptions in new settings is one that Shake raises; this is appropriate to ask in the case of the RSJI and its descendants as well. Arguably, the context of institutional racism and legacies of persistent disparities throughout U.S. society mean that unsettling whiteness would have profound and positive impacts for cultivating social justice everywhere. The precise form that unsettling whiteness might

UNSETTLING WHITENESS

take, however, should vary based on the specificities of each place and policy application.

In making the case for examining the movement of policies between places through the frame of policy mobilities rather than policy transfers, geographer Jamie Peck (2011, 775, emphasis in the original) affirms that "context matters, in the sense that policy regimes and landscapes are more than empty spaces across which borrowing and learning take place; they are dynamically remade through the traffic in policy norms and practices, the flows of which *reflect* (and remake) particular policy regimes." This conclusion echoes the points made by other geographers contributing to this growing literature. Effacing the salience and significance of place reduces the applicability and power of a policy. Ideally, urban governance is attentive to the realities of context. Examining the traveling of the RSJI to other contexts through the frame of policy mobilities makes sense, as this is an initiative that is informing important work in several urban contexts. For instance, cities such as Madison, Wisconsin, St. Paul, Minnesota, and Portland, Oregon, have copied core elements of the RSJI (Nelson et al. 2015). The incorporation of facets of the RSJI into GARE suggests that this number most likely will grow. Consequently, identifying the mobility of the RSJI to diverse places could illuminate how unsettling whiteness and keeping a sharp focus on dismantling institutional racism and race-based disparities produces social change in urban governance. Rather than a wholesale replication of the RSJI and a lack of attention to the particular histories, communities, and daily material realities that give meaning to a place, as is the case with standard policy transfers, the policy mobility of the RSJI could mean that city governments tailor their social justice initiatives to particular struggles and contexts while using the tools, practices, strategies, and advice of the RSJI to guide the work. There is acknowledgment that one size does not fit all and that racial inequities can assume particular context-dependent forms. Thus, although there is a simultaneous push and desire for the successes of the RSJI and the measurable changes in Seattle to emerge in other municipalities, it is important to recognize that merely reinstating the RSJI under a new name in a new place would not produce that outcome. Unsettling whiteness to produce social transformation requires substantive work.

Examining the development of the ESJI in King County and the national alliance GARE in light of the RSJI illustrates that this initiative has had ripple effects beyond the scope of Seattle. People from the RSJI have moved to different organizations and institutions, which helps the translation of key principles of the RSJI into new contexts and settings. Additionally, the incorporation of capacity building practices (sometimes the very same RSJI training modules), racial equity toolkits, and exercises for organizational change illuminate that the RSJI as a forum for addressing race-based disparities and institutional racism has been and continues to be transformative. I suggest that this is largely because of a sustained focus on unsettling whiteness. As the tenets and practices of the RSJI and the network of local jurisdictions engaged with this work gain momentum, the possibility for equitable and just cities throughout the United States comes into sharper focus.

Conclusions

According to Gooden (2014), there are ten key tenets for inculcating equity work within government: making plain the responsibility of government to address inequities; attending to historical racialized disparities as an important context for contemporary work; catalyzing the response to a racialized trigger; gaining senior leadership involvement; ensuring that individual government workers understand their role in reproducing racialized disparities, or not; embedding social equity work throughout government; striving for structural equity in all decisions; providing accountability; maintaining leadership in work toward race-based equity; and believing that racial equity is possible (Gooden 2014, 196–201). Importantly, the success of urban governance in addressing inequities and producing social justice also corresponds with the degree of investment in unsettling whiteness. Without unsettling whiteness, the depth of engagement with institutional racism and race-based disparities within local governments is lessened. Unsettling whiteness is crucial to achieving social justice and institutional change.

Through implementing practices for unsettling whiteness, the RSJI shows how institutions can shift norms and push employees to evolve and grow, thereby expanding and nuancing urban governance. The RSJI blends top down mandates and community organizing strategies to instill systems for institutional change. The core and change team model of the RSJI enabled the initiative to take on a life of its own within each city department. While this approach does not necessarily produce total coherence, it allowed the initiative to take root and become fully incorporated into the daily work of individuals throughout city government. This model has also permitted the RSJI to shift and grow in response to new learning, evidence, and understandings of institutional racism. The designers of the RSJI have had to collaboratively create an initiative that is flexible and enduring. As city employee Sierra remarked, "We're figuring out how to do this while we're doing it, so that makes it really challenging, especially for those of us here in this office that are building the bus as it's rolling, or changing the tires on the bus as it's rolling." This comment is a prescient reminder that working toward racial justice within urban governance is not a well-traveled or straightforward path. Creativity and innovation remain crucial assets in making and sustaining the translation of social justice as a value into practice.

Studying the RSJI makes clear that part of the power of the initiative is that it traverses spatial scales, from capacity building exercises that evolved individual understandings of racism to broader policy shifts that fundamentally remade how budgeting occurs throughout municipal government. Small changes were supported and guided by broader ethics and processes so that systemic transformation began to unfold. A high degree of self-reflexivity, collaboration, adaptability, and belief in the possibility for transformation is built into the RSJI, which has become a powerful shaper of Seattle's urban governance. This model for social change demonstrates the power of a relational approach as there was an effort made to understand legacies of disenfranchisement and the barriers that have been constructed between certain communities and city government. Through the RSJI, city employees, as Marta described, "are really trying to figure out how to live in this world where there are no borders, where languages are getting mixed all the time, where populations change from week to week." The theory of change and associated actions compelled by the RSJI departs from other institutional responses to racism where a tacit assumption is that writing a good policy solves, or at least effectively deflects attention away from, racialized inequities (Ahmed 2012, 101). In contrast, the RSJI delves into the impacts of institutional racism and race-based disparities.

The RSJI drew upon the self-perception and imaginative geographies of Seattleites and Seattle as progressive and liberal to then demonstrate how within this urban race-light context racism ensures differential health, education, and livelihood outcomes for residents. City employee Sierra spoke to the importance of cohering Seattle's reputation with its material practices:

> That narrative that you see in the [RSJI] materials is also part of our internal narrative about raising awareness of the impacts of race and racism on outcomes in people's lives, and shifting us away from the idealized view that we have of ourselves to be one that takes into consideration the outcomes that we are creating, as a community, as a city. . . . It's not really trying to make people feel bad about being unaware Seattleites; it's to, actually, try to enliven or engage people in the idea . . . because the next part of the narrative is we could change this. [*Laughter*] . . . You know that thing, that vision in our head, that idea of who we are? We could actually be working to achieve that. Would you like to join us? Wouldn't *that* be exciting? [*Laughter*]

Positioning social change as an invitation to actualize many shared values and aspirations assists in the building of a base for and sustenance of the RSJI, as Sierra indicates. The RSJI helped unmask the institutional racism within city government and highlight how not all residents benefited from current practices of urban governance. Identifying these realities and then offering tools and strategies for city employees to learn about and engage with whiteness and challenge the status quo enabled significant numbers of city employees to understand the realities of racism and work to diminish its impact and effects. This genuine investment in equity and the unsettling of whiteness in the RSJI helped pave the way for greater alignment, especially compared to the inculcation of sustainability and creativity in Seattle, between the value and practice of social justice in urban governance.

Conclusion

"The City Lives in Us"

With the aid of Google maps, I sit absorbed in visual representations of Seattle's changing urban landscape. A rush of excitement floods my stomach when I see a favorite small restaurant or shop still in existence, and a disorientation that makes my head hurt emerges whenever I cannot locate any identifiable landmarks within once familiar neighborhoods. I surge between silent declarations of "I lived there!" and "Where am I?" I am physically far from Seattle now, yet the indelible presence of the city remains. "A Corner to Love," by Claudia Castro Luna (2017), Seattle's first official civic poet, suggests that I am not alone in my persistent and visceral encounters with the city. She writes,

> Maps of this city
> number in the thousands
> unique and folded
> neatly inside each citizen's
>
> heart. We live in the city
> and the city lives in us

Castro Luna's words affirm that Seattle as a place both constitutes and is constituted. Myriad political, social, cultural, economic, and environmental processes form the substance of everyday experiences, policy decisions, and interpretations of this particular place. Seattle is not abstracted from its multi-species residents and would not hold the contours it does without human interventions. From racialized residential regulations to the regrading of Seattle's hills to the green roof on City Hall, people have modified the biophysical and built environments in the name of power, prestige, politics, and profit. Such legacies shape the making and remaking of Seattle in a continuous fashion.

Within this context, residents, past and present, craft lives and carry knowledge about this city tucked in their hearts, as Castro Luna suggests. These maps are specific, informed by positionalities and life experiences in Seattle. Some features on these maps are widely known, while others remain hidden, veiled, and familiar only to some. This differentiation often breaks along lines of racialized and classed power. Boundaries, exclusions, and borders are etched into the maps alongside spaces of relationships and movement. Inhabitants, past, present, or future, have a stake in Seattle, in its aspirational possibilities as a city and in its current complex lived realities. These are the dynamics of the city as compared to perceptions of the City as a homogenous locus of power. Regardless of whether the tie to Seattle is tenuous or robust, Castro Luna intimates that such connections matter. We collectively carry our maps of Seattle. We fiercely protect the spaces that we love in the city. We tenderly cradle memories of the place. We tell stories about our encounters and experiences. We elevate or erase sites in the urban landscape. We inhabit the city, and it resides within us.

The depictions of Seattle as sustainable, creative, and socially just promote certain expectations for and understandings of the place and its residents. Investigating the work of these social values within urban governance compelled this book. Because the city is often upheld as a leader in progressive politics, Seattle was an important and influential setting for my study of how the social values of sustainability, creativity, and social justice translated into policies, programs, and processes and, paradoxically, how such translations often extended racialized and classed inequities. A place that regularly tops the lists of sustainable, innovative, and livable U.S. cities, Seattle is "the darling among cities" because "Seattle has it all," said Wes, who worked in economic development. Although Wes was talking about the popular place perceptions that arose alongside grunge rock and gourmet coffee in the 1990s, the imaginative geographies of Seattle as progressive and the routine emphasis on the quality of life in the city suggest that Seattle is a well-loved city, one that embodies the wide gamut of urban joys and challenges and enacts values-driven urban governance.

Since the time of my fieldwork, the social values of sustainability, creativity, and social justice have gained even more prominence within Seattle. For example, newly elected Mayor Jenny Durkan, the second woman mayor in Seattle's history, in her State of the City address in February 2018 emphasized Seattle's renowned position as a leader in environmental sustainability. She expressed her steadfast commitment to racial equity and social justice and described the city as a place focused on creating opportunity and building innovation. The crises of homelessness and housing affordability, the need for greater public transportation access, and the imperative of equitable educational opportunities and job creation as the city continues to grow were other notable topics in her address (Derrick 2018).[1] She concluded her speech by saying, "Let us resolve together that next year, we can look each other in the eye and say: The state of our City is more just. The state of our City is even stronger. That life for all who call Seattle home is better because of our resolve, our actions, and our love" (Derrick 2018, 20). The place attachment, daily work, and departmental and personal aspirations that interviewees shared with me, that I observed throughout the city, and that I read in the Seattle Municipal Archives mirrored the affective domains of governance and change to which Mayor Durkan alluded years later.

The arc of *Imagining Seattle* moved from blinkered engagement with sustainability that affirmed classed privilege to efforts to dismantle institutional racism with the RSJI. I considered three social values, sustainability, creativity, and social justice, one by one while fully recognizing their imbricated nature conceptually and in practice. I separated them out, though, to identify crucial factors that contributed to the distance or coherence between social values in concept and social values as practiced in urban governance. I foregrounded the impacts of classism and racism, especially whiteness, for analytical clarity, while fully recognizing that discrimination pertaining to other social identities persistently shapes policies and programs. In terms of sustainability, I posited that latent class privilege exhibited through an assumption of choice propelled the exclusive inclusion of sustainability efforts. I framed the discussion within the sustainability imagination that coats Seattle and examined exclusive inclusion in the Way to Go transportation initiative and the Green Fee debate about plastic and paper bags. The promotional video *We're So Green* helped demonstrate the class privilege built into the sustainability programs and the prominent attachment to a "green" urban identity.

Next, I contended that economic development plans based on conceptions of creativity as tied to people and products can commodify diversity and compel gentrification and displacement. In contrast, the translation of creativity as a value into processes can facilitate equitable results. The equitable transit-oriented development (eTOD) in Southeast Seattle bore out the practice of creativity as a process. A proposed retail revitalization plan for Rainier Valley, on the other hand, showed the potential negative impacts of tying notions of creativity with certain products. The cultural arts district designation in Capitol Hill demonstrated the possible repercussions of operationalizing creativity as principally linked to people, namely those designated as the creative class.

An analysis of the RSJI allowed the investigation of social justice as translated into practice. I suggested that unsettling whiteness was vital to the institutional change brought forth by the RSJI. Looking at this citywide initiative, I examined how unsettling whiteness unfolded through capacity building exercises, a range of policy revisions, the implementation of equity tools, and the expansion of community engagement. I discussed how the institutionalization of the RSJI throughout urban governance has contributed to the persistent focus on institutional racism, race-based disparities, and racial equity. I also showed how the RSJI has informed county and national equity governance ambitions. Revamping structures and processes with an equity focus can contribute to both imaginative geographies and material practices in Seattle, a place that works to achieve congruence between values and practices and enable the thriving of human and non-human residents.

Social values matter for city employees and residents, and these values shape Seattle's reputation nationally and globally. As city employee James plainly stated when I asked why he worked in local government, "It really is the fact that we have all of those values that we're trying to put together." It is imperative, therefore, to think critically about how social values assume tangibility through urban governance because, as my research demonstrates, merely naming a policy creative or sustainable does not mean it necessarily or fully bears out such values. By addressing the translation of values into practice within urban governance, *Imagining Seattle* emphasizes three main points: the extensive impacts of racism and classism and the fundamental need for centering equity; the importance of a geographic perspective; and the salience of ethnographic encounters and narratives.

Classism, Racism, and Equity

The importance of identifying the ways in which classism and racism, particularly whiteness, are built into structures, institutions, and interpersonal engagements and therefore shape all aspects of urban governance is a core focus of this book. Actions premised upon sustainability, creativity, and social justice can be put to work for social change and for the reproduction of classed and racialized privilege. Such a finding disabuses the common assumption that liberal values-driven politics necessarily contribute to equity. Moreover, when measurable benchmarks emerge as the dominant format for assessing success with policy interventions, attention to inequities often falls out of view. Counting how many arts organizations exist in a neighborhood or how many cars travel on a street each day, for instance, provides useful data for understanding aspects of life in Seattle. Yet such information cannot capture the lived experiences that accompany the arts organizations and transportation access and can sidestep questions of racialized or classed inequities. When city government quantifies its realization of social values in such a fashion, the scope shrinks for relational interpretations of power and conceptualizations of different future pathways. The template for inculcating values thus remains relatively limited and can become bound up with unmitigated economic growth, place branding, and the marketing of Seattle. Therefore, it is vitally important that intersectional policy generation and implementation processes, awareness of different forms of knowledge production, and varied metrics and time scales for assessment become more thoroughly rooted within urban governance.

The work of the RSJI is markedly different, and arguably more successful, than the sustainability and creativity examples largely due to the focused attention on racism and equity in the context of institutional transformation. As a mayoral initiative with mandatory citywide application, the RSJI emerged with more staff support and mayoral leadership than the sustainability and creativity programs and policies during my fieldwork. In the practice of social change, it mattered that the person at the top of the local government hierarchy asked for the RSJI to come into existence. The RSJI was not a small program relevant to just one office; on the contrary, it signified a fundamental retooling of urban governance. As a second point of comparison, the RSJI began with mandatory compliance on the part of city employees and an internal focus on ameliorating disparities within municipal government. Not an initiative motivated by the promise of national prestige or the latest trend for economic development, the RSJI stemmed from a deep conviction that the level of racialized disparities in the city was intolerable and that structural change needed to happen. Over time, the RSJI established mechanisms for assessing accountability internally. This system pushed institutional shifts. The sustainability and creativity work, on the other hand, was mostly public facing and had little to modest impact in terms of internal accountability measures. For instance, an individual resident could opt into the efforts to reduce GHG emissions in the city or not or comply with or rebel against bag regulations. Similarly, a resident could engage with marketing strategies and visit Southeast Seattle for "exotic" culinary experiences or set up an art studio in Capitol Hill to be a part of the creative buzz. Creativity and sustainability efforts included some internal elements, such as shifting the city's fleet to energy-efficient vehicles and advocating for the city's creativity index, but many of the efforts looked outward and were not required. As a result, the power for transformation was less.

Third, the RSJI solidified around a common understanding of why the initiative would lead with race and racism and what these concepts mean. Such a focused conceptualization of the initiative positively contributed to the persistent unsettling of whiteness in the execution of the RSJI. In contrast, efforts around creativity and innovation, sustainability and a green identity, did not exhibit a similar kind of coherence or fluency of shared understanding. As a result, the terms slipped around, linked to disparate programs and policies with varying applications. The question of what constitutes sustainability beyond a pat answer about the three E's—environment, economy, and equity—remains unanswered, and the substance of actionable creativity is illusory. Fourth, the RSJI illustrates the power that emerges from the entwining of social values in the pursuit of equity. Specifically, the RSJI exemplifies innovation and creativity at every step: rethinking employee training, reimagining budgeting processes, changing policies, communicating about racialized disparities, unsettling whiteness. These are all venues wherein the work of creating, generating, and innovating are fundamental to success. Put differently, the RSJI engages with creativity as a process for responding to feedback, evolving the initiative, and advancing the work. Similarly, the institutionalization of the RSJI assures the longevity of the initiative. Sustaining the focus on racial equity and social justice in this fashion enables systemic transformation to occur over the long term. Additionally, the RSJI demonstrated economic sustainability. Addressing disparities in educational opportunities and job prospects, for instance, usually requires immediate budgetary outlay. Over time, however, such investments pay off as all people do better work in a context where human dignity and worth are respected. Such a shift can improve the bottom line for the city, thereby enhancing economic sustainability. The ties between environmental degradation and contamination and questions about social justice are obvious in everything from the siting of hazardous waste sites and the disproportionality of environmental health risk exposure to access to green space. Within Seattle's urban governance, the RSJI contributed to the development of the Equity and Environment Initiative, which addresses environmental injustices throughout the urban landscape and within city practices. The RSJI has provided guidance for advancements in the environmental, economic, and equity fronts of sustainability. In short, weaving together creativity, sustainability, and social justice through the RSJI has provoked significant institutional changes in Seattle's urban governance.

While these successes are notable, the near invisibility within my data about Seattle's setting on the traditional territories of the Coast Salish people ripples through my examination as a powerful silence. The elucidation of such erasures affirms how reparations and healing need to accompany the inculcation of social values in urban governance. The RSJI has addressed inequities and worked toward systemic change, yet this obvious silence about indigenous communities makes it clear that urban governance needs to address the impacts of settler colonialism more pointedly and challenge dominant narratives that subsume or commodify indigeneity. Addressing the multi-faceted impacts of racism, particularly whiteness, and classism through such endeavors is fundamental to disrupting the reproduction of inequities.

The Lens of Geography

A geographic perspective animated my examination of social values in urban governance as well. For example, investigating how the geographical imagination of Seattle as a place with liberal social values shaped activities within and beyond the city focused my attention on expectations for the City. Assorted imaginative geographies—centered on, for instance, Seattle's purported greenness, innovation and creativity, and social agenda—further animated prevailing perspectives of the city as a dynamic place. Digging into imaginative geographies assisted in my analysis of how social values assumed tangibility through urban governance and how they could be constituted differently. Identifying how imaginative geographies contribute to core assumptions driving policy generation and implementation highlights why and how racialized and classed inequities arose within social values-driven urban governance. I found that on the one hand, imaginative geographies shaped policy development and interpretation as city employees, for example, relied upon well-worn narratives of the entrepreneurial spirit of Seattleites to emphasize the significance of recruiting the creative class. At other times, such as in the RSJI, city employees marshaled the imaginative geography of Seattle as a beacon of progressive values to encourage colleagues to work toward closing the gap between ideal and practice. Rifling through boxes upon boxes of municipal documents in the archives further illuminated the interweaving of people and place within imaginative geographies. Stakeholder meeting notes, policy drafts, internal memos, and news articles articulated the realities of Seattle as a place and suggested what it could be. In such documents, the hopes of people for themselves and the City as politically progressive, socially just, innovative, sustainable, and globally minded, at least in name, came to the forefront. Imaginative geographies are core parts of making—and making sense of—place. Holding up such imagery for scrutiny, therefore, helps reveal prevailing patterns and noted impacts.

The frequent discursive representation of Seattle as a leader in sustainability pervades local and national contexts. This is the stuff of city boosterism, resident urban pride, and policy focus. Analyzing sustainability in Seattle through the lens of imaginative geographies thus helps reveal the disjunctures and overlaps between aspirational sustainability and "actually existing sustainability," which sustainability scholars Rob Krueger and Julian Agyeman (2005, 411) define as "those existing policies and practices not explicitly linked to the goals of or conceived from sustainable development objectives but with the capacity to fulfill them." I honed in on examples of actually existing sustainability within Seattle through my analysis of the Way to Go initiative and the Green Fee debate. While these programmatic and policy interventions held the possibility of achieving sustainable development goals,

I elucidated how the latent classism built into these expressions of actually existing sustainability curtailed the execution of these programs and the realization of sustainability aims. I also emphasized how the racialized context of the environmental movement, from which mainstream sustainability efforts spring, further constrained the possibilities for achieving just sustainabilities. The prevailing imaginative geographies of Seattle as green and sustainable gloss over the pervasive impact of such disparities. Studying sustainability through the angle of imaginative geographies and the practices on the ground contributes to understandings of actually existing sustainability in particular and urban sustainability more generally.

Thinking across spatial scales, from the individual through to county-level policy and national relevance, assisted in my efforts to craft an urban analysis focused on relationality within *Imagining Seattle*. I adopt this stance because "a relational perspective recognizes the indelible connectedness of urban residents with their material surroundings" (Karvonen 2011, ix) and, therefore, shows how ideas and issues co-arise within urban governance. Using a relational perspective helped illuminate how the view of a policy often shifted by scale of analysis. For example, the Green Fee made sense to the City Council when they envisioned Seattle's urban future, while it made little sense to individual small business owners as they considered daily expenditures, a perspective change that exposes the work of urban governance as processual. Consistently probing the co-constitution of society and space, whether it be in the *We're So Green* video or a multiracial work group training, further highlighted the relational making of the city. The spatial and the social are deeply implicated in each other within expressions of the city and the City.

The dynamism of places drove my analysis as well. I chronicled stubborn points of continued inequity and excavated sites of social transformation. The ways in which boosters promote Seattle, the activities deemed in and out of place in the city, and the evolving structures of municipal government uncover the significance of thinking critically about the meanings of place. Anthropologist

Keith Basso (1996, 7, emphasis in the original) writes, "What people make of their places is closely connected to what they make of themselves as members of society and inhabitants of the earth, and while the two activities may be separable in principle, they are deeply joined in practice.... We *are*, in a sense, the place-worlds we imagine." These linkages between interpretations of place and understandings of society and the earth undoubtedly informed how I conducted research. These ties also came to bear in how participants narrated urban governance and themselves and how textual references described Seattle. For instance, the group Vanishing Seattle "documents displaced and disappearing institutions, businesses, communities & cultures of Seattle—often due to growth, development, and gentrification" (#Vanishing Seattle 2018). Noting that gentrification is not inevitable and that an equity focus in urban development would support "spaces [that] have significance to our local culture and social fabric" (Schlosser 2018), Vanishing Seattle aims to speak to the continued onslaught of economic growth pressures and the ensuing elimination of sites throughout Seattle's urban landscape. A tribute to places and spaces of the city facing redevelopment, Vanishing Seattle calls for activism, commemoration, and resistance. Place enters our imagination as so much more than a mere description of location. My examination of Seattle's urban governance as a locus of social values draws on a rich geographical framework to amplify the multiple meanings of place, the power of imaginative geographies, the insights of multiscalar analyses, and the mutual constitution of society and space.

Ethnographic Encounters and Narratives

Centering everyday actions and narratives marks a key way that I enlivened urban governance in Seattle. Persistently dwelling in such an analytical space marks the third primary focus of this book. Attending to urban narratives is important because, as urban planning professor Leonie Sandercock (2003, 182) explicates, "In order to imagine the ultimately unrepresentable space, life and languages of the city, to make them legible, we translate them into narratives. The way we narrate the city becomes constitutive of urban reality, affecting the choices we make, the ways we then might act." Narratives can describe systems and complexity or can simplify and present sound bites. Through narratives I learned about the processes of change driven by social values and witnessed the contingencies and contextualities of urban governance. Focusing on a granular sense of place and the narratives people shared about their work, their values, and their aspirations made Seattle's urban governance transcend the moniker and come alive. The city and City became legible as a result.

Henry, an unabashed fan of Seattle who works in city government, exemplified Sandercock's point about narrative and actions. For example, when I asked Henry about the future of Seattle, as I asked all interviewees, he noted that the city government was "just so hell bent on being a world-class city" that it was hard to envision much beyond that stance for many years. Now, though, he felt that city government, residents, and boosters alike could "relax" and "stay focused on the good work that we're doing" because, as he explained, "I think a lot of people are looking to us now for some of the answers or for replication in their own communities because we've done a lot of things right. And I think the biggest fears are—you know more than 100 years ago, Cleveland was that city. [*Pause*] It's precarious. . . . I think it's easy to take for granted what we have and lose, or possibly even worse is failure to adapt. And so, I think it's going to take some vigilance to make sure that we don't coast and relax on our laurels." Henry's narration of success paired with ongoing attention to relevance struck me as outwardly about Seattle and its rank within the urban pantheon and internally about Henry's department and its abiding role in urban governance. He narrated the perceived precarity of being on the forefront, an urban leader, and stated that if Seattle hopes to retain its edge it must be alert to activities in other cities. Henry told a story of urban accomplishments and status while hinting at the costs and fears that come from that fame. Such a station, perhaps for himself and the city, is fleeting, he intimated. Still feeling the impacts of the economic recession in 2009 meant there was no time or space to go easy and ride the tide of past successes. An understanding of city employees as nimble, responsive, and agile underpinned Henry's depiction of Seattle's urban governance as the same. He wove together his interpretations of Seattle's future with subtle commentary about his role in this unfolding narrative.

I too participated in the storytelling about this city and the establishment and rupturing of normative discourses about specific social values. As I sat in the foyer of City Hall watching people move in and out, attended department trainings, and participated in business group meetings, I learned about the centrality of sustainability, creativity, and social justice to Seattle residents and institutions alike and crafted this narrative about *Imagining Seattle*. My methods for data collection encouraged a focus on narratives as I searched the Seattle Municipal Archives, interviewed people with varied affiliations, and conducted participant observation within and beyond the halls of formal municipal government. My research design also produced blindnesses through the partiality of my exposure and interactions. I certainly did not engage with all city or county departments or all residents of Southeast Seattle, for example. People volunteered to speak with me, so there were inherent constraints posed by my methodology. My analyses and interpretations filter through my own implicit biases and positionality. Acknowledging the layers upon layers of narratives embedded within the process and study of urban governance emphasizes the situated partiality of knowledge production and the work of rendering cities legible through narratives.

Some narratives revealed how interviewees imagined themselves and Seattle as part of global processes. Janice, who moved to Seattle as a young adult and raised her children there, concluded our interview with a pointed reference to the reservoir of meaning bound up with storytelling. When I asked Janice what she envisioned for the future of the region, she took an extended pause, repeatedly sipped her coffee, and then replied:

> Well, the world is in a lot of trouble, and it's bigger than whether or not you can rent a house or live in a house or buy it or have a job. I think that if we have a future, there needs to be a confluence

of invention and a willingness to change that involves both science and the culture. We need to admit the things that we need to do as a human race in order to save our a**. It may be too late. I think there are whole areas of the world that are going to be lost. The oceans are rising, you know. New Orleans will be gone. Lots of Florida will be gone. Manhattan might be gone ... what I believe the function of the artist is ... we're storytellers, and we're flexible thinkers.

Janice described the impacts of climate change vis-à-vis the submergence of coastal areas of the United States. She mentioned the need for thinking differently, for sharing stories, and for directly confronting the realities of this moment in planetary history. She pinned human survival on these factors. The urgency of the situation she described felt muted, though, in the Central Area District independent coffee shop where we sat. A steady flow of people purchased drinks, their daily rituals unperturbed by our conversation. Janice's pensive gaze eased as she began to describe the role of artists in the making of a future that is less catastrophic. Inasmuch as narratives and an "ethnographer's findings are shaped by a larger structural context" (Duneier et al. 6), narratives also create an important space for envisioning and detailing alternative pathways forward.

Lessons and Linkages

The deep impacts of racism and classism, the influence of a geographic perspective, and the power of narratives matter not only in Seattle. Indeed, this study of social values in urban governance connects with broader macro-structural considerations, such as the production of inequities, the resource limits of the planet, and the practices and processes of social change more generally. Considering these issues within Seattle generates insights into approaches utilized to advance systemic transformation, with varying effects, which can inform understandings of urban spaces in the twenty-first century. As the United States witnesses further contractions in the modern welfare state, local governments are increasingly taking the lead in the materialization of progressive values. Cities increasingly represent the sites of greatest possibility for focused leadership on social change. Thus learning from a city that is, by image and some practices, engaged in values-driven urban governance can shed light on and provide guidance for other places seeking to evolve. Centering the power of narratives, the assumptions of people and place circulated and promoted through imaginative geographies, and the ways in which racism, especially whiteness, and classism thread through urban governance in Seattle indicates both the particularities of this study and the lessons writ large for cities.

The examples I analyze, such as the cultural district designations, which represent a route taken for infusing the creative class into urban policy, were particular to Seattle but also link up with trends visible in cities throughout the world. Investigating how the creative class concept informed urban governance in Seattle and with what effects, therefore, contributes to ongoing conversations about the gentrifying pressures embedded in the creative class theory. Querying how a city expresses what it means to be "green" has widespread relevance. Sustainability ambitions are evident in many cities and lifestyles, as the ubiquitous advertising of "natural" products and the performance of "green" places and institutions attest. Centering equity and shifting processes accordingly is a crucial part of combating structural, institutional, and interpersonal racism. Analyzing the steps taken in Seattle and drawing out the leverage points that augment systemic institutional change can positively inform related efforts in other settings.

A further commonality between Seattle and other urban spaces is the context of neoliberalism and the challenges posed to the enactment of social values by this economic and political system. In a long monologue on the general status of the United States and world, city employee Derek outlined this key issue:

> The problem is that we do live in a capitalist consumer society. That's how our society works, and it's a real problem on all sorts of different levels because if we say that we want people to use less and consume less and do that, the net effect of that is the economy goes down. People worry about we're in a recession [in 2009]. We're in

a recession because people are using less and consuming less. But that's our goal to cut carbon emissions. But if you cut carbon emissions, then our economy actually is failing. So what's the balance? This is the huge societal question.

Highlighting, as Derek does, how the current mandate of endlessly pursuing economic growth contradicts the execution of sustainability goals foregrounds the need for city governments to reckon with the prevailing logics of capital. I certainly met the neoliberal city in Seattle in the pressures to increase revenues, gentrify neighborhoods, and generate public-private partnerships. The intense impacts of Amazon in the SLU—from extensive changes in the built environment to rising housing prices due to the influx of amenities in the area—serve as potent reminders of the persistence of neoliberalism and its effects. I also encountered the influences of neoliberalism during interviews. For example, Lance, who worked in the for-profit sector, described the necessity of education and informed involvement in politics due to the pervasive exploitation in a capitalist system. As he stated, "There is a whole philosophy of consumption around suckerfication—selling people stuff they don't need with money they don't have." He contended that businesses of all sizes and in many different communities operate within a scarcity capitalist model and "suckerfy" as a result. Shifting away from this model, in Seattle and beyond, can help repudiate the core assumptions of neoliberalism.

Ignoring the implications of unchecked economic growth means that efforts to enact sustainability, creativity, and social justice within urban governance will not be fully realized. A revamping of economic processes and an acknowledgement of resource limits, however, could create space for a deeper inculcation of these values and the manifestation of equity. While such a dramatic change in economic philosophies and practices seems unlikely in the near future and perhaps revolutionary in scope, the stark income inequalities and concerns about the enhanced power of corporations serve as potent reminders of widespread discontent with neoliberalism. Amplifying the intersectionality of social values and a process-based understanding of urban governance can augment efforts toward systemic transformation while pushing back against the individualized economic rationales of neoliberalism. This is the case in Seattle and in cities more broadly.

Thinking in Systems

Imagining Seattle offers a view of urban governance as process based, as lived, as manifested through everyday encounters, positionalities, and socializations, and as rife with power relations. Governing is neither easily predictive nor linear. Instead, it is dynamic, which brings me to the utility of systems thinking, a multi-scalar and relational approach to and philosophy for understanding complexity. Ludwig von Bertalanffy developed general systems theory from his biological research in the mid-1900s (Macy and Brown 1998, 40). Since that time, systems thinking has grown as a field and has been applied to settings as diverse as ecosystems, management structures, and interpersonal conflicts. Within the framework of systems thinking, a collection of interdependent parts that form a whole and produce their own pattern of behavior over time, rather than a random set of items, constitutes a system. The interconnections and synergies within systems mean that the entirety of a system is always more than the sum of its parts. The human body is a complex system made up of many subsystems. Seattle's urban governance is another system constituted by many smaller systems, such as department norms, the implementation plans for specific policies, and the interface between individuals and institutions beyond City Hall and the SMT. Systems can be biological, such as a forest system, or can be entirely constructed by humans, such as management structures in an organization. Systems have purposes and functions, include inputs and outputs, and can change or rebalance if a part of a system is removed, altered, or added. Systems adapt to produce equilibrium and are far from static as they respond to feedback. Stocks, meaning here "elements of the system that you can see, feel, count or measure at any given time" (Meadows 2008, 17), and flows, the actions that can change levels of a stock, make up and modify systems.

Building on this conceptualization of systems, systems thinking is a non-linear philosophy, applied practice, and language that aims to make visible the many dimensions of complex relationships and the root causes for unwanted outcomes (Senge 1990; Kim 1999; Meadows 2008). In other words, systems thinking represents a holistic and relational "way of seeing" (Macy and Brown 1998, 40). Emphasizing interdependencies, systems thinking focuses on cycles and circles rather than linear cause and effect. As a field of study and practice, systems thinking deploys special vocabulary and a set of modeling tools, such as reinforcing and balancing feedback loop diagrams, behavior over time graphs, stock and flow diagrams, and simulation models. These tools are meant to counter reductionist problem-solving interpretations and locate modes of interaction between different elements of a system through the identification of interdependencies. Aiming to avoid "solutions" that ultimately create new problems in organizations, ecosystems, or communities, systems thinking assesses situations to apprehend when a result strays from expectations and to ascertain leverage points that can contribute to closer alignment between desired and witnessed outcomes (Meadows 2008). The long temporal view is a key element of systems thinking. Rather than commit to short term "fixes that fail"—that alleviate some immediate issues but do not address root causes—a systems approach focuses on mapping out the processes that produce the problem and addressing the interconnected factors that can shift the outcome. Exploring dynamic complexity across spatial scales and temporalities in this way helps illustrate how and why small changes in a system can produce big results.

The language, applied practice, and perspective of systems thinking resonates particularly with the RSJI. By way of example, the RSJI intervened at leverage points within the ambit of urban governance, such as policy briefing memos and neighborhood planning, to reimagine fundamentally how these practices worked. These changes pushed forward wider engagement with racial equity because policy generation now emerged through an equity lens, for example, and the updated neighborhood plans revealed, for instance, what a more inclusive participatory planning approach could entail. The RSJI also honed in on employees as sites of change within the urban governance system. The mandatory capacity building exercises ensured growing racial literacy among employees and encouraged people to evolve the ways they performed their jobs. While integration of the RSJI throughout city departments was not uniform, its widespread diffusion meant that actions toward eliminating institutional racism and race-based disparities unfolded in many sites throughout the system of urban governance. Rather than dwell on the illusory construct of a perfectly designed institution, the RSJI prompted systemic investigation into the multiple factors contributing to conditions of injustice and identified sites and strategies for intervention to generate capacities for justice (Agyeman 2013). The unsettling of whiteness through this systems approach is leading to structural, institutional, and interpersonal transformation in Seattle's urban governance.

Humans crafted the inequitable systems currently in use, so it is possible, and necessary, to alter course. Systems thinking provides tools, concepts, and applications for engaging with social change in many domains, not just social justice. Political scientists Seaton Patrick Tarrant and Leslie Paul Thiele (2016, 54), for example, argue that developing "critical thinking and systems thinking skills, communication skills and collaboration skills in students" is essential in contemporary sustainability education and efforts. Drawing on educational philosopher John Dewey's ideas about problem solving and learning, Tarrant and Thiele emphasize that understanding one's role within complex socio-ecological communities is fundamental to advancing sustainability in society. In other words, applying a systems lens to sustainability endeavors contributes positively to the realization of sustainability aspirations because thinking in systems encourages acknowledgment of desired outcomes and forces consideration of the unintended consequences, such as the extension of racialized and classed inequities. While a systems approach was most notable in the RSJI during my fieldwork, Tarrant and Thiele underscore its centrality in sustainability work too.

Poet and author Mary Oliver (2016, 154) writes about mutual-ity and interdependence in ways that intersect with understandings of systems thinking. She states, "I would say that there exist a thousand unbreakable links between each of us and everything else, and that our dignity and our chances are one." Oliver moves through time and space to note, "The farthest star and the mud at our feet are a family; and there is no decency or sense in honoring one thing, or a few things, and then closing the list. The pine tree, the leopard, the Platte River, and ourselves—we are at risk together, or we are on our way to a sustainable world together." To underscore this point, she concludes, "We are each other's destiny." This recognition of our shared future and extensive connections affirms the importance of systems thinking and of acknowledging that humans are not separate from each other or other species and biophysical systems. Oliver speaks directly to the links that bind us together and to the significance of expanding an ethic of care to spaces and species familiar and unknown. She attunes her readers to the need for accompaniment, a method and mode for working, knowing, and living together that does not require harmony but signifies a profound acknowledgment of interconnections (Tomlinson and Lipsitz 2013). Through this lens, Oliver invites us into a holistic engagement with the world.

Frameworks for the Future

Working to produce conditions that extend the possibilities for interdependent sustainability, creativity, and social justice and imagining such a future are fundamental to reducing the gap between value in concept and in practice. To this point, Julian Agyeman (2013, 7), professor of urban and environmental policy and planning, conceptualized the framework of just sustainabilities because this "approach to policy, planning, and practice has an analysis and theory of change" that can "transform the way in which we treat each other and the planet." Agyeman (2013, 7) convincingly demonstrates that focusing on well-being and quality of life, intergenerational and intragenerational equity, justice, and ecosystem limits contributes to the creation of just sustainabilities. Drawing attention to the co-production of wasted biophysical resources and the wasting of human capacity and potential through mass incarceration, for instance, Agyeman emphasizes the intricate interweaving of sustainability and justice. The framework of just sustainabilities persistently elucidates the interdependencies of human and ecological systems. Thematically related, urban scholar Andrew Karvonen (2011, 188) contends that cities need new politics and "civic imaginaries" that encompass all species to address their systemic ecological and social challenges effectively. Karvonen suggests that relational politics can contribute to the increased generation of urban governance rooted in equity for humans and nonhumans.

Law professor Maxine Burkett (2011, 345) also considers alternative approaches to normative legal structures as she interrogates the seemingly immutable, namely the coupling of a state with defined territory, in response to a "post-climate era, in which the very structure of human systems—be they legal, economic, or socio-political—are irrevocably changed and ever-changing." Burkett tackles what is often presented as fixed and opens up such systems for re-articulation. For instance, she proposes the concept of the nation *ex-situ* as a reformulation of international law that addresses the landlessness produced through the impacts of climate change. *Ex-situ* nationhood "would be a status that allows for the continued existence of a sovereign state, afforded all the rights and benefits of sovereignty amongst the family of nation-states, in perpetuity" (Burkett 2011, 346) after climate change has rendered a nation-state uninhabitable. The governing of a geographically disparate group of people no longer cohered around a shared territory would emerge through a trusteeship model, Burkett suggests. The goal for reimagining governance and the state in this manner is to advance thinking about international law, migration, citizenship, and rights in an era of increasing endangered states, as Burkett calls nation-states at risk of losing territorial existence largely due to climate change. Burkett's proposal for the nation *ex-situ* shows what climate responsiveness and adaptive capacities could look like in a legal system. She conceptualizes alternative legal frameworks, such as the nation *ex-situ*, to highlight how laws could evolve and in so doing offers insights into other possible systemic changes. Her analysis also demonstrates how changing structures can contribute to greater equity. While revamping systems to respond to climate disturbances is a key motivation, her method of holding up a seemingly incontrovertible system for revision elicits a reconsideration of systems established to perpetuate whiteness, for instance, and other forms of systemic oppression. Building upon such work in the urban governance context indicates why and how questioning current practices and intervening for different outcomes is so vital.

The "Great Turning," the epochal shift under way from industrial growth societies to life-sustaining ones, as explained by Buddhist eco-philosopher and systems thinker Joanna Macy, relies on the kinds of reconceptualization of structures and systems that Burkett advances (Macy and Brown 1998, 17). Macy describes the Great Turning as akin in scope to the agricultural and industrial revolutions. Macy and colleagues highlight three key areas of engagement that contribute to the Great Turning, namely efforts to reduce the devastation of the Earth, examination of the structural causes for such damage and the creation of structural alternatives, and a fundamental shift in consciousness (Macy and Brown 1998, 17). Participation in these different areas by individuals and organizations may shift over time, yet collectively helps usher in the seismic transformations of the Great Turning. Inspired by Macy, author David Korten (2006, 251) accentuates the "epic choice" underlying the Great Turning, which he sees as a decision between empire and economic exploitation or a commitment to "the joys of Earth Community." Korten outlines cultural, political, and economic "turnings" that can contribute to the transformations encompassed within the Great Turning. Much like Macy and colleagues, Korten (2006, 316–18) advocates for shifts in consciousness, strategies of resistance against systems of empire, nurturing community connections, and building a majoritarian political base and coalition. Systems thinking and efforts to produce greater equity are crucial elements to the Great Turning. These approaches can provide strategies for engaging in social transformation and ensuring that life-sustaining societies focus on the thriving of all species, not just a select few.

Participating in the Great Turning, imagining alternative structures and systems, and instantiating just sustainabilities are all venues for working to align values with practices. While scholars, activists, community members, and individuals may use different languages to describe current actions, policies, and mobilizations undertaken, I see shared investment in equity, common humanity, intergenerational learning and healing, and efforts to reduce the negative impacts of climate change. An element of what philosopher Jonathan Lear (2006, 103) calls "radical hope," a perspective "directed toward a future goodness that transcends the current ability to understand what it is," accompanies many of these actions and concepts as well. Radical hope requires participating in a "courageous life" (Lear 2006, 107) and exercising "imaginative excellence" (Lear 2006, 117). It is a continual practice and a perspective engendered in the face of catastrophic change. Radical hope can provide a forum for grieving all that is lost, recognizing all that has been endured, and working in common cause for the future. In the context of Seattle's urban governance, radical hope—for a more responsive urban government, for different systems of governing, for greater attunement between immediate and long-term needs and challenges, for a city wherein all beings thrive—surfaced time and again. People cared, through anger, frustration, enthusiasm, and celebration, about Seattle, the city and the City. Such affective ties offer the impetus and space for envisioning and enacting systemic transformation.

By 2025 it is estimated that over five billion people worldwide will live in cities (Keith 2005, 1). The projection is for 120,000 more residents in Seattle by 2035 (City of Seattle 2015a). The concomitant pressures on existing urban infrastructures will be vast. As we respond to the growth of cities, climate change, and associated challenges, it behooves us to keep in mind that cities reside within us and that we are woven into dense webs of shared existence. We all have a role to play in collectively and creatively crafting more equitable and adaptive places. Taking this to heart helps catalyze our imaginations and build our inner resolve as we struggle to actualize real change.

APPENDIX 1

Research Methods

I drew upon a triad of established qualitative methods to examine how social values translated into practice in Seattle's urban governance. I describe the three methods below.

Archival Research

My archival research centered upon reading documents at the Seattle Municipal Archives located on the third floor of Seattle's City Hall (see map 2). At times I traced a particular theme, such as sustainability, through archival documents and noted the diverse meanings and sites where this topic emerged. In other instances I searched archival files to learn more about a specific organization in Seattle and to see how the group advocated for its causes over time. These targeted investigations shed light on the recorded interactions between community groups and city departments and employees, which helped me understand processes of urban governance. In addition to specific thematic or organizational research, in the archives I studied developments in city planning, structures of governance, community relations, and neighborhood revitalization programs from the mid-1950s to the early 2000s to inform my overall understanding of the inclusion of social values in contemporary urban governance and of the relevant historical antecedents. The archives I examined were all hard copy and varied in form from correspondence between city employees and constituents to departmental publications to legislative actions.

Research in the archives prompted the creation of new interview questions and shaped the direction of interviews as well. Simultaneously, specific legislation or local controversies mentioned in interviews would send me back to the archives to learn more about the larger context of and historical precedence for a bill or battle. Through this recursive process, I found myself both following assorted leads and generating new ones as I deepened my engagement with Seattle through the archives. The archives provided a wider historical and temporal context for my investigations.

Participant Observation

Participant observation extends from the assumption that participating with others in various situations is a productive way of gathering data. It is a fundamental part of ethnography. Scholars tend to use three types of participant observation: observer-as-participant, participant-as-observer, and complete participation (Kearns 2000, 110). I used the first two types in my research. In each of these forms of participant observation, researchers negotiate insider/outsider statuses and usually spend significant time chronicling multi-sensory perceptions of places and people. These field notes make up an important source of data for ethnographic research (Emerson et al. 1995). I wrote more than one hundred single-spaced typed pages of field notes. These immediate impressions and recollections about interviews and the numerous settings where I conducted research both instantly re-immerse me in the materiality of fieldwork and nuance interpretations of my data.

In my roles as observer-as-participant and participant-as-observer, I attended meetings for district councils, neighborhood associations, planning commissions, business associations, and city and county departments. I also participated in training sessions for the Race and Social Justice Initiative. I joined neighborhood tours and took note of new housing developments, contested projects (such as proposed new businesses and designs for the light rail stations), and the changes wrought in the built environment. I went to local conferences and lectures on sustainable cities and equitable development to engage further with local constituents focused on these issues. In each of these settings I both participated in the conversations and recorded the ways in which people grappled with Seattle's urban issues. My level of explicit involvement via participant observation varied by venue. At the conferences, for instance, I actively participated in breakout sessions, small group discussions, and visioning exercises. In contrast, at large meetings I often just listened and learned, speaking only to introduce myself or to share a few thoughts with fellow attendees. Collecting data via participant observation disrupts reified interpretations and provides an opportunity to notice difference and question tensions. It offers a powerful lens for understanding and studying Seattle's urban governance.

Semi-Structured Interviews

In-depth semi-structured interviews rely upon a select number of key questions and leave room for spontaneous developments in the conversation. I initially recruited voluntary research participants whose names I found within archival materials, such as the project managers for initiatives, the heads of departments, and community activists who communicated with city employees about salient urban issues. Once the interviews started and I began to build a network, I employed a snowball sampling technique (Biernacki and Waldorf 1981), which involved asking interviewees for ideas about other people who might be willing to participate in my study, to locate additional research participants within county and city government, for-profit and non-profit organizations, and Southeast Seattle neighborhoods. I interviewed a diverse group of people who all had some type of connection to sustainability, creativity, or social justice. In total I interviewed fifty-eight people with ages ranging from twenties to seventies. Some interviewees were born and raised Seattleites, and others were relatively new to the city. Similarly, some had made a career out of working in city or county government and could share perspectives on different administrations, whereas others found themselves recently hired. Many of the people employed in city and county government positions during my fieldwork have since moved on. People's affiliations at the time of my research parsed out in the following ways:

twelve were a part of what I call the for-profit sector. The majority of these people (nine) were involved in some aspect of economic development; seventeen were community leaders in Southeast Seattle or in the non-profit sector. Of this group, the interviewees worked in organizations oriented toward sustainability, housing, and social justice; twenty-one were City Council members and Seattle city government employees from thirteen departments. Despite this range of departmental affiliations, interviewees thematically represented interests in sustainability, the arts, economic development, planning, neighborhoods, and equity; and eight were employees in seven departments of King County government. All of the county employees focused their work on equity and/or sustainability. I interviewed a total of thirty-three women and twenty-five men. I did not ask directly how people racially self-identified. The interviews generally lasted about an hour, and I held all but four interviews in person. Scheduling conflicts required these four interviews to be held on the phone. I did not record the phone interviews but used a digital recorder for nearly all the in person interviews. Interviewees spoke in both official and unofficial capacities. The focus on social values and the complexity of urban governance as a contested process emerged within and materialized through people's words and actions.

My research design offered pathways for encountering the heterogeneity of the city amidst reified discourses of the City. These three qualitative methods encouraged me to notice patterns and trends unfolding at different spatial scales, from the micro-geographies of daily life to the broader realm of policy implementation, and to attend to the ways in which values were construed through urban governance. Interviews, archival research, and participant observation revealed prominent imaginative geographies and signaled how racism and classism wove through sustainability, creativity, and social justice endeavors. Narratives surfaced as potent depictions of values and place through this research design as well. Clearly, these methods for data collection privilege certain kinds of knowledge production, elucidating some social processes and details while obscuring others. I illustrate the benefits of qualitative methods for research on social values in urban governance throughout *Imagining Seattle*, while fully acknowledging that other forms of insights could arise through different data and analyses.

Primary Sources

Pseudonym	Affiliation
Adam	non-profit sector
Adi	city employee
Alex	city employee
Amiko	city employee
Anna	city employee
Beth	for-profit sector
Bob	for-profit sector
Brian	county employee
Chantal	for-profit sector
Daniel	non-profit sector
Dave	city employee
Deepesh	city employee
Derek	city employee
Eliza	non-profit sector
Emi	county employee
Geneva	city employee
George	for-profit sector
Hannah	county employee
Harry	for-profit sector
Henry	city employee
Hilary	for-profit sector
James	city employee
Janice	non-profit sector
Jesse	non-profit sector
Jill	community leader
Joanna	for-profit sector
John	non-profit sector
Julian	community leader

Kathy	for-profit sector
Lance	for-profit sector
Leslie	county employee
Lila	city employee
Liz	city employee
Lucy	city employee
Makela	community leader
Malcolm	community leader
Marta	city employee
Matt	non-profit sector
Melanie	city employee
Miles	county employee
Miranda	non-profit sector
Patty	non-profit sector
Raquel	county employee
Reiko	for-profit sector
Rick	community leader
Roger	city employee
Sal	city employee
Sarah	city employee
Sebastian	city employee
Sheila	for-profit sector
Sid	for-profit sector
Sierra	city employee
Sophie	county employee
Val	county employee
Wes	non-profit sector
Whitney	city employee
Xavier	non-profit sector
Zan	non-profit sector

APPENDIX 2

Recent Mayors of Seattle

Norman Rice: January 1990–January 1998

Paul Schell: January 1998–January 2002

Gregory Nickels: January 2002–January 2010

Michael McGinn: January 2010–January 2014

Edward Murray: January 2014–September 13, 2017

Bruce Harrell: September 13, 2017–September 18, 2017

Timothy Burgess: September 18, 2017–November 28, 2017

Jenny Durkan: November 28, 2017–present

APPENDIX 3

We're So Green Lyrics

Last summer was great, though it's up for debate,
Eighty days with no rain is kind of insane.

We are Seattle, and we're leading the change,
It feels so good to be clean, you know who you are, and we're talking
to you, we're so green!

We lead with our feet, we're so green!
We plug in our cars, we're so green!
We check the bus from our phones.

It's hard to move when you're under a thumb,
They got you wondering where the power comes from.
It comes from people making use of the sun,
It feels so good to be clean, you know who you are, and we're talking
to you, we're so green!

We grow our own food, we're so green!
We compost our forks, we're so green!
We make use of the rain.

We got it wired by using our wires,
We got it dialed by removing the dials.
We get a rebate 'cause we insulate.
It feels so good to be clean, you know who you are, and we're talking
to you, we're so green!

We recycle our trash, we're so green!
We bring our bags to the store, we're so green!

There's so much more we can do.
We're talking to you, we're so green.
So much more we can do, we're so green.
We're talking to you, we're so green.
So much more we can do!

Source: Office of Sustainability & Environment 2013a, *We're So Green* (video), Seattle: Capitol Media and Punch Drunk, https://punch-drunk.com/our-work/were-so-green-animated-video. Transcription of lyrics for the present volume by author.

NOTES

Introduction

1. The name Sebastian, as with all names given to people I interviewed, is a pseudonym.

2. For more information on urbanization trends, see Frantzeskaki et al., "Advancing Urban Environmental Governance"; and UN Habitat, *National Urban Policy*.

3. For more on urban governance, see Buizer et al., "Governing Cities Reflexively"; Gupta et al., "Theorizing Governance"; and Häikiö, "Expertise, Representation and the Common Good."

4. For more on the history, theory, practice, and significance of translation and translation studies, see Bassnett, *Translation*; Fawcett et al., *Translation*; Hatim and Munday, *Translation*; and Weissbort and Eysteinsson, *Translation—Theory and Practice*.

5. For more on racism and race, see Alexander, *The New Jim Crow*; Bonilla-Silva, *Racism Without Racists*; Bonilla-Silva, "Rethinking Racism"; Feagin, *Racist America*; Gilmore, *Golden Gulag*; Golash-Boza, *Race and Racisms*; Lipsitz, *How Racism Takes Place*; Pulido, "Rethinking Environmental Racism"; and Sensoy and DiAngelo, *Is Everyone Really Equal?*

6. For more on urban governance and neoliberalism, see Brenner and Theodore, "Neoliberalism and the Urban Condition"; Hubbard and Hall, "The Entrepreneurial City"; Leitner et al., *Contesting Neoliberalism*; McKendry and Janos, "Greening the Industrial City"; and Wilson, "Towards a Contingent Urban Neoliberalism."

7. It is important to note that neighborhood boundaries do not necessarily align with census tract designations. Thus Seattle's city government aggregates census data into community reporting areas, which are groups of census tracts that loosely represent neighborhoods. The community reporting areas generally approximate on the ground neighborhood boundaries (City of Seattle 2011b).

1. Urban Ambitions and Anxieties

1. *Dyspepsia* is another name for indigestion.

2. For information on the class politics surrounding the AYP and the Progressive Era in Seattle more generally see Putnam, *Class and Gender Politics*.

3. See Gibson, *Securing the Spectacular City*, for more on revitalization efforts in downtown Seattle, and associated exclusionary practices, during the 1990s.

4. See@L marked the next chapter in a long history of city brands. In 1869 a pair of real estate agents dubbed Seattle the "Queen City of the Pacific Northwest," thereby coining the first largely agreed upon nickname for the city (Wilma, "Seattle Becomes the Emerald City in 1982"). This name stuck around for a while, although Gateway to Alaska, a livable city, and others briefly held favor over the subsequent one hundred years. Jet City gained prominence during the 1950s and 1960s and paid homage to the powerful presence of Boeing. In 1981 SCVB held a contest for a new city slogan. Several people submitted Emerald City as an idea, but an entrant from California, Sarah Sterling-Franklin, ultimately won the contest and gained fame as the founder of the new brand (Wilma, "Seattle Becomes the Emerald City in 1982"). The new moniker elicited some ridicule, given the Wizard of Oz connotations, but it was chosen as an appropriate brand because of the perceived relevance of this description. To this point, Wes explained that the Emerald City moniker has "really has been indoctrinated into the city . . . people have actually come to like it. In fact, now it's hard to get rid of." Related, a January 2017 travel article about Seattle sported the title "Exploring the Emerald City" showing the persistence of the Emerald City brand (Pfeuffer, "Exploring the Emerald City"). Although this description of Seattle still pops up, the dot.com boom ushered in See@L as the official city brand in 2001.

5. Derek is referring to the urban forest and urban canopy projects in Seattle.

2. Exclusive Inclusion

1. The initial generation of environmental governance in the United States emerged in the form of the Clean Air and Clean Water Acts of the 1970s (Romolini et al., "Toward an Understanding of Citywide Urban Environmental Governance"). Over time environmental governance practices expanded to include incentives for compliance with resource regulations alongside punishment for noncompliance. More recently, the language and lens of ecosystem services has become a key focal point in environmental governance, especially at the urban scale (Frantzeskaki et al., "Advancing Urban Environmental Governance"). Given that cities both endure the impacts of climate change, ranging from rising sea levels to severe storms to desertification and the attendant rural to urban migration, *and* drive climate change through, for example, greenhouse gas emissions, municipal and county governments increasingly focus on urban environmental governance practices. Discussions about urban resilience and adaptation, urban planning strategies, and alternative modalities for conceptualizing human-environment relations are focal points in these efforts (Frantzeskaki et al., "Advanc-

ing Urban Environmental Governance"; Gupta et al., "Theorizing Governance").
The sustainability conversations within Seattle echo these general developments
and illustrate how urban environmental governance assumes situated meaning
and context-specific contingency and legitimacy (Wilson, "Towards a Contingent Urban Neoliberalism").

2. The Green Ribbon Commission, a group of governmental and non-
governmental members, was originally founded in 2005 to help guide the implementation of the CAP. Reconvened in 2012 to offer more explicit implementation
suggestions for the updated CAP, the commission laid out extensive implementation suggestions within five broad categories: shared prosperity, vibrant communities, health and communities, social equity, and sustainable environment
(Office of Sustainability & Environment, *Seattle Climate Action Plan*, 13). While
acknowledging that the necessary transformations within these categories are
wide-ranging and daunting, the report also emphasizes the qualities of Seattle,
namely innovation, economic wealth, and a history of environmental leadership, that purportedly make such transformation possible (Office of Sustainability & Environment, *Seattle Climate Action Plan*, 18). Stating that the city "should
be the national proving ground for important advancements in climate action"
(Office of Sustainability & Environment, *Seattle Climate Action Plan*, 18) speaks
to the frequently promulgated identity of Seattle as a leader in green. This status
of being on the leading edge of environmental work resonates with the sustainability imagination of Seattle and indicates once again the continued investment in a green status.

3. See Lawhon, "Relational Power in the Governance," for an analysis of relational power in sustainability.

4. See McKendry and Janos, "Greening the Industrial City"; and Moore, *Alternative Routes to the Sustainable City* for more on collaborative and non-linear
pathways towards sustainable cities.

5. In 2016 then mayor Murray released the agenda for the Equity and Environment Initiative (EEI) (Office of Sustainability & Environment, *Equity & Environment Agenda*). Conceptualized by the Community Partners Steering Committee,
this agenda seeks to translate the three goals of the EEI into action steps. Recognizing the complexity and interdependence of these issues and setting up systems of
accountability are key themes for this agenda. Educating historically white-led environmental organizations in the city and inviting them to integrate a collaborative
equity approach authentically into their work is also a central focus on this agenda.
Other concrete action steps include developing an environmental justice screening
process for all city projects; increasing opportunities for young people to participate
in and shape environmental programs for the city; helping the city design environmentally focused policies that also address the interwoven economic and cultural
needs of communities; and building on oral cultural traditions within communities to make space for storytelling as a venue for environmental justice work (Office
of Sustainability & Environment, *Equity & Environment Agenda*, 12–18).

6. The April 2017 environment progress report entitled *Moving the Needle* (Office of Sustainability & Environment) is a prescient example of the changes under way and the substantial shifts still needed. On the one hand, the report cites the equity and environment agenda and emphasizes the need for a holistic environmental justice approach to sustainability work in Seattle. On the other, a fascinating discursive pattern threads through the report in the frequent superficial mention that people of color and low-income people disproportionately bear the burden of inequities. An example of this pattern is the following: "Large parts of Seattle—notably where our communities of color, immigrants, refugees, and residents with low incomes tend to live, learn, work and play—have less tree canopy cover than neighborhoods that are home to a majority of white, upper income residents" (Office of Sustainability & Environment, *Moving the Needle*, 12). This kind of reality has been well documented in environmental justice literature for years, and yet it seems like a new insight within the OSE as the same phrase is peppered throughout the report. As such, the language of the report does not convey a deep understanding of imbricated systems of oppression and privilege that contour the city and instead seems primarily to indicate the addition of the "right" words. Language signals awareness of issues and makes visible contexts and perspectives. It is certainly an important first step to have attention paid to the experiences of "communities of color, immigrants, refugees, and residents with low incomes" (Office of Sustainability & Environment, *Moving the Needle*, 12). Yet there is still more work ahead to reach discursively and materially beyond listing categories of people to re-imagining systems and processes for just sustainabilities.

3. People, Products, and Processes

1. The role of the arts and cultural organizations in Seattle's economy remains a prominent focus. By way of example, the 2012 *Arts & Economic Prosperity IV* report, put out by Americans for the Arts and described as the most comprehensive study of its type to date, examined the economic impacts of the arts in 182 study regions (Americans for the Arts, *Arts & Economic Prosperity IV*). The report caused quite a buzz in Seattle. Arts- and culture-related non-profit organizations employed 10,000 full-time workers in Seattle and represented a nearly $450 million industry in 2012. Non-profit arts and culture organizations also produced over $38 million in local and state taxes the same year (Americans for the Arts, *Arts & Economic Prosperity IV*, 3). To summarize such numbers, the report enthusiastically concludes, "The arts mean business!" (Americans for the Arts, *Arts & Economic Prosperity IV*, 11). The quantifying of creative endeavors into numbers in this report indicates the push to specify the monetary value of arts and cultural organizations.

2. CODAC teamed up with the Capitol Hill Chamber of Commerce to examine this possibility.

3. In 2015 the Central Area District, the historic African American neighborhood, became Seattle's second arts and cultural district. The Uptown arts and

cultural district designation happened in 2017 to recognize the 1962 World's Fair history of this area and the multitude of festivals, concerts, performances, and arts spaces in the neighborhood (Office of Arts & Culture, "Arts & Cultural Districts).

4. See Dávila, *Barrio Dreams*, for an analysis of the commodification of Puerto Rican and Latinx experiences and related gentrification in El Barrio, New York.

5. Accounts for the number of languages spoken in Southeast Seattle vary from forty to ninety.

6. The regional collaborations are funded largely by the Sustainable Communities Initiative and known as the Growing Transit Communities office of the Puget Sound Regional Council.

4. Unsettling Whiteness

1. See Bhabha, "The White Stuff," for an analysis of whiteness as an unsettled "form of authority." See Johnston, "Unsettling Whiteness," for an examination of unsettling whiteness in Australian cinema. See Straker, "Unsettling Whiteness," for a discussion of unsettling whiteness in the context of the Apartheid Archives Project in South Africa.

2. The aspirational tagline "Together we can achieve racial justice in Seattle" for the SOCR, the office that oversees the RSJI, reflects the simultaneous hope for a future of racial justice and acknowledgment of the enormity of inequities. This description is an evolution from the original "We all belong" slogan for the SOCR, which indicated an inclusive stance but did not explicitly acknowledge the structures and systems of racialized inequities that prevent belonging. In contrast, the revised tagline names more directly the focused goal of racial justice. By claiming racial justice as the destination, the tagline also indicates that such a reality is not present in Seattle yet.

3. Now called the Office of Planning and Community Development.

4. Just as the translation policy took root, then mayor Nickels changed the name of the primary public-facing office of municipal government from the Citizen Service Bureau to the Customer Service Bureau. This linguistic revision was meant to offer greater inclusivity to residents who might not be U.S. citizens. Yet this name change also hints at the neoliberalization of city government as residents became located within the frame of customers and clients. Such entanglements between social justice values and economic growth mandates as principally expressed through neoliberalism indicate some of the limits to unsettling whiteness that arose adjacent to the RSJI.

5. Parallel to these three plan updates, the Seattle Planning Commission and DPD worked on status reports for twenty-four additional neighborhoods. The goal of the status reports was to solicit a range of perspectives from residents, through both virtual and actual meetings, on the current state of their neighborhoods. In total more than five thousand people participated in these discussions (Seattle Planning Commission, "Status Check," 5). The status reports were then

used to shape "decisions about whether or how to update neighborhood plans" and to delineate "emerging priorities" (City of Seattle, *Draft Neighborhood Plan*, 1).

6. The recent ETOD efforts discussed in chapter 3 used a different method for establishing the steering committee for the Multicultural Center in Southeast Seattle for precisely the reasons that Joanna described.

7. Upzone refers to changes in land use regulations such that an area becomes more densely developable. In this case concerns were voiced about changing the zoning from single-family homes to multi-story, mixed-use buildings.

8. Also in 2009, the RSJI received support and official backing from the entire suite of elected officials in the Executive, Legislative, and City Attorney's Offices of City Hall (Seattle Office for Civil Rights, *Race and Social Justice Initiative: Accomplishments 2009–2011*, 1).

9. The year 2015 marked the launch of the first ESJ strategic plan process in light of a self-study on the extensiveness of inequities within King County (Beatty and Foster, *The Determinants of Equity*; King County, *King County Equity and Social Justice Annual Report*, 8). This report established a baseline analysis of equity conditions in King County to provide a reference point for future ESJ work. Although there have been advancements since 2009, the self-study stressed that significant disparities exist in educational, economic, and health outcomes for low-income communities, people with limited English proficiency, and people of color in King County (Beatty and Foster, *The Determinants of Equity*, 4). As the report states, "people of color generally do not experience the same quality of life as white residents" (Beatty and Foster, *The Determinants of Equity*, 8). From a higher percentage of household income paid on childcare to lower graduation rates, higher unemployment rates, and food insecurity, communities of color in King County disproportionately bear the burden of social inequities.

10. See Mountz and Curran, "Policing in Drag"; Peck, "Geographies of Policy"; and Swyngedouw et al., "Neoliberal Urbanization in Europe" for more on policy transfers.

Conclusion

1. See Gibson, *Securing the Spectacular City*, for more on the politics surrounding endeavors to end homelessness in Seattle.

REFERENCES

Abel, Troy T., and Jonah White. 2011. "Skewed Riskscapes and Gentrified Inequities: Environmental Exposure Disparities in Seattle, Washington." *American Journal of Public Health* 101 (Supplement 1) (December): S246–54.

Abello, Oscar Perry. 2016. "Seattle Starts $21M Loan Fund to Promote Affordable Housing Near Transit." NextCity.org. https://nextcity.org/daily/entry/seattle-equitable-transit-oriented-development-loan-fund.

Adelman, Larry, and Llewellyn Smith. 2008. *Place Matters* (video). In *Unnatural Causes* (video series) produced by Larry Adelman and Llewellyn Smith. San Francisco: California Newsreel.

Agnew, John. 1987. *Place and Politics: The Geographical Mediation of State and Society.* Boston: Allen and Unwin.

Agyeman, Julian. 2013. *Introducing Just Sustainabilities: Policy, Planning, and Practice.* New York: Zed Books.

Agyeman, Julian, Robert D. Bullard, and Bob Evans, eds. 2003. *Just Sustainabilities: Development in an Unequal World.* Cambridge MA: MIT Press.

Ahmed, Sara. 2007. "A Phenomenology of Whiteness." *Feminist Theory* 8, no. 2 (August): 149–68.

———. 2012. *On Being Included: Racism and Diversity in Institutional Life.* Durham NC: Duke University Press.

Alexander, Michelle. 2012. *The New Jim Crow: Mass Incarceration in the Age of Colorblindness.* New York: New Press.

Alkon, Alison Hope, and Christie Grace McCullen. 2011. "Whiteness and Farmers Markets: Performances, Perpetuations . . . Contestations?" *Antipode* 43, no. 4 (November): 937–59.

Allen, Dave. 2010. *WALK BIKE RIDEr* (newsletter of Way to Go, Seattle!). http://archive.constantcontact.com/fs051/1103565212781/archive/1103696813552.html.

All Home. 2017. *Seattle/King County Point-in-Time Count of Persons Experiencing Homelessness, 2017: Count Us In.* San Jose: Applied Survey Research.

Americans for the Arts. 2012. *Arts & Economic Prosperity IV: The Economic Impact of Nonprofit Arts and Culture Organizations and Their Audiences in the City of Seat-*

tle, Washington. Washington DC: Americans for the Arts. https://www.seattle
.gov/Documents/Departments/Arts/Downloads/Reports/wa_CityOfSeattle
_aep4_FinalReport-Local.pdf.

Anand, Rohini, and Mary-Frances Winters. 2008. "A Retrospective View of Corporate Diversity Training from 1964 to the Present." *Academy of Management Learning & Education* 7, no. 3 (September): 356–72.

Apartments.com. 2018. Capitol Hill—Seattle, WA. https://www.apartments.com
/capitol-hill-seattle-wa/2/?bb=1-hvhqzrtq89__L.

Atkinson, Rowland, and Hazel Easthope. 2009. "The Consequences of the Creative Class: The Pursuit of Creativity Strategies in Australia's Cities." *International Journal of Urban and Regional Research* 33, no. 1 (November): 64–79.

Barnett, Erica. 2017. "Anchors against Displacement: Seattle Experiments with Community-Owned Hubs and Job Incubators." Sightline.org. http://www
.sightline.org/2017/05/25/anchors-against-displacement/.

Barraclough, Laura. 2011. *Making the San Fernando Valley: Rural Landscapes, Urban Development, and White Privilege.* Athens: University of Georgia Press.

Bassnett, Susan. 2014. *Translation.* New York: Routledge.

Basso, Keith H. 1996. *Wisdom Sits in Places: Landscape and Language Among the Western Apache.* Albuquerque: University of New Mexico Press.

Beatty, Abigail, and Dionne Foster. 2015. *The Determinants of Equity: Identifying Indicators to Establish a Baseline of Equity in King County.* Seattle: King County Office of Performance, Strategy and Budget.

Bernard, Sara. 2015. "Tent Cities: Seattle's Unique Approach to Homelessness." *Grist Magazine.* http://grist.org/cities/tent-cities-seattles-unique-approach-to
-homelessness/?iframe=true&preview=true.

Bernardo, Richie. 2017. "2017's Greenest Cities in America." WalletHub. https://
wallethub.com/edu/most-least-green-cities/16246/.

Bhabha, Homi. 1998. "The White Stuff." *Artforum International* 36, no. 9 (May): 21–25.

Biernacki, Patrick, and Dan Waldorf. 1981. "Snowball Sampling: Problems and Techniques of Chain Referral Sampling." *Sociological Methods and Research* 1, no. 2 (November): 141–63.

Bledsoe, Adam, Latoya E. Eaves, and Brian Williams. 2017. "Introduction: Black Geographies in and of the United States South." *Southeastern Geographer* 57, no. 1 (Spring): 6–11.

Bonilla-Silva, Eduardo. 1997. "Rethinking Racism: Toward a Structural Interpretation." *American Sociological Review* 62, no. 3 (June): 465–80.

———. 2018. *Racism Without Racists: Color-Blind Racism and the Persistence of Racial Inequality in America, Fifth Edition.* New York: Rowman & Littlefield Publishers.

Brenner, Neil, and Nik Theodore. 2005. "Neoliberalism and the Urban Condition." *City* 9, no. 1 (April): 101–7.

Bronstein, Elliot, Glenn Harris, Ron Harris-White, and Julie Nelson. 2011. "Eliminating Institutional Racism within Local Government: The City of Seattle

Race and Social Justice Initiative." In *Government Is Us 2.0.*, edited by Cheryl Simrell King, 157–73. Armonk NY: M. E. Sharpe.

Brown, Michael, Sean Wang, and Larry Knopp. 2011. "Queering Gay Space." In *Seattle Geographies*, edited by Michael P. Brown and Richard Morrill, 155–64. Seattle: University of Washington Press.

Buizer, Marleen, Birgit Elands, and Kati Vierikko. 2016. "Governing Cities Reflexively: The Biocultural Diversity Concept as an Alternative to Ecosystem Services." *Environmental Science & Policy* 62 (March): 7–13.

Burgess, Timothy, Carlos de Imus, Bruce Heller, Dorothy Mann, Eric Schnapper, and Ruth Schroeder. 2000. *Report to the Seattle City Council WTO Accountability Committee by the Citizens' Panel on WTO Operations.* Seattle: City of Seattle.

Burkett, Maxine. 2011. "The Nation *Ex-Situ*: On Climate Change, Deterritorialized Nationhood and the Post-Climate Era." *Climate Law* 2, no. 3: 345–74.

Bush, Melanie E. L. 2011. *Everyday Forms of Whiteness: Understanding Race in a "Post-Racial" World, Second Edition.* New York: Rowman & Littlefield Publishers.

Carbado, Devon W. 2005. "Racial Naturalization." *American Quarterly* 57, no. 3 (September): 633–58.

Carlson, Daniel, Elizabeth Johnson, and Rachel Garshick Kleit. 2014. *City of Seattle HUD Community Challenge Grant: Community Cornerstones Program, Annual Evaluation Report.* Seattle: Evans School of Public Affairs, University of Washington.

Castro Luna, Claudia. 2017. "A Corner to Love." Seattle Poetic Grid. https://seattlepoeticgrid.com/.

Chin, Dennis. 2015. "National Groups Join Forces to Center Racial Equity in Government." Center for Social Inclusion website. http://www.centerforsocialinclusion.org/national-groups-join-forces-to-center-racial-equity-in-government/.

Cidell, Julie. 2017. *Imagining Sustainability: Creative Urban Environmental Governance in Chicago and Melbourne.* New York: Routledge.

Citizens' Panel. 2000. *Lost Opportunities: The Budget for the Seattle Meeting of the World Trade Organization. Report of the Citizens' Advisory Panel on WTO Invitation, Part Two.* Seattle: City of Seattle.

City of Seattle. 1995. *Resolution 29215 Attachment 1 to Resolution 29215: The Vision for the City of Seattle Comprehensive Plan.* Seattle: City of Seattle.

———. 2008a. *Ordinance 122752.* Seattle: City of Seattle—Legislative Department.

———. 2008b. *Budget and Policy Filter: Supplemental Toolkit.* Seattle: City of Seattle. http://racialequitytools.org/resourcefiles/nelson.pdf.

———. 2009a. *Resolution 31155.* Seattle: City of Seattle—Legislative Department.

———. 2009b *Resolution 31164.* Seattle: City of Seattle—Legislative Department.

———. 2009c. *Draft Neighborhood Plan: Status Reports 2009.* Seattle: City of Seattle.

———. 2011a. *Basic Population and Housing Unit Characteristics.* Seattle: City of Seattle—Department of Planning and Development.

———. 2011b. "Census Tracts and Community Reporting Areas." http://www.seattle.gov/Documents/Departments/opcd/Demographics/AboutSeattle/2010censusSeattleCommunityReportingAreasandCensus2010tracts.pdf.

————. 2011c. *Resolution 31312*. Seattle: City of Seattle—Legislative Department.

————. 2011d. *Ordinance 123775*. Seattle: City of Seattle—Legislative Department.

————. 2014. *Resolution 31555*. Seattle: City of Seattle—Legislative Department.

————. 2015a. *Seattle 2035, Your City, Your Future: A Comprehensive Plan for Managing Growth 2015–2035, Draft*. Seattle: Department of Planning and Development.

————. 2015b. *Resolution 31577*. Seattle: City of Seattle—Legislative Department.

————. 2016. *Ordinance 125165*. Seattle: City of Seattle—Legislative Department.

————. 2018a. "Equitable Development Initiative." Office of Planning & Community Development. https://www.seattle.gov/opcd/ongoing-initiatives/equitable-development-initiative.

————. 2018b. "Language Access." Office of Immigrant and Refugee Affairs. https://www.seattle.gov/iandraffairs/la.

Clark, Sally, Glenn Harris, Sebhat Tenna, Janice Kong, and Nora Liu. 2010. *A Revolutionary Approach: Bringing an Equity Focus to Smart Growth by Engaging Marginalized Populations*. PowerPoint presentation given at the conference New Partners for Smart Growth: Building Safe, Healthy and Livable Communities, February 3–6, 2010, Seattle. https://newpartners.org/2010/docs/presentations/thursday/np10_liu_clark_harris_tenna_kong.pdf.

Cloke, Paul, Philip Crang, and Mark Goodwin, eds. 2014. *Introducing Human Geographies, Third Edition*. New York: Routledge.

CODAC. 2009. *Preserving and Creating Space for Arts and Culture in Seattle: Final Recommendations*. Seattle: Lund Consulting.

Cohen, Aubrey. 2009. "Proposed Bus Cuts Unfair, Rainier Valley Service Provider Says." *Seattle Post-Intelligencer*. http://www.seattlepi.com/local/transportation/article/Proposed-bus-cuts-unfair-Rainier-Valley-service-1303969.php.

Community Land Use and Economics (CLUE) Group. 2009. *Retail Development Strategy for Rainier Valley: Final Report*. Arlington VA: CLUE Group.

Compton, Jim, Jan Drago, and Nick Licata. 2000. *Report of the WTO Accountability Review Committee Seattle City Council*. Seattle: Seattle City Council.

Crenshaw, Kimberle, ed. 1995. *Critical Race Theory: The Key Writings That Formed the Movement*. New York: New Press.

Cresswell, Tim. 2006. *On the Move: Mobility in the Modern Western World*. New York: Routledge.

————. 2014. "Place." In *Introducing Human Geographies*, edited by Paul Cloke, Philip Crang, and Mark Goodwin, 249–61. New York: Routledge.

Crowley, Walt. 2003. "Native American Tribes Sign Point Elliott Treaty at Mukilteo on January 22, 1855." HistoryLink.org. http://www.historylink.org/File/5402.

Daily Journal of Commerce. 2017. "Mercy Othello Plaza Opens, Adding 108 Affordable Units Near Station." http://www.djc.com/news/re/12102095.html.

Davidson, Mark. 2010. "Social Sustainability and the City." *Geography Compass* 4, no. 7 (August): 872–80.

Dávila, Arlene. 2004. *Barrio Dreams: Puerto Ricans, Latinos, and the Neoliberal City*. Berkeley: University of California Press.

Delgado, Richard, and Jean Stefancic, eds. 2017. *Critical Race Theory: An Introduction, Third Edition.* New York: New York University Press.

DeMay, Daniel. 2016. "Seattle Among Greenest Cities in America." *Seattle Post-Intelligencer.* https://www.seattlepi.com/local/article/Seattle-among-greenest-cities-in-America-9967861.php.

Derrick, Anthony. 2018. "Mayor Jenny A. Durkan's 2018 State of the City Address." http://durkan.seattle.gov/2018/02/state-of-the-city-2018/.

DiAngelo, Robin. 2011. "White Fragility." *International Journal of Critical Pedagogy* 3, no. 3: 54–70.

———. 2012. *What Does It Mean to Be White? Developing White Racial Literacy.* New York: Peter Lang.

Diers, Jim A. 2004. *Neighbor Power: Building Community the Seattle Way.* Seattle: University of Washington Press.

Dierwechter, Yonn. 2013. "Smart City-Regionalism across Seattle: Progressing Transit Nodes in Labor Space?" *Geoforum* 49 (February): 139–49.

Driver, Felix. 2014. "Imaginative Geographies." In *Introducing Human Geographies, Third Edition,* edited by Paul Cloke, Philip Crang, and Mark Goodwin, 234–48. New York: Routledge.

Duncan, Don. 2009. "A Fair to Remember." *Seattle Times, AYP Exposition 100th Anniversary.* https://www.seattletimes.com/pacific-nw-magazine/100-years-later-seattles-first-worlds-fair-remembered/.

Duneier, Mitchell, Philip Kasinitz, and Alexandra Murphy. 2014. "An Invitation to Urban Ethnography." In *The Urban Ethnography Reader,* edited by Mitchell Duneier, Philip Kasinitz, and Alexandra Murphy, 1–8. New York: Oxford University Press.

Elias, Sean, and Joe R. Feagin. 2016. *Racial Theories in Social Science: A Systemic Racism Critique.* New York: Routledge.

Emerson, Robert M., Rachel I. Fretz, and Linda L. Shaw. 1995. *Writing Ethnographic Fieldnotes.* Chicago: University of Chicago Press.

Enterprise. 2018. "Regional Equitable Development Initiative (REDI) Fund." http://www.enterprisecommunity.org/financing-and-development/community-loan-fund/redi-fund.

Fawcett, Antoinette, Karla Guadarrama García, and Rebecca Parker, eds. 2010. *Translation: Theory and Practice in Dialogue.* New York: Continuum International Publishing Group.

Feagin, Joe R. 2014. *Racist America: Roots, Current Realities, and Future Reparations, Third Edition.* New York: Routledge.

Findlay, John M. 1997. "A Fishy Proposition: Regional Identity in the Pacific Northwest." In *Many Wests: Place, Culture and Regional Identity,* edited by David Wrobel and Michael Steiner, 37–70. Lawrence: University Press of Kansas.

Finney, Carolyn. 2009. "What's Race Got to Do with It? Climate Change, Privilege, and Consciousness." *Whole Thinking Journal* 4 (Winter): 21–24.

First National People of Color Environmental Leadership Summit. 1991. "Principles of Environmental Justice." https://www.nrdc.org/resources/principles -environmental-justice-ej.

Florida, Richard. 2001. "The Rise of the Creative Class." *Washington Monthly*. https://washingtonmonthly.com/2001/05/01/the-rise-of-the-creative-class/.

———. 2002. *The Rise of the Creative Class and How It's Transforming Work, Leisure, Community, and Everyday Life*. New York: Basic Books.

———. 2012. *The Rise of the Creative Class, Revisited*. New York: Basic Books.

Frantzeskaki, Niki, Nadja Kabisch, and Timon McPhearson. 2016. "Advancing Urban Environmental Governance: Understanding Theories, Practices and Processes Shaping Urban Sustainability and Resilience." *Environmental Science & Policy* 62 (August): 1–6.

Freire, Paulo. 2000 [1970]. *Pedagogy of the Oppressed*. New York: Continuum International Publishing Group.

Friends of Seattle's Olmsted Parks. 2009. *Olmsted Centennial News*. Seattle: Friends of Seattle's Olmsted Parks.

Gardheere, Ubax, and Lauren Craig. 2015. *Community-Supported Equitable Development in Southeast Seattle*. Seattle: Puget Sound Sage.

Gibson, Chris. 2003. "Cultures at Work: Why Culture Matters in Research on the 'Cultural' Industries." *Social and Cultural Geography* 4, no. 2 (June): 201–15.

Gibson, Chris, and Natascha Klocker. 2004. "Academic Publishing as 'Creative' Industry, and Recent Discourses of 'Creative Economies': Some Critical Reflections." *Area* 36, no. 4 (December): 423–34.

Gibson, Timothy A. 2004. *Securing the Spectacular City: The Politics of Revitalization and Homelessness in Downtown Seattle*. New York: Lexington Books.

Gieseking, Jen Jack 2017. "Geographical Imagination." In *The International Encyclopedia of Geography*, edited by Douglas Richardson, Noel Castree, Michael F. Goodchild, Audrey Kobayashi, Weidong Liu, and Richard Marston, 1–5. Hoboken NJ: John Wiley & Sons.

Gilliam, Shawn. 2015. "Green Cities." *Sky* magazine (Minneapolis MN: Delta Airlines) (April): 72–79.

Gilmore, Ruth Wilson. 2007. *Golden Gulag: Prisons, Surplus, Crisis, and Opposition in Globalizing California*. Los Angeles: University of California Press.

Golash-Boza, Tanya Maria. 2015. *Race & Racisms: A Critical Approach*. New York: Oxford University Press.

Gooden, Susan T. 2014. *Race and Social Equity: A Nervous Area of Government*. Armonk NY: M. E. Sharpe.

Goodman, Alan H., Yolanda T. Moses, and Joseph L. Jones. 2012. *Race: Are We So Different?* Malden MA: Wiley-Blackwell.

Government Alliance on Race and Equity (GARE). 2018a. "Our Approach." http://www.racialequityalliance.org/about/our-approach/.

———. 2018b. "Map." https://www.racialequityalliance.org/where-we-work /jurisdictions/.

———. 2018c. "Leadership and Staff." https://www.racialequityalliance.org/about /who-we-are/leadership-and-staff/.

———. 2018d. "Why Working for Racial Equity Benefits Everyone." http://www .racialequityalliance.org/about/our-approach/benefits/.

Greenwich, Howard, and Margaret Wykowski. 2012. *Transit Oriented Development That's Healthy, Green & Just: Ensuring Transit Investment in Seattle's Rainier Valley Builds Communities Where All Families Thrive.* Seattle: Puget Sound Sage. http://pugetsoundsage.org/research/research-equitable-development /healthy-green-just-tod/.

Gregory, Derek. 2009a. "Imaginative Geographies." In *The Dictionary of Human Geography, Fifth Edition*, edited by Derek Gregory, Ron Johnston, Geraldine Pratt, Michael Watts, and Sarah Whatmore, 369–71. Malden MA: Wiley-Blackwell.

———. 2009b. "Geographical Imagination." In *The Dictionary of Human Geography, Fifth Edition*, edited by Derek Gregory, Ron Johnston, Geraldine Pratt, Michael Watts, and Sarah Whatmore, 282–85. Malden MA: Wiley-Blackwell.

Grygiel, Chris. 2009a. "Plastic Industry Aims for 'Greener' Bags." *Seattle Post-Intelligencer.* http://www.seattlepi.com/local/article/Plastic-industry-aims -for-greener-bags-1303424.php.

———. 2009b. "Seattle Says 'No' to Grocery Bag Tax: Plastic Industry Spent $1.4 Million to Defeat First-of-Its Kind Measure." *Seattle Post-Intelligencer.* http://www.seattlepi.com/local/article/Seattle-says-no-to-grocery-bag-tax -1305800.php.

Gupta, Joyeeta, Hebe Verrest, and Rivke Jaffe. 2015. "Theorizing Governance." In *Geographies of Urban Governance: Advanced Theories, Methods and Practices*, edited by Joyeeta Gupta, Karin Pfeffer, Hebe Verrest, and Mirjam Ros-Tonen, 27–43. New York: Springer International.

Hackworth, Jason, and Josephine Rekers. 2005. "Ethnic Packaging and Gentrification: The Case of Four Neighborhoods in Toronto." *Urban Affairs Review* 41 (November): 211–36.

Häikiö, Liisa. 2007. "Expertise, Representation and the Common Good: Grounds for Legitimacy in the Urban Governance Network." *Urban Studies* 44, no. 11 (October): 2147–62.

Harris, Leila. 2014. "Imaginative Geographies of Green: Difference, Postcoloniality, and Affect in Environmental Narratives in Contemporary Turkey." *Annals of the Association of American Geographers* 104, no. 4 (April): 801–15.

Harris, Cheryl. 1993. "Whiteness as Property." *Harvard Law Review* 106, no. 8: 1707–91.

Hartmann, Douglas, Joseph Gerteis, and Paul R. Croll. 2009. "An Empirical Assessment of Whiteness Theory: Hidden from How Many?" *Social Problems* 56, no. 3 (August): 403–24.

Harvey, David. 1989. "From Managerialism to Entrepreneurialism: The Transformation of Urban Governance in Late Capitalism." *Geografiska Annaler* 71, no. 1: 3–17.

———. 1990. *The Condition of Postmodernity*. Malden MA: Blackwell Publishers.

Hatim, Basil, and Jeremy Munday. 2004. *Translation: An Advanced Resource Book.* New York: Routledge.

Herbert, Steve. 2007. "The 'Battle of Seattle' Revisited: Or, Seven Views of a Protest-Zoning State." *Political Geography* 26, no. 5 (June): 601–19.

Herrera Environmental Consultants. 2008. *Alternatives to Disposable Shopping Bags and Food Service Items, Volume 1.* Seattle: Seattle Public Utilities.

Heynen, Nik, and Paul Robbins. 2005. "The Neoliberalization of Nature: Governance, Privatization, Enclosure and Valuation." *Capitalism Nature Socialism* 16, no. 1 (March): 5–8.

Heynen, Nik, Harold A. Perkins, and Parama Roy. 2006. "The Political Ecology of Uneven Urban Green Space: The Impact of Political Economy on Race and Ethnicity in Producing Environmental Inequality in Milwaukee." *Urban Affairs Review* 42, no. 1 (September): 3–25.

HistoryLink and Friends of Olmsted Parks. 2004. "Olmsted Park Plans for Seattle Cybertour." HistoryLink.org. http://www.historylink.org/index.cfm?DisplayPage=output.cfm&file_id=7054.

Hoelscher, Steve. 2006. "Imaginative Geographies." In *Encyclopedia of Human Geography,* edited by Barney Warf, 244–45. Thousand Oaks CA: Sage Publications.

Hoerner, J. Andrew, and Nia Robinson. 2008. *A Climate of Change: African Americans, Global Warming, and a Just Climate Policy for the U.S.* Oakland CA: Environmental Justice and Climate Change Initiative.

Holden, Meg. 2006. "Revisiting the Local Impact of Community Indicators Projects: Sustainable Seattle as Prophet in Its Own Land." *Applied Research in Quality of Life* 1 (September): 253–77.

HomeSight. 2018a. "Othello Square." https://homesight-my.sharepoint.com /personal/michelle_homesightwa_org/_layouts/15/onedrive.aspx?id= %2Fpersonal%2Fmichelle_homesightwa_org%2FDocuments%2FOthello %20Square%202%20Pager_Updated%20April%202018%2Epdf&parent= %2Fpersonal%2Fmichelle_homesightwa_org%2FDocuments&slrid=ee1e689e -f060-5000-e241-50c125fbb63b.

———. 2018b. "Othello Square: Master Plan." https://issuu.com/weberthompson /docs/othello_square_master_plan_180425_4.

Hou, Jeffrey, and Isami Kinoshita. 2007. "Bridging Community Differences through Informal Processes: Reexamining Participatory Planning in Seattle and Matsudo." *Journal of Planning Education and Research* 26 (March): 301–14.

Houston, Serin. 2009. "Scales of Whiteness and Racial Mixing: Challenging and Confirming Racial Categories." *Geographical Bulletin* 50 (November): 93–110.

Hoyman, Michele, and Christopher Faricy. 2009. "It Takes a Village: A Test of the Creative Class, Social Capital, and Human Capital Theories." *Urban Affairs Review* 44, no. 3 (January): 311–33.

Hubbard, Phil, and Tim Hall. 1998. "The Entrepreneurial City and the 'New Urban Politics.'" In *The Entrepreneurial City: Geographies of Politics, Regime and Representation,* edited by Tim Hall and Phil Hubbard, 1–26. New York: John Wiley and Sons.

Huberman, Bond. 2009. "The Great White Fair." *Eastside City Arts* 1, no. 11 (May): 20–23.

James, Paul. 2015. *Urban Sustainability in Theory and Practice: Circles of Sustainability.* New York: Routledge.

Johnston, Meg Elizabeth. 2008. "Unsettling Whiteness: The Slippage of Race and Nation in Clara Law's *Letters to Ali.*" *Studies in Australasian Cinema* 2, no. 2: 103–19.

Jornlin, Emma. 2013. "Consumers React to Seattle's Plastic Bag Ban." Environment Washington website. http://www.thestranger.com/images/blogimages /2013/01/15/1358276856-luc20130115_3a.pdf.

Kaika, Maria. 2006. "Dams as Symbols of Modernization: The Urbanization of Nature between Geographical Imagination and Materiality." *Annals of the Association of American Geographers* 96, no. 2 (June): 276–301.

Karvonen, Andrew. 2010. "Metronatural: Inventing and Reworking Urban Nature in Seattle." *Progress in Planning* 74, no. 4 (November): 153–202.

———. 2011. *Politics of Urban Runoff: Nature, Technology, and the Sustainable City.* Cambridge MA: MIT Press.

Kearns, Robin. 2000. "Being There: Research through Observing and Participating." In *Qualitative Research Methods in Human Geography*, edited by Iain Hay, 103–21. New York: Oxford University Press.

Keith, Michael. 2005. *After the Cosmopolitan? Multicultural Cities and the Future of Racism.* New York: Routledge.

Kelsey, Norma, Sister Kathleen Pruitt, Clark Pickett, and Angela Toussaint. 2000. *Report to the Seattle City Council WTO Accountability Review Committee: Preparations and Planning Panel.* Seattle: Seattle City Council.

Kim, Daniel. 1999. "Introduction to Systems Thinking." https://thesystemsthinker .com/introduction-to-systems-thinking/.

King County. 2010a. *Ordinance 16948.* Seattle: Metropolitan King County Council.

———. 2010b. *2009 Equity and Social Justice Commitments by Department: Year-End Tracking.* Seattle: King County Equity and Social Justice Initiative.

———. 2015. *King County Equity and Social Justice Annual Report.* Seattle: Office of Equity and Social Justice and Office of King County Executive Dow Constantine.

———. 2018. "Tools and Resources." Equity and Social Justice. http://www .kingcounty.gov/elected/executive/equity-social-justice/tools-resources.aspx

Klingle, Matthew. 2006. "Changing Spaces: Nature, Property, and Power in Seattle, 1880–1945." *Journal of Urban History* 32, no. 2 (January): 197–230.

———. 2007. *Emerald City: An Environmental History of Seattle.* New Haven CT: Yale University Press.

Korten, David. 2006. *The Great Turning: From Empire to Earth Community.* Bloomfield CT: Kumarian Press.

Krueger, Rob, and Julian Agyeman. 2005. "Sustainability Schizophrenia or 'Actually Existing Sustainabilities?' Toward a Broader Understanding of the Politics and Promise of Local Sustainability in the U.S." *Geoforum* 36, no. 4 (July): 410–17.

Krueger, Rob, and Susan Buckingham. 2009. "Creative-City Scripts, Economic Development, and Sustainability." *Geographical Review* 99, no. 1 (January): iii–xii.

Lange, Greg. 1999. "Billboard Reading 'Will the last person leaving SEATTLE—Turn out the lights' Appears Near Sea-Tac International Airport on April 16, 1971." HistoryLink.org. http://www.historylink.org/File/1287.

Larner, Wendy. 2000. "Neoliberalism: Policy, Ideology, Governmentality." *Studies in Political Economy* 63 (Autumn): 5–25.

Lawhon, Mary. 2012. "Relational Power in the Governance of a South African e-Waste Transition." *Environment and Planning A* 44, no. 4 (April): 954–71.

Lear, Jonathan. 2006. *Radical Hope: Ethics in the Face of Cultural Devastation.* Cambridge MA: Harvard University Press.

Lee, Shelley. 2007. "The Contradictions of Cosmopolitanism: Consuming the Orient at the Alaska-Yukon-Pacific Exposition and the International Potlatch Festival, 1909–1934." *Western Historical Quarterly* 38, no. 3 (Autumn): 277–302.

Lees, Loretta, Tom E. Slater, and Elvin Wyly. 2008. *Gentrification.* New York: Routledge.

Lefebvre, Henri. 1991 [1974]. *The Production of Space*, trans. Donald Nicholson-Smith. Malden MA: Blackwell Publishing.

Leitner, Helga, Jamie Peck, and Eric Sheppard, eds. 2007. *Contesting Neoliberalism: Urban Frontiers.* New York: Guilford Press.

Ley, David. 2003. "Artists, Aestheticisation, and the Field of Gentrification." *Urban Studies* 40, no. 12 (November): 2527–44.

Lipsitz, George. 2006. *The Possessive Investment in Whiteness: How White People Profit from Identity Politics, Revised and Expanded Edition.* Philadelphia: Temple University Press.

———. 2011. *How Racism Takes Place.* Philadelphia: Temple University Press.

Lloyd, Sarah. 2011. "There Is No Other Option: We Need to Approve the $20 'Congestion Reduction' Fee." Seattlest.com. http://seattlest.com/2011/07/08/there_is_no_other_option_we_need_to.php.

Lyons, James. 2004. *Selling Seattle: Representing Contemporary Urban America.* New York: Wallflower Press.

———. 2005. "'Think Seattle, Act Globally': Specialty Coffee, Commodity Biographies and the Promotion of Place." *Cultural Studies* 19, no. 1 (January): 14–34.

Macy, Joanna, and Molly Young Brown. 1998. *Coming Back to Life: Practices to Reconnect Our Lives, Our World.* Gabriola Island BC: New Society Publishers.

Markusen, Ann. 2006. "Urban Development and the Politics of a Creative Class: Evidence from a Study of Artists." *Environment and Planning A* 38, no. 10 (October): 1921–40.

Massey, Doreen. 2005. *For Space.* London: Sage Publications.

McCarthy, Ronald M., and Associates. 2000. *An Independent Review of the World Trade Organization Conference Disruptions in Seattle, Washington November 29–December 3, 1999.* San Clemente CA: R. M. McCarthy and Associates.

McKendry, Corina, and Nik Janos. 2015. "Greening the Industrial City: Equity, Environment, and Economic Growth in Seattle and Chicago." *International Environmental Agreements: Politics, Law, and Economics* 15, no. 1 (March): 45–60.

McKittrick, Katherine, and Clyde Woods, eds. 2007. *Black Geographies and the Politics of Place.* Toronto: Between the Lines.

Meadows, Donella. 2008. *Thinking in Systems: A Primer.* Edited by Diana Wright. White River Junction VT: Chelsea Green Publishing.

Mercy Housing. 2017. "Mercy Housing Northwest-Washington." https://www.mercyhousing.org/washington/mercy-othello-plaza-apartments.

Minard, Anna. 2013. "Murray Fires Civil Rights Director Julie Nelson." *Stranger.* http://slog.thestranger.com/slog/archives/2013/12/11/rumor-alert-murray-fires-civil-rights-director-julie-nelson.

Mitchell, Katharyne, Mikail Aydyn Blyth, Ethan Boyles, Sofia Gogic, et al. 2011. "Cultural Geographies." In *Seattle Geographies,* edited by Michael P. Brown and Richard Morrill, 165–82. Seattle: University of Washington Press.

MLK Business Association. 2018. "Home Page." http://www.mlkba.org/.

Moody, Fred. 2003. *Seattle and the Demons of Ambition: A Love Story.* New York: St. Martin's Press.

Moore, Steven. 2007. *Alternative Routes to the Sustainable City: Austin, Curitiba, and Frankfurt.* New York: Lexington Books.

Morrill, Richard, William Beyers, and Michael P. Brown. 2011. "Introducing Seattle Geographies." In *Seattle Geographies,* edited by Michael P. Brown, and Richard Morrill, 3–18. Seattle: University of Washington Press.

Mountz, Alison, and Winifred Curran. 2009. "Policing in Drag: Guiliani Goes Global with the Illusion of Control." *Geoforum* 40, no. 6 (December): 1033–40.

Mulady, Kathy. 2008. "City OKs 20-Cent Fee on Plastic, Paper Bags." *Seattle Post-Intelligencer.* http://www.seattlepi.com/local/article/City-OKs-20-cent-fee-on-plastic-paper-bags-1280533.php.

Municipal Research and Services Center. 2018. "Growth Management Act." http://mrsc.org/getdoc/37359eae-8748-4aaf-ae76-614123c0d6a4/Comprehensive-Planning-Growth-Management.aspx.

Murray, Edward. 2015. "Mayor Murray Launches First-of-Its-Kind Equity and Environment Initiative." Office of the Mayor. http://murray.seattle.gov/mayor-murray-launches-first-of-its-kind-equity-environment-initiative/#sthash.gTX02jTC.dpbs.

Nafziger, Rich, Susan Crane, Ellen Greene, Judith Olsen, and Lance Matteson. 2014. *Case for Creating the SE Seattle Economic Opportunity Center, Community Cornerstones: Commercial Stability-Opportunity Center Feasibility.* Seattle: Skill Up Washington. https://skillupwa.org/wp-content/uploads/EOC_Final_Report.pdf.

Nelson, Gerald B. 1977. *Seattle: The Life and Times of an American City.* New York: Alfred Knopf.

Nelson, Julie, Glenn Harris, Sandy Ciske, and Matias Valenzuela. 2009. "How Seattle and King County Are Tackling Institutional Inequities." *Poverty and Race Research Action Council. 18, no. 5 (September–October): 5–9.*

Nelson, Julie, Lauren Spokane, Lauren Ross, and Nan Deng. 2015. *Advancing Racial Equity and Transforming Government: A Resource Guide to Put Ideas into Action.* Government Alliance on Race and Equity. https://www.racialequityalliance .org/wp-content/uploads/2015/02/GARE-Resource_Guide.pdf.

Nickerson, Peter. 2008. "Comments on the Proposed 'Green Fee.'" http://www .seattlebagtax.org/lettertocitycouncil.html.

Office of Arts & Culture. 2019. "Arts and Cultural Districts." www.seattle.gov/arts /programs/cultural-space/arts-and-cultural-districts.

———. 2018b. Current Districts: Central Area. https://www.seattle.gov/arts/arts -and-cultural-districts#centralarea.

———. 2018c. Current Districts: Uptown. https://www.seattle.gov/arts/arts-and -cultural-districts#uptown.

Office of Economic Development. 2018. "Income." https://www.seattle.gov /economicdevelopment/data/income.

Office of Financial Management. 2018. "April 1 Official Population Estimates." https://www.ofm.wa.gov/washington-data-research/population-demographics /population-estimates/april-1-official-population-estimates.

Office of Housing. 2013. *A New Model for Development in Southeast Seattle: A Study and Proposal for an Equitable Transit-Oriented Development Loan Program.* Seattle: City of Seattle.

Office of Sustainability & Environment. 2001. *Sustaining Seattle: Our Defining Challenge.* Seattle: Office of Sustainability & Environment.

———. 2012. *Seattle Climate Action Plan: Green Ribbon Commission Recommendations.* http://www.seattle.gov/Documents/Departments/Environment /ClimateChange/GRCReport_forweb-1-29–13.pdf.

———. 2013a. *We're So Green* (video). Seattle: Capitol Media and Punch Drunk. https://punch-drunk.com/our-work/were-so-green-animated-video.

———. 2013b. *Action: Seattle Climate Action Plan.* http://www.seattle.gov /Documents/Departments/Environment/ClimateChange/2013_CAP _20130612.pdf.

———. 2016a. *2014 Seattle Community Greenhouse Gas Emissions Inventory.* https:// www.seattle.gov/Documents/Departments/Environment/ClimateChange /2014GHG%20inventorySept2016.pdf.

———. 2016b. *Equity and Environment Agenda.* https://www.seattle.gov/Documents /Departments/Environment/EnvironmentalEquity/SeattleEquityAgenda.pdf.

———. 2017. *Moving the Needle: City of Seattle Environmental Progress Report.* https://www.seattle.gov/Documents/Departments/OSE/Reports/MTN2.0 _Final_Web.pdf.

Office of the Mayor. 2007. *Executive Order 01–07: Translation and Interpretation Policy.* Seattle: City of Seattle.

———. 2014. *Executive Order 2014-02: Race and Social Justice Initiative.* Seattle: City of Seattle.

Office of the Press Secretary. 2014. "Fact Sheet: 16 U.S. Communities Recognized as Climate Action Champions for Leadership on Climate Change." White House website. https://obamawhitehouse.archives.gov/the-press-office/2014/12/03/fact-sheet-16-us-communities-recognized-climate-action-champions-leaders.

Oliver, Mary. 2016. *Upstream: Selected Essays.* New York: Penguin Press.

Omi, Michael, and Howard Winant. 1994. *Racial Formation in the United States: From the 1960s to the 1990s, Second Edition.* New York: Routledge.

Peck, Jamie. 2005. "Struggling with the Creative Class." *International Journal of Urban and Regional Research* 29, no. 4 (December): 740–70.

———. 2007. "The Creativity Fix." *Eurozine.* https://www.eurozine.com/the-creativity-fix/.

———. 2011. "Geographies of Policy: From Transfer-Diffusion to Mobility-Mutation." *Progress in Human Geography* 35, no. 6 (December): 773–97.

Peters, Ajayi Abayomi. 2015. "Environmental Justice—A Three Dimensional Parts." *International Journal of Scientific Research and Innovative Technology* 2, no. 5 (May): 27–36.

Pfeuffer, Charyn. 2017. "Exploring the Emerald City." *Sky* magazine (Minneapolis MN: Delta Airlines) (January): 70–71.

Portney, Kent. 2005. "Civic Engagement and Sustainable Cities in the United States." *Public Administration Review* 65, no. 5 (September–October): 579–91.

———. 2013. *Taking Sustainable Cities Seriously: Economic Development, the Environment, and Quality of Life in American Cities, Second Edition.* Cambridge MA: MIT Press.

Pounder, C. C. H., Larry Adelman, Jean Cheng, Christine Herbes-Sommers, Tracy Heather Strain, Llewellyn Smith, and Claudio Ragazzi. 2003. *Race: The Power of an Illusion* (video series). San Francisco: California Newsreel.

Price, Patricia L. 2004. *Dry Place: Landscapes of Belonging and Exclusion.* Minneapolis: University of Minnesota Press.

———. 2010. "At the Crossroads: Critical Race Theory and Critical Geographies of Race." *Progress in Human Geography* 34, no. 2 (April): 147–74.

Pulido, Laura. 2000. "Rethinking Environmental Racism: White Privilege and Urban Development in Southern California." *Annals of the Association of American Geographers* 90, no. 1 (March): 12–40.

Putnam, John C. 2008. *Class and Gender Politics in Progressive-Era Seattle.* Reno: University of Nevada Press.

Race to Democracy. 2018. "Multicultural Community Center Coalition." https://racetodemocracy.wordpress.com/portfolio/multicultural-community-center-coalition/.

Raco, Mike, Steven Henderson, Sophie Bowlby. 2008. "Changing Times, Changing Places: Urban Development and the Politics of Space-Time." *Environment and Planning A* 40, no. 11 (November): 2652–73.

Rainier Chamber of Commerce. 2018. "About Southeast Seattle." https://www.rainierchamber.com/southeast-seattle/.

Ramírez, Margaret Mariette 2015. "The Elusive Inclusive: Black Food Geographies and Racialized Food Spaces." *Antipode* 47, no. 3 (June): 748–69.

Rantisi, Norma M., Deborah Leslie, and Susan Christopherson. 2006. "Guest Editorial." *Environment and Planning A* 38, no. 10 (October): 1789–97.

Rice, Jennifer. 2010. "Climate, Carbon, and Territory: Greenhouse Gas Mitigation in Seattle, Washington." *Annals of the Association of American Geographers* 100, no. 4 (October): 929–37.

Romolini, Michele, J. Morgan Grove, Curtis L. Ventriss, Christopher J. Koliba, and Daniel H. Krymkowski. 2016. "Toward an Understanding of Citywide Urban Environmental Governance: An Examination of Stewardship Networks in Baltimore and Seattle." *Environmental Management* 58, no. 2 (August): 254–67.

Rucker, Randal R., Peter H. Nickerson, and Melissa P. Haugen. 2008. "Analysis of the Seattle Bag Tax and Foam Ban Proposal." Northwest Economic Policy Seminar website. http://www.seattlebagtax.org/RuckerReport.pdf.

Russo, Antonio P., and Jan van der Borg. 2010. "An Urban Policy Framework for Culture-Oriented Economic Development: Lessons from the Netherlands." *Urban Geography* 31, no. 5 (July): 668–90.

Saha, Devashree. 2008. "Empirical Research on Local Government Sustainability Efforts in the USA: Gaps in the Current Literature." *Local Environment* 14, no. 1 (January): 17–30.

Said, Edward. 1978. *Orientalism.* London: Routledge.

Saldaña, Rebecca, and Margaret Wykowski. 2012. "Racial Equity: New Cornerstone of Transit-Oriented Development." *Race, Poverty, and the Environment: The National Journal for Social and Environmental Justice* 19, no. 2: 13–15.

Sale, Roger. 1976. *Seattle: Past to Present.* Seattle: University of Washington Press.

Sandercock, Leonie. 2003. *Cosmopolis II: Mongrel Cities of the 21st Century.* New York: Continuum.

Sanders, Jeffrey Craig. 2010. *Seattle and the Roots of Urban Sustainability: Inventing Ecotopia.* Pittsburgh PA: University of Pittsburgh Press.

Schlosser, Kurt. 2018. "Geek of the Week: 'Vanishing Seattle' Creator Cynthia Brothers on Why the City's Loss of 'Soul' Is about More Than Nostalgia." https://www.geekwire.com/2018/cynthia-brothers/

Seattle City Council. 2012. "Plastic Bag Ban." https://www.seattle.gov/council/meet-the-council/mike-obrien/plastic-bag-ban.

Seattle Civil Rights and Labor History Project. 2018. "Restrictive Covenants Database." http://depts.washington.edu/civilr/covenants_database.htm.

Seattle Climate Protection Initiative. 2009. *Progress Report.* Seattle: Office of Sustainability & Environment.

Seattle's Convention and Visitors Bureau. 2006. *Seattle Metronatural.*™ Seattle: Seattle's Convention and Visitors Bureau.

Seattle Department of Neighborhoods. 2018. "Outreach and Engagement." http://www.seattle.gov/neighborhoods/outreach-and-engagement.

Seattle–King County Coalition on Homelessness. 2015. "2015 Results." http://www.homelessinfo.org/what_we_do/one_night_count/2015_results.php.

Seattle Office for Civil Rights. 2008. *Report 2008: Looking Back, Moving Forward.* Seattle: Seattle Office for Civil Rights.

———. 2012. *Race and Social Justice Initiative: Accomplishments 2009–2011.* Seattle: Seattle Office for Civil Rights.

———. 2013. *Race and Social Justice Initiative: Employee Survey 2012.* Seattle: Seattle Office for Civil Rights.

———. 2014a. *City of Seattle Racial Equity Community Survey.* Seattle: Seattle Office for Civil Rights.

———. 2014b. *Race and Social Justice Initiative: Vision and Strategy 2015–2017.* Seattle: Seattle Office for Civil Rights.

———. 2016. *Race and Social Justice Initiative Annual Report.* Seattle: Seattle Office for Civil Rights.

———. N.d. *RSJI Training and Education.* https://www.seattle.gov/Documents/Departments/RSJI/RSJI-Training-and-Education.pdf.

Seattle Planning Commission. 2009. *Status Check: How Is Your Neighborhood Doing?* http://www.seattle.gov/Documents/Departments/SeattlePlanningCommission/IntroNhoodPlanning.pdf.

Seattle Police Department. 2000. *The Seattle Police Department After Action Report.* Seattle: City of Seattle.

Seattle Post-Intelligencer. 1902. "'Let Us Make a Beautiful City of Seattle,' Say the Park Commissioners." *Olmsted Centennial NEWS–2009 A-Y-P Edition.* Seattle: Friends of Seattle's Olmsted Parks.

Seattle Public Utilities. 2009. *CurbWaste & Conserve.* Seattle: City of Seattle.

———. 2013. *Plastic Carryout Bag Ban: Retail Business Survey and Six-Month Progress Report.* Seattle: City of Seattle.

———. 2016. *Bag Requirements.* Seattle: City of Seattle.

Senge, Peter. 1990. *The Fifth Discipline: The Art and Practice of the Learning Organization.* New York: Doubleday.

Sensoy, Özlem, and Robin DiAngelo. 2017. *Is Everyone Really Equal? An Introduction to Key Concepts in Social Justice Education.* New York: Teachers College Press.

Shake, Joshua. 2015. "Ideas Out of Context and the Contextualization of Ideas: The Transference of Jane Jacobs to São Paulo." *Geoforum* 65 (October): 201–8.

Silva, Catherine. 2009. "Racial Restrictive Covenants: Enforcing Neighborhood Segregation in Seattle." Seattle Civil Rights and Labor History Project. http://depts.washington.edu/civilr/covenants_report.htm.

Simonton, Dean Keith. 2011. "Big-C Creativity in the Big City." In *Handbook of Creative Cities*, edited by David Andersson, Åke Andersson, and Charlotta Mellander, 72–84. Northampton MA: Edward Elgar.

Sirianni, Carmen. 2007. "Neighborhood Planning as Collaborative Democratic Design." *Journal of the American Planning Association* 73, no. 4 (Autumn): 373–87.

Smith, Bruce. 2009. *The Key of Green: Passion and Perception in Renaissance Culture.* Chicago: University of Chicago Press.

Southeast Economic Opportunity Center. 2017. "Community Meeting Presentation." https://homesight-my.sharepoint.com/personal/michelle_homesightwa _org/_layouts/15/WopiFrame.aspx?docid=0edbd13e01234458cb269e35d458ef61e &authkey=AfjqCDFcIRr7RMP4_E6IC_o&action=view&slrid=54721b9e-403a -4000-4a1c-42393e9a2fa6.

SouthEast Effective Development. 2018. "About Southeast Seattle." http://www .seedseattle.org/about-southeast-seattle/.

Sparke, Matthew. 2011. "Global Geographies." In *Seattle Geographies*, edited by Michael P. Brown and Richard Morrill, 48–70. Seattle: University of Washington Press.

Stein, Garth. 2009. "Seattle: City of the Year." FastCompany.com. http://www .fastcompany.com/magazine/135/seattle-grace.html.

Stephens, Alexis. 2015. "Shifting Planning from Pretty Renderings to Affordability and Inclusion." NextCity.org. https://nextcity.org/daily/entry/urban -planning-affordability-inclusion-seattle-model.

Straker, Gillian. 2011. "Unsettling Whiteness." *Psychoanalysis, Culture and Society* 16, no. 1 (April): 11–26.

Swyngedouw, Erik, Frank Moulaert, and Arantxa Rodriguez. 2002. "Neoliberal Urbanization in Europe: Large-Scale Urban Development Projects and the New Urban Policy." *Antipode* 34, no. 3 (July): 542–77.

Tarrant, Seaton Patrick, and Leslie Paul Thiele. 2016. "Practice Makes Pedagogy: John Dewey and Skills-Based Sustainability Education." *International Journal of Sustainability in Higher Education* 17, no. 1: 54–67.

Tatum, Beverly Daniel. 2017. *Why Are All the Black Kids Sitting Together in the Cafeteria? And Other Conversations about Race.* New York: Basic Books.

Taylor, Quintard. 1994. *The Forging of a Black Community: Seattle's Central District from 1870 through the Civil Rights Era.* Seattle: University of Washington Press.

Thrift, Nigel. 2009. "Space: The Fundamental Stuff of Geography." In *Key Concepts in Geography*, edited by Nicholas J. Clifford, Sarah L. Holloway, Stephen P. Rice, and Gill Valentine, 85–96. Los Angeles: Sage Publications.

Thrush, Coll. 2007. *Native Seattle: Histories from the Crossing-Over Place.* Seattle: University of Washington Press.

Tomlinson, Barbara, and George Lipsitz. 2013. "American Studies as Accompaniment." *American Quarterly* 65 (March): 1–30.

Ueda, Reed. 1994. *Postwar Immigrant America: A Social History.* Boston: Bedford Books.

UN Habitat. 2015. *National Urban Policy: Framework for a Rapid Diagnostic.* Nairobi: UN Habitat.

United Nations World Commission on Environment and Development. 1987. *Report of the World Commission on Environment and Development: Our Common Future.* http://www.un-documents.net/our-common-future.pdf.

Urban Design Advisory Board. 1965. *Designing a Great City: Report of the Urban Design Advisory Board to the Seattle City Planning Commission.* Seattle: The Commission.

U.S. Census Bureau. 2011. "Income, Poverty and Health Insurance Coverage in the United States: 2010." https://www.census.gov/newsroom/releases/archives/income_wealth/cb11-157.html

———. 2018. "QuickFacts: Seattle City, Washington; United States." https://www.census.gov/quickfacts/fact/table/seattlecitywashington,US/PST045216.

U.S. Conference of Mayors. 2018. "Mayors Climate Protection Center." https://www.usmayors.org/mayors-climate-protection-center/.

#Vanishing Seattle. 2018. "About." https://www.vanishingseattle.org/copy-of-about.

Van Riper, Tom. 2008. "America's Cleanest Cities." *Forbes Magazine.* https://www.forbes.com/2008/03/17/miami-seattle-orlando-biz-logistics-cx_tvr_0317cleanest.html.

Wainwright, Joel, Scott Prudham, and Jim Glassman. 2000. "Guest Editorials." *Environment and Planning D: Society and Space* 18, no 1. (February): 1–13.

Walker, Gordon. 2012. *Environmental Justice: Concepts, Evidence and Politics.* New York: Routledge.

Walsh, Katherine Cramer. 2006. "Communities, Race, and Talk: An Analysis of the Occurrence of Civic Intergroup Dialogue Programs." *Journal of Politics* 68, no. 1 (February): 22–33.

Ward, Kevin. 2003. "Entrepreneurial Urbanism, State Restructuring and Civilizing 'New' East Manchester." *Area* 35, no. 2 (June): 116–27.

Way to Go, Seattle! Team. 2012. *WALK BIKE RIDEr* newsletter. http://archive.constantcontact.com/fs051/1103565212781/archive/1110608910822.html.

Weber Thompson. 2018. "Othello Square HomeSight Opportunity Center: Arrangement Studies." https://homesight-my.sharepoint.com/personal/michelle_homesightwa_org/_layouts/15/onedrive.aspx?id=%2Fpersonal%2Fmichelle_homesightwa_org%2FDocuments%2FBuilding%20Concept%20Presentations%2FWeber%20Thompson%20-%20Building%20A%20and%20Site%20Wide%2Epdf&parent=%2Fpersonal%2Fmichelle_homesightwa_org%2FDocuments%2FBuilding%20Concept%20Presentations&slrid=36dd9c9e-5059-7000-4cd1-132ec723b9a6.

Weissbort, Daniel, and Astradur Eysteinsson, eds. 2006. *Translation—Theory and Practice: A Historical Reader.* New York: Oxford.

Welch, Nicholas. 2013. *City for All? A Geospatial Approach to Equity, Sustainability, and Gentrification in Seattle, Washington.* Unpublished master's thesis. Tufts University.

Williams, David B. 1999. "The Olmsted Legacy: The Fabled Massachusetts Landscape Firm Got to Seattle Early, and That Has Made All the Difference." *Seattle Times.* http://community.seattletimes.nwsource.com/archive/?date=19990502&slug=2958185.

Wilma, David. 2001. "Seattle Becomes the Emerald City in 1982." HistoryLink.org. http://www.historylink.org/index.cfm?DisplayPage=output.cfm&file_id=3622.

Wilson, David. 2004. "Towards a Contingent Urban Neoliberalism." *Urban Geography* 25, no. 8: 771–83.

World Trade Organization Accountability Review Committee. 2000. *Report of the Citizens' Advisory Panel One to the WTO Accountability Review Committee of the Seattle City Council.* Seattle: City of Seattle.

WTO History Project. 2018. http://depts.washington.edu/wtohist/index.htm.

Yardley, William. 2008. "Seattle Takes Steps to Recognize Minorities' Role in Shaping Region." *New York Times.* http://www.nytimes.com/2008/02/06/us/06seattle.html.

Zajac, Ina. 2009. "A Fair to Remember: What Would Seattle Be without the AYPE?" *Columns, University of Washington Alumni Magazine* (June): 28–31.

Zillow. 2018a. "Seattle Home Prices and Values." https://www.zillow.com/seattle-wa/home-values/.

———. 2018b. "Capitol Hill Market Overview." https://www.zillow.com/capitol-hill-seattle-wa/home-values/.

Zimmerman, Jeffrey. 2008. "From Brew Town to Cool Town: Neoliberalism and the Creative City Development Strategy in Milwaukee." *Cities* 25, no. 4 (August): 230–42.

INDEX

equitable transit-oriented development (eTOD), 100, 124–32, 186, 222n6

equity: in city government, 147–48, 161; on county and national level, 169–78; focus on, 8; in planning and development, 148; and racial anxieties, 59; and RSJI, 31; social, 44, 110, 168, 172, 174, 175; and sustainability, 92. *See also* racial equity

Equity and Environment Initiative (EEI), 95, 96, 190, 219n5

Equity and Social Justice (ESJ), 173, 174, 222n9

Equity and Social Justice Initiative (ESJI), 169–78

ethnic businesses, 100, 115, 118, 123–25, 128

eTOD program. *See* equitable transit-oriented development (eTOD)

exclusive inclusion frame, 64–67, 74–76, 80, 86–87, 92–93, 186

ex-situ nationhood, concept of, 203

Fair Housing Act, 45

field notes, 28, 208

Florida, Richard, 7, 98–99, 101, 102, 103, 107, 108, 113, 131

for-profit sector, 77, 134, 162, 198, 210

for-profit sector interviewees: Beth, 20, 77, 79; Hilary, 134; Joanna, 29, 83–85, 161, 222n6; Lance, 26, 27, 51–52, 101, 198; Sheila, 56

Gentlemen's Agreement, 38

gentrification: and creativity, 109–10; and displacement, 111, 112, 113, 121–23; and economic development, 99; negative connotation of, 111; predictors of, 108; and Vanishing Seattle group, 193; vicious circle of, 109

geographical imagination, 13, 146, 190

globalization, 25, 49, 93

"Go Live!" campaign, 155

Government Alliance on Race and Equity (GARE), 174, 175, 176, 178

Great Turning, 204–5

green, being: collective identity of, 65; and green spaces, 40; and race overlays, 40; as a "relationship," 63; video and lyrics about, 61–63, 65, 79, 90, 186, 215–16. *See also* sustainability

Green Fee: about, 30, 64; and assumptions of choice, 92–93; City Council's role in, 80, 83–85, 87, 90, 192; class privilege issue, 86; conclusion about, 186, 192; cost issues, 86; defeat of, 82; ordinance, 81, 82; repeal of, 82, 85; and reusable bags, 80–82, 89–90; revenue from, 81–82; and small businesses, 83, 84, 89; and solid waste management, 81, 82, 89, 90; and sustainability, 80–90, 95

greenhouse gas (GHG) emissions, 67, 70, 75, 81, 83, 91

Green Ribbon Commission, 219n2

Growth Management Act, 158

homelessness, 152, 154, 170, 185

Home Owners' Loan Corporation (HOLC), 44

HomeSight, 129

home values, median, 25, 26, 109

imaginative geographies: about people and place, 12–13, 17, 191, 193, 197, 210; concept of, 13; and policy development issues, 191; of risk taking, 53; of Seattle, 20, 23–24, 36, 97, 98, 136, 185, 190, 191; sustainability through, 186, 191–92

immigrants: Chinese and Japanese, 38, 39; in Rainier Valley, 117, 120; and refugee communities, 134, 152, 156, 173; in Southeast Seattle, 28

indigenous peoples, 37, 38, 41, 43, 154, 190

inequalities, 94, 95, 198

inequities: about, 6; and creative class theory, 99; racialized and classed, 5, 11, 25, 147, 169, 172, 184, 187, 190, 191, 220n6; and resource allocation issues, 22, 154; structural, 29; systemic, 5, 8, 147; through exclusive inclusion, 66, 67

institutional racism: about, 7, 11, 31; capacity building exercises for, 148–49; within city government, 95; conclusion about, 179–81, 201; and RSJI, 135, 140–41, 143–45, 165, 176, 186

International District (ID), *map 1*, 43, 119

International Potlatch festivals, 42, 43

international trade, 48, 50

interpersonal racism, 11, 197

To order or obtain more information on these or other University of Nebraska Press titles, visit nebraskapress.unl.edu.

CPSIA information can be obtained
at www.ICGtesting.com
Printed in the USA
LVHW091946120419
613990LV00005B/120/P